THE GOSPELS IN BRIEF

THE BARNES & NOBLE LIBRARY OF ESSENTIAL READING

THE GOSPELS IN BRIEF

LEO TOLSTOY

TRANSLATED BY LEO WIENER

INTRODUCTION TO THE NEW EDITION
BY EDWARD ROSLOF

EDITED BY GREG OVIATT

BARNES & NOBLE
NEW YORK

THE BARNES & NOBLE
LIBRARY OF ESSENTIAL READING

Introduction and Suggested Reading
© 2004 by Barnes & Noble, Inc.

Originally published in 1904

This 2004 edition published by Barnes & Noble, Inc.

ISBN-13: 978-0-7607-5762-8
ISBN-10: 0-7607-5762-3

Printed and bound in the United States of America

3 5 7 9 10 8 6 4 2

CONTENTS

EDITOR'S NOTE

IN 1891, AT THE BEHEST OF HIS FRIENDS AND ADMIRERS, TOLSTOY AGREED to the publication of his harmonization and translation of the Gospel. That work, as it was originally published, consisted of three parallel Biblical texts: the New Testament Greek, the King James Version, and Tolstoy's translation of the New Testament Greek into colloquial Russian. The original publication also included Tolstoy's rational for his interpretation of the translation as well as Tolstoy's commentary on the Scriptural text. In 1904, Leo Wiener, late Professor of Slavic Languages at Harvard University, was commissioned by the Dana Estes & Company, of Boston, to translate this work from the colloquial Russian to modern English.

The Barnes & Noble edition of *The Gospels in Brief* has retained the Wiener translation of Tolstoy's harmonized biblical text, and Tolstoy's commentary, but excludes the ancillary New Testament Greek and King James translations.

K. G. O.

INTRODUCTION TO THE
NEW EDITION

LEO TOLSTOY'S *THE GOSPELS IN BRIEF* (1881) IS A DARING ATTEMPT BY Russia's greatest novelist to rewrite "the greatest story ever told." This book appeared soon after the writer experienced a period of deep despair that led to a conversion in his personal life. Following what might best be described as a midlife crisis, Tolstoy devoted himself to a rational religion for the masses based on the moral teachings of Jesus Christ. He rejected all the mystery and miracles in Christianity and focused instead on the powerful truth in Jesus' words—a truth he believed that the church's emphasis on mystery, miracles, and the divinity of Jesus had long obscured. In order to show the true essence of what Jesus taught, Tolstoy resolved to make a new translation of the four Gospels from Greek into Russian. He rejected anything that he considered not part of Jesus' original teaching, including all references to the Resurrection, and then rearranged these teachings in a way that highlighted Tolstoy's own understanding about the divine purpose for human existence. The combined forces of the Russian government and the Orthodox Church in the late nineteenth century would surely have succeeded in silencing anyone else who might have tried such a radical revision of the core teachings of Christianity, but Tolstoy's reputation, both in Russia and abroad, together with his social status as a member of the nobility, protected him. His ideas became the foundation for a new religious movement bearing his name (Tolstoyism) and influenced such political activists as Mohandas Gandhi and Martin Luther King, Jr.

This side of Tolstoy's life is little known to today's reading public, in part because Tolstoyism ceased to exist as an organized movement soon after the 1917 communist revolution in Russia. Tolstoy himself did not live to see the communists come to power. He died at the age of eighty-two in 1910. Nonetheless, he did witness many changes in Russia over a long life that had as many subplots and characters as one of his novels. He was more than a great writer, although his literary talent brought him celebrity status and wealth, which in turn fueled much of his subsequent success as a religious philosopher, critic of the political and religious establishment, and champion of social reform. He was born in 1828 at his family's estate in Yasnaya Polyana, which is located approximately 130 miles south of Moscow. By the time he was ten both his parents had died and, together with his sister and three brothers, he came under the care of various relatives. Being a member of the wealthy Russian aristocracy meant that Tolstoy received his elementary and secondary education from foreign tutors. He then began but never completed studies at the University of Kazan. By the age of thirty-three, Tolstoy had squandered a large portion of his inheritance through gambling and partying. He also had served as an officer in the army and seen the horrors of combat during the Crimean War (1853–56). While in the artillery corps, Tolstoy began writing a series of semi-autobiographical works, including the trilogy *Childhood* (1852), *Boyhood* (1854), and *Youth* (1857), as well accounts of a soldier's life in war time (*Sevastopol Sketches*, 1855–56).

Tolstoy enjoyed a dramatic shift in fortune between 1862 and 1877. In 1862, he fell in love with seventeen-year-old Sofya Andreyevna Bers ("Sonya"). They married that same year, and Sonya promptly took charge of running Yasnaya Polyana and caring for their rapidly expanding family. The couple became parents to thirteen children in all, nine of whom lived to adulthood. Tolstoy's concern for the financial wellbeing of his wife and children pushed him to a more serious attitude toward writing. With Sonya's encouragement, he began *War and Peace* (1867–69), an epic historical novel on the Napoleon wars, which was initially published in six volumes. His other great novel, *Anna Karenina*, appeared first as a serialized work in the early 1870s and then as a book in 1878. In both of these works, Tolstoy questions conventional wisdom and social norms even as he probes the inner lives of his main characters. *War and Peace* rejects the idea that great individuals make history. Forgotten masses of common people acting together, not individual "heroes" like Napoleon, determined the course of that epic conflict. The novelist addresses personal upheavals with the same skepticism toward traditional explanations in *Anna Karenina*, the tragic story of a noblewoman who is destroyed by a belief in romantic love that leads her to commit adultery and abandon her family. The novel reveals the emptiness of Russian high society whose artificial standards for behavior lack any moral foundation. Hope for marital and personal happiness is found in the subplot of Kitty and Levin, who abandon aristocratic society for a simple life modeled on peasant values. The worldview presented in Tolstoy's two great novels later became part of the writer's religious philosophy.

By the age of fifty, Tolstoy was at the pinnacle of personal and professional success. He had great wealth, good health, a loving family, and international acclaim. But he also was dogged by doubts about the long-term significance of his achievements. He became acutely aware of his own mortality and wondered what would be left of all his seemingly splendid achievements after his death. This existential crisis led him initially to an intellectual search for answers in the works of great thinkers and an attempt to embrace the rites and rituals of Russian Orthodoxy. Neither of these paths provided the answers he sought. Resolution came from two other sources: an idealized vision of peasant life that he combined with a radical interpretation of biblical teachings. Both of these ideas had long been part of Tolstoy's life and were widely accepted by his contemporaries. The first was distinctively Russian, the second markedly European. Prior to his midlife crisis, Tolstoy had often commented on the simple virtues of the peasants on his estate and undertaken projects to improve their material conditions through education. Many Russian intellectuals turned to the peasantry for answers during the era of the Great Reforms that took place for some twenty years after the emancipation of the serfs by Tsar Alexander II in 1861. Tolstoy's unique contribution was to combine this Russian love of the peasantry with a version of humanistic Christianity that had emerged during the European Enlightenment. Philosophers such as England's John Locke (1632–1704) and Ireland's John Toland (1670–1722), along with many of their contemporaries, argued for a version of Christianity based on logic as opposed to mystery, on human reason rather than divine revelation. Tolstoy embraced their quest over a century later.

Tolstoy was unsuccessful in his attempts to have *The Gospels in Brief* published in Russia during his lifetime. Manuscript versions and foreign editions, however, circulated among his followers and intellectual circles in Russia. Its purpose was simple: to present the teachings of Jesus as clearly as possible so that every person could know how to live in this earthly world. Tolstoy believed that God existed but could never be proven. He also believed that the Church was an obstacle to living life in harmony with humanity's limited place in the world because dogmatic Christianity emphasized the divinity of Christ and promised future happiness for believers rather than providing useful guidance for fulfillment in life in the present. By retranslating and reorganizing the Gospels and adding his own commentary, Tolstoy intended to provide a practical guide for every life based on the solution he had discovered to his own spiritual despair.

As a result, the Christian teaching that emerges from this book is based on the author's personal experiences and his own understanding of the meaning of truth. Every person is a creation of the "infinite principle" (that is, God), which means that every person has the ability to recognize truth and order his or her life around it. In other words, every reasonable person can follow Tolstoy's path to see the truth in Jesus' words. The pure teaching of Jesus, although surrounded by "mud and ooze" from centuries of misguided interpretation, shines out with brightness and clarity from the Gospels and the Gospels alone. All other sections of the Bible, including the Old Testament and the rest of the New Testament, obfuscate the purity of Jesus' ideas. According to Tolstoy, Jesus provided five simple rules for living as children of the Father of life and not as a slave to the whims of the flesh. In their simplest form, these rules say to avoid anger, avoid lust, do not swear oaths, meet evil with non-resistance, and treat everyone—both the just and the unjust—with goodness. The authority of church and state alike becomes superfluous as a consequence of Tolstoy's rules for living. Poverty is a virtue, since all property could be held only through the use of force. Church rituals add nothing to following these rules and so are dismissed as useless. The supreme law for human behavior is love. Tolstoy's vision of a perfectly fulfilled life—a personal utopia as it were—is based on individuals who follow the internal summons to love one another. Nothing else matters.

Tolstoy spent the last thirty years of his life attempting to spread the teachings in *The Gospels in Brief* and to live them out in his own life. In works like *The Death of Ivan Ilich* (1886) and *The Kingdom of Heaven Is Within You* (1893), Tolstoy dwells on the meaning of death and the power of nonviolent resistance. His last novel, *Resurrection* (1899), is practically a sermon against all the evils of Russian society and religion. During these years, Tolstoy adopted vegetarianism and the simple garb of the Russian peasantry. He also embraced a peasant's life of physical labor dictated by nature's rhythms as the way to live in the present moment. He stopped drinking and smoking. He also made repeated unsuccessful attempts to give up all sexual relations. Ironically, his pursuit of the ideals of Tolstoy-ism led to conflicts in his personal life. Sonya rejected both his attempts at total chastity and at relinquishing copyrights to the works he produced prior to 1880. She acted out of concern for their marriage and the financial needs of their large family. The struggle between the formerly close husband and wife continued until his death.

The last decade of Tolstoy's life was a time of troubles and productivity for the great writer. The Russian Orthodox Church excommunicated him in 1901 for his attacks on the church and denial of the divinity of Christ. Tolstoy responded with a statement that rallied public opinion to his support. He wrote several plays, stories, and novels, and international acclaim for his genius grew. Yet, his family quarreled over property and the rights to his works. They did not renounce their upper-class lifestyle and were embarrassed by his eccentricities. Relations between Leo and Sonya worsened, and she came to resent the constant stream of disciples who sought guidance from the great writer and philosopher. Tolstoy did not understand her unwillingness to accept the rules for living that seemed so obvious to him. In the end, Tolstoy wanted to enter a monastery in order to be free from possessions, but the Church refused to lift its edict of excommunication. His health in decline, Tolstoy fled Yasnaya Polyana and spent his last days in a futile attempt to get to the Caucasus. He died in Astopovo, a small town in Riazan province, in 1910. The Church refused to allow any of its priests to conduct a Christian funeral when Tolstoy's body was buried on the edge of his estate. A century after his death, Leo Tolstoy's writings attract new generations of readers thanks to the beauty of his prose, his insights into the human condition, and the power of his ideas.

Edward Roslof holds a Ph.D. in Russian history from the University of North Carolina at Chapel Hill. He has taught at Harvard University, the University of North Carolina at Chapel Hill, and United Theological Seminary, and he currently serves as the Director of the Fulbright Program in Russia.

PREFACE

THIS SHORT EXPOSITION OF THE GOSPEL IS AN EXTRACT FROM A LARGE work which is lying in manuscript and cannot be printed in Russia. This work consists of four parts:

1. AN EXPOSITION OF THAT COURSE OF MY PRIVATE LIFE AND OF MY THOUGHTS WHICH HAVE LED ME TO THE CONVICTION THAT THE TRUTH IS TO BE FOUND IN THE CHRISTIAN TEACHING.

2. AN EXPOSITION OF THE CHRISTIAN TEACHING ACCORDING TO THE INTERPRETATIONS OF THE CHURCH IN GENERAL—THE APOSTLES, THE COUNCILS, AND THE SO-CALLED FATHERS OF THE CHURCH, AND PROOFS OF THE FALSENESS OF THESE INTERPRETATIONS.

3. AN INVESTIGATION OF THE CHRISTIAN TEACHING, NOT ACCORDING TO THESE INTERPRETATIONS, BUT ACCORDING TO WHAT HAS REACHED US FROM THE TEACHING OF CHRIST, AS ASCRIBED TO HIM AND RECORDED IN THE GOSPELS, AND A TRANSLATION AND HARMONIZATION OF THE GOSPELS.

4. AN EXPOSITION OF THE REAL MEANING OF THE CHRISTIAN TEACH-ING, OF THE CAUSES WHY IT WAS DISTORTED, AND OF THE CONSEQUENCES WHICH ITS PREACHING WAS TO HAVE.

This Short Exposition of the Gospel is an abbreviation of the third part. The harmonization of the four gospels is made in accordance with the meaning of the teaching. In this harmonization I had hardly to depart from the order in which the gospels are expounded, so that in my harmonization there are rather fewer transpositions of the verses of the Gospel than in the majority of concordances known to me, and fewer than in the harmonization of the four gospels by Grechulévich.

In the gospel of John there are no transpositions in my harmonization: it is expounded in the same order as in the original.

The division of the Gospel into twelve chapters, or six (if each two be united), resulted naturally from the meaning of the teaching.

Here is the meaning of these words:

1. MAN IS THE SON OF THE INFINITE PRINCIPLE, THE SON OF THIS FATHER, NOT IN THE FLESH, BUT IN THE SPIRIT.

2. THEREFORE MAN MUST SERVE THIS PRINCIPLE IN THE SPIRIT.

3. THE LIFE OF ALL MEN HAS A DIVINE BEGINNING. IT ALONE IS HOLY.

4. THEREFORE MAN MUST SERVE THIS PRINCIPLE IN THE LIFE OF ALL MEN. SUCH IS THE WILL OF THE FATHER.

5. ONLY THE MINISTERING TO THE WILL OF THE FATHER OF LIFE GIVES THE TRUE, THAT IS, THE RATIONAL, LIFE.

6. THEREFORE THE GRATIFICATION OF ONE'S WILL IS NOT NECESSARY FOR THE TRUE LIFE.

7. THE TEMPORAL, CARNAL LIFE IS A FOOD FOR THE TRUE LIFE—A MATERIAL FOR THE RATIONAL LIFE.

8. THEREFORE THE TRUE LIFE IS OUTSIDE OF TIME—IT IS ONLY IN THE PRESENT.

9. THE DECEPTION OF THE LIFE OF TIME, OF THE LIFE OF THE PAST AND OF THE FUTURE, CONCEALS FROM MEN THE TRUE LIFE—OF THE PRESENT.

10. THEREFORE MAN MUST STRIVE TO DESTROY THE DECEPTION OF THE TEMPORAL LIFE OF THE PAST AND OF THE FUTURE.

11. THE TRUE LIFE IS NOT ONLY OUTSIDE OF TIME—A LIFE OF THE PRESENT, BUT IT IS ALSO OUTSIDE OF PERSONALITY—IT IS THE COMMON LIFE OF MEN.

12. THEREFORE HE WHO LIVES IN THE PRESENT THE COMMON LIFE OF ALL MEN UNITES WITH THE FATHER, THE BEGINNING AND FOUNDATION OF LIFE.

Each two chapters have between them the connection of cause and effect. In addition to the twelve chapters there are added to the exposition: the introduction from the first chapter of John, in which the writer speaks in his own name about the meaning of the whole teaching, and a conclusion from the epistle of the same writer (written, no doubt, before the gospels), which contains a general deduction from everything which precedes. The introduction and conclusion do not form any essential part of the teaching. They are only general views of the whole teaching. Although the introduction and the conclusion may be omitted without any loss to the meaning of the teaching (the more so since these two parts were written in the name of John, and not of Jesus), I have retained them, because in a simple and rational understanding of Christ's teaching these parts, confirming one another and the whole teaching, in contradistinction to the queer interpretations of the church, furnish the simplest indication of the meaning which ought to be ascribed to the teaching.

In the beginning of each chapter I have placed, besides a short definition of the contents, the words of the prayer, which Jesus taught his disciples to recite, and which befit the particular chapters.

When I finished my work, I discovered to my surprise and joy that the so-called Lord's prayer is nothing but a briefly expressed exposition of the teaching of Jesus in the very order in which the chapters were arranged by me, and that each expression of the prayer corresponded to the meaning and order of the words.

1. Our Father	Man is the son of God.
2. Which art in heaven,	God is the infinite spiritual principle of life.
3. Hallowed be thy name.	Let this principle of life be holy.
4. Thy kingdom come.	May his power be realized in all men.
5. Thy will be done, as in heaven,	May the will of this infinite principle be done in himself,
6. So in earth.	So also in the flesh.
7. Give us our daily bread	The temporal life is the food for the true life.
8. Today.	The true life is in the present.
9. And forgive us our debts, as we forgive our debtors.	And let not our transgressions and errors conceal the true life from us.
10. And lead us not into temptation,	Let them not lead us into deception,
11. But deliver us from evil:	And so there will be no evil.
12. For thine is the kingdom, and the power, and the glory.	And let there be thy dominion, and power, and reason.

In the extensive exposition of the third part, which is in manuscript, the Gospel, according to the four evangelists, is translated and explained in full, without the least omissions; but in the present exposition the following verses are left out: The procreation and birth of John the Baptist, his imprisonment and death, the birth of Jesus, his genealogy, his flight with his mother to Egypt, the miracles of Jesus in Cana and Capernaum, the casting out of the devils, the walking on the waters, the drying up of the fig-tree, the healing of the sick, the resurrection of Christ himself, and the indications of the prophecies which took place in Christ's life.

These verses are omitted in the present short exposition because, not containing any teaching, but only describing events which took place before, during, and after the preaching of Jesus, they add nothing, and complicate and surcharge the exposition. No matter how these verses may be understood, they contain neither contradictions to the teaching, nor confirmations of it. The only significance of these verses for Christianity was this, that they proved the divinity of Christ to him who did not believe in it. But for a man who does not see the convincingness of the story of the miracles, and who besides does not doubt the divinity of Jesus, according to his teaching, these verses fall off, of their own accord, as being unnecessary. In the large exposition every deviation from the usual translation, every added explanation, every omission is explained and proved by the collation of the different variants of the gospels, by contexts, and by philological and other considerations. In this Short Exposition all such proofs, and the rejections of the false understanding of the church, as also the detailed notes with the quotations, are omitted on the ground that the reflections on each separate passage, which at times are very long, are not the chief proofs of the true understanding of the teaching. The main proof of the truth of the understanding is the unity, clearness, simplicity, fulness of the teaching and its correspondence with the inner feeling of every man who is seeking the truth.

In respect to all the departures in my exposition from the text as accepted by the churches, the reader must not forget that the customary conception that all four gospels, with all their verses and letters, are sacred books, is, on the one hand, a very gross error, and on the other, a very gross deception.

The reader must remember that Jesus never wrote any book himself, as did Plato, Philo, or Marcus Aurelius; nor did he ever, like Socrates, transmit his teaching to educated people; he spoke to those uneducated men whom he met in life, and only much later, long after his death, did people come to realize that what he had said was very important, and that it would not be bad if they jotted down a few of the things which he said and did, and it was nearly a hundred years later that they began to write down what they had heard about him.

The reader must remember that there was a large, a very large number of such notes; that many have disappeared; that many were very bad, and that the Christians made use of all of them, and by degrees picked out what to them seemed to be better and more sensible; that, in selecting these best gospels, out of the enormous literature about Christ, the churches, according to the proverb which says, "You can't cut a stick without knots," could not help but take in some knots also; that there are many places in the canonical gospels which are as bad as in the rejected apocrypha, and that in the apocryphal literature there is some good.

The reader must remember that what can be sacred is Christ's teaching, but by no means a certain number of verses and letters, and that certain books cannot become sacred from the first to the last line for the very reason that men say that they are sacred. Only our Russian readers of the educated class can, thanks to the censorship, ignore the labors of the historical criticism of the last hundred years, and say naïvely that the Gospels of Matthew, Mark, and Luke, as they are, were written by the evangelists, each separately and in full.

The reader must remember that to say this in the year 1880, ignoring everything which science has worked out in this matter, is the same as when in the past century they spoke of the sun as turning around the earth.

The reader must remember that the synoptical gospels, as they have reached us, are the fruit of slow accretion by means of copying and interpolation, and reflections of thousands of different minds and hands, and by no means the productions of the Holy Ghost who spoke to the evangelists.

The reader must remember that the ascribing of the gospels in their present form to the apostles is a fable, which not only cannot stand any criticism, but has even no foundation but the desire of pious people, who want it to be so. The gospels were selected, complemented, and expounded through the ages. All the gospels of the fourth century that have reached us are written in a continuous script, without signs of punctuation, and so were after the fourth and fifth centuries subject to most varied readings; that they count as many as fifty thousand such different evangelical books.

All this the reader must remember, in order that we may not be driven to that customary view that the gospels, as they are now understood, have come to us in that form from the Holy Ghost.

The reader must remember that there is nothing prejudicial in rejecting from the gospels the useless passages and in illuminating some of them by others, that, on the contrary, it is prejudicial and godless not to do so, but to consider a given number of verses and letters holy.

On the other hand, I beg the reader of my exposition of the Gospel to remember that, if I do not look upon the gospels as upon sacred books, I at the same time do not look upon them as upon mere documents of the history of religious literature. I understand both the theological and the historical view of the gospels, but I look differently at them, and so I beg the reader, in reading my exposition, not to be switched off on the church view, nor on the historical view of the gospels, which of late has become the fashion with cultivated people, a view which I did not hold and which I find equally incomplete.

I look on Christianity not as on an exclusive divine revelation, nor as on a historical phenomenon, but as on a teaching which gives us the meaning of life. I was led to Christianity, not by theological or historical investigations, but by this, that when, being fifty years old, I asked myself and the people close to me what I am, and wherein lies the meaning of my life, and received the answer, "Thou art an accidental concatenation of particles—there is no meaning in life, and life itself is evil"—I was brought to the point of despair and wanted to commit suicide; but, recalling that formerly, in my childhood, when I believed, there had been for me a meaning in life, and that the believing men around me, the majority of men, who are not corrupted by wealth, believed and lived an actual life, I doubted the correctness of the answer given me by the wisdom of men of my class, and I tried to understand the answer which Christianity gave to those who live a real life.

But, while I studied Christianity, I found, together with this source of the pure water of life, mud and ooze, which is illegitimately connected with it, and which alone concealed its purity from me; by the side of the profound Christian teaching I found connected with it the early teaching of the Jews and invalid doctrines of the church. I was in the position of a man who has received a bag of stinking mud, and who only after prolonged struggle and labor discovers that in this dirty bag there lie costly pearls, and yet he does not know what to do with the pearls that he has found mixed with the mud. I was in an agonized state, until I discovered that the pearls were not grown over with mud, but could be cleared of it.

I did not know the light, and thought that there was no truth in life, but, having convinced myself that men live by that light alone, I began to look for its source, and found it in the gospels, in spite of the false interpretations of the churches. And when I reached this source, I was blinded by the light, and received full answers to my questions as to the meaning of my life and of the life of other men, answers which fully agreed with those I knew of the other nations, and which, in my opinion, surpassed them all.

I was looking for an answer to the question of life, and not to the theological and historical questions, and so it did not make any difference to me whether Jesus Christ was a God, or not, or from whom the Holy Ghost descended, and so forth; and equally unimportant and unnecessary it was for me to know when and by whom the gospel or this or that parable was written, and whether it may be ascribed to Christ, or not. What was important to me was the light, which for eighteen hundred years has been illuminating humanity, and which has illuminated me; but what I should call this source of light, and what its materials are, and by whom it was lighted, were a matter of indifference to me.

And I began to look closely at this light and to discover everything that was opposed to it, and the farther I proceeded on this path, the more indubitable did the difference between truth and untruth become to me. In the beginning of my labor I had doubts and attempts at artificial explanations, but the farther I proceeded, the clearer and more undoubted did the matter become to me, and the more unquestionable the truth. I was in the position of a man who is picking up a statue that is broken in pieces. In the beginning there can be some doubt whether this or that piece is a part of the leg or the arm, but when the legs are put together, and the piece certainly does not belong to the leg, and when, besides, it fits in with another side piece and with its curves coincides with a lower part, there can be no doubt as to where it belongs. This I felt in proportion as my work proceeded, and if I am not insane, the same feeling will overcome the reader of the longer exposition of the Gospel, where each proposition is at the same time confirmed by philological considerations, and by variants, and by contexts, and by agreement with the fundamental idea.

The preface would have ended here, if the gospels were books that were revealed at the present time, if Christ's teaching had not been subject to the false interpretations of eighteen hundred years. But now, that we may understand the true teaching of Christ, as he himself must have understood it, it is necessary to recognize the chief causes of the false interpretations, which have distorted the teaching, and the chief methods employed by the false interpretations. The chief cause of those false interpretations, which have so distorted Christ's teaching that it is difficult to see under their thick crust, consists in this, that Paul, who did not properly understand Christ's teaching and did not know it as it was later expressed in the gospel of Matthew, connected it with the teaching of the Pharisaic tradition and so with all the teachings of the Old Testament. Paul is generally regarded as an apostle of the Gentiles, as a protestant apostle. Such he was indeed externally in respect to the circumcision, and so forth. But the doctrine of the tradition, of the connection of the Old Testament with the New, was introduced into Christianity by Paul, and this doctrine of the tradition, this principle of the tradition, was the chief cause of the distortion of the Christian teaching and of its misunderstanding.

From the time of Paul begins the Christian Talmud, which is called the doctrine of the church, and Christ's teaching becomes, not the one, divine, and full teaching, but one of the links of the chain of revelation, which begins with the beginning of the world and which lasts in the church up to the present time.

These false interpreters call Jesus a God; but the fact that they recognize him as a God does not cause them to ascribe a greater significance to the words and teachings, which are ascribed to God, than to the Pentateuch, the Psalms, the Acts of the Apostles, the Epistles, the Revelation, and even the Ecumenical Decrees and the writings of the Holy Fathers of the church.

These false interpreters do not admit any other understanding of the teaching of Jesus Christ than such as are in agreement with the preceding and the subsequent revelation, so that it is not their aim to explain the significance of Christ's preaching, but only to find the least contradictory meaning in the most diversified writings, the Pentateuch, the Psalms, the Gospels, the Acts, the Epistles, and everything which is regarded as Holy Scripture.

It is evident that with such a view of Christ's teaching the understanding of it is unthinkable. From this same false view results an endless diversity in the understanding of the Gospel.

Naturally there can be an endless number of such explanations, which have for their aim, not the truth, but the harmonization of what cannot be harmonized, that is, of the writings of the Old and the New Testaments, and there is a large number of them. And so, all that is necessary in order to acknowledge a certain harmonization as true, is to have recourse to external means, to miracles, to the descent of the Holy Ghost, and such like.

Different men have harmonized in their own way; but each in his harmonization affirms that his harmonization is the continued revelation of the Holy Ghost. Such are the epistles of Paul, the decrees of the councils, which begin with the phrase, "It pleased us and the Holy Ghost"; such are the decrees of the Popes, the synods, the Arians, the Paulicians, and all the false interpreters, who affirm that the Holy Ghost speaks through their mouths. All of them use the same crude method of confirming the truth of their harmonization by saying that their harmonization is not the fruit of their thoughts but a confirmation by the Holy Ghost.

Without entering into the analysis of the creeds themselves, each of which calls itself the true one, we cannot help but see that in their common method of recognizing the enormous quantity of the so-called Scriptures of the Old and the New Testaments as equally sacred lies the insurmountable, self-set obstacle to the understanding of Christ's teaching, and, also, that from this error results the possibility, and even the necessity, of endlessly diversified hostile sects.

Only the harmonization of an immense number of revelations can be endlessly diversified; but the interpretation of one person, considered as God, cannot lead to the evolution of sects. The teaching of God descended upon earth cannot be understood differently. If God descended upon earth to reveal the truth to men, then the least which he could do was to reveal it in such a way that all might understand it; and if he did not do so, he was not God; but if the divine truths are such that even God could not make them understandable to men, men certainly will not be able to do so.

If Jesus is not God, but a great man, his teaching can to a still lesser degree be the cause of sects. The teaching of a great man is great even because it is understandable and clearly enunciates what others have not enunciated clearly and intelligibly. What is not understandable in the teaching of a great man is not great, and so the teaching of a great man cannot bring forth sects. The teaching of a great man is great in that it unites all in the one truth.

Only the interpretation which affirms that it is the revelation of the Holy Ghost, that it is the only, true revelation, and that all the rest are false, produces hatred and the so-called sects. Let the sectarians of all the creeds say as much as they please that they do not condemn another creed, that they are praying for their union with the others, and that they do not hate them, they are not telling the truth. Never has any assertion of any dogma, beginning with Arius, resulted from anything but an accusation of falsehood against a contrary dogma. But the proclamation that the expression of a given dogma is divine, of the Holy Spirit, is the highest degree of pride and stupidity: of the highest pride, for nothing more haughty can be said than that the words which I utter God himself spoke through me, and of the highest stupidity, because nothing more stupid can be said than to reply to the assertion of a man that God is speaking through his mouth, "No, God is not speaking through your mouth, but through mine, and he says the very opposite of what your God has said." And yet it is precisely this that all the councils, all the symbols of faith, all the churches say, and from this has resulted all the evil which has been committed in the world in the name of religion. But, besides this external evil of the sects, there is also another important, internal defect, which is inherent in all the sects, and which invests them with an indistinct, indefinite, and unscrupulous character.

This defect consists in this, that, having recognized as the last revelation the Holy Ghost, who came down on the apostles and has passed over a specially chosen people, the false interpreters nowhere show directly, definitely, and conclusively wherein this revelation of the Holy Ghost consists, and yet continue to base their faith on this supposed revelation, and call it Christ's.

All the sectarians who acknowledge the revelation of the Holy Ghost, like the Mohammedans, assume three revelations: the Mohammedans have Moses, Jesus, and Mohammed; the church men have Moses, Jesus, and the Holy Ghost. But according to the Mohammedan religion Mohammed is the last prophet, the one who explained the meaning of the revelations of Moses and of Jesus, and he is the last revelation, which explains everything which precedes, and every righteous believer has this revelation before him. It is not so with the faith of the church: like the Mohammedan, it accepts three revelations—that of Moses, of Jesus, and of the Holy Ghost; but it does not call itself the Holy Ghost religion, from the name of the last revelation, but affirms that the basis of its religion is Christ's teaching. Thus they confess one doctrine, and ascribe the authority of this doctrine to Christ.

The Holy Ghost sectarians, who recognize as the last revelation—which explains everything which precedes—some Paul, others these or those councils, or the Popes, or the epistles of the patriarchs, or the private revelations of the Holy Ghost, ought to say so and call their faith by the name of him who had the last revelation, and if the last revelation is the fathers, or the epistle of the Eastern patriarchs, or the decrees of the Popes, or the syllabus, or Luther's or Filarét's catechism, they ought to say so and call their faith accordingly, for the last revelation, which explains everything which precedes, will always be the chief revelation.

But they do not do so and, instead, preach doctrines which are foreign to Christ, affirming that Christ preached these doctrines. Thus it turns out from their doctrine that Christ announced that he redeemed with his blood the human race which fell through Adam; that God is a Trinity; that the Holy Ghost descended on the apostles and passed through the laying on of hands to the clergy; that seven sacraments are needed for salvation, etc. It turns out that all this is the teaching of Christ, whereas there is not as much as a hint of all this in the teaching of Jesus. These false teachers ought to call their teaching and their faith the teaching and the faith of the Holy Ghost, and not of Christ, for we can call Christ's faith only the faith which recognizes Christ's revelation, which has come down to us in the gospels, as the last revelation, even as they must recognize it according to Christ's words, Call no one teacher but Christ.

One would think that this is so simple that no mention ought to be made of it; but, strange to say, up to the present men have not come to see this. Instead of directing all their attention to separating Christ's teaching from all the artificial, unjustifiable harmonization with the Old Testament, and with those arbitrary additions to his teaching, which have been made in the name of the Holy Ghost, all the efforts are directed toward finding the greatest possible meaning in this harmonization. And, strange to say, in this error two extreme camps meet: the camp of the churchmen and of the free thinking historians of Christianity. The first, by calling Jesus the second person of the Trinity, understand his teaching only in connection with the supposed revelations of the third person, which they find in the Old Testament, in the epistles of the councils, in the decrees of the fathers, and preach the strangest faiths, asserting that they are Christ's.

The second, who do not regard Jesus as God, understand the teaching in the same way, not as it may have been preached by him, but as it is understood by Paul and the other interpreters. While regarding Jesus as a man, and not as God, these interpreters deprive Jesus of the most legitimate human right of being responsible for his own words, and not for those of his false interpreters. While trying to explain the teaching of Jesus, these learned misinterpreters foist on Jesus what he never had in his mind to say. The representatives of this school of interpreters, beginning with the most popular among them, Renan, have not troubled themselves about sifting out of Christ's teaching that which Christ himself taught, and not that which his interpreters have lied about him; they have not tried to understand the teaching more profoundly than the churchmen, but attempt to understand the meaning of the appearance of Jesus and of the dissemination of his teaching from the events of his life and the conditions of his time.

One would, however, think that the historians ought not to make this mistake. The problem which they ought to solve is like this: eighteen hundred years ago there appeared a poor man who said so and so. He was flogged and hanged, and all forgot about him, as millions of similar incidents have been forgotten, and for two hundred years the world did not hear anything about him. But it turns out that some one had made a note of what he had said, and had told it to a second and a third person. And so it went on, until billions of wise and foolish men, of the learned and the unlearned, cannot get rid of the idea that this man, and no other, was God. How is such a remarkable phenomenon to be explained? The churchmen say that that was due to the fact that Jesus was really God. If so, everything is intelligible. But if he was not God, how are we to explain that this simple man was acknowledged by all to be God?

The learned men of this school carefully investigate all the details of the conditions of this man's life, without noticing that no matter how many details they may discover (in reality they have discovered nothing but what is given in Josephus Flavius and in the gospels), no matter how they may reconstruct Jesus' life down to the minutest details, and may find out what he ate and where he slept, the question as to why he and no one else had such an influence on people still remains without an answer. The answer is not this, in what circle Jesus lived, who educated him, and so forth, and still less, what was going on in Rome, and that the people were predisposed to superstitions, and so forth, but only in this, what this man preached that was so peculiar as to cause people to separate him from all the others and to recognize him as God at that time and even now.

One would think that if we want to understand this, the first thing which we must do is to try to understand the teaching of this man, to understand, of course, his own teaching, and not those coarse interpretations of his teachings which have been disseminated since his day. But this they do not do. These learned historians of Christianity were so glad to find that Jesus was not God, and they are so anxious to show that his teaching is not divine, and so not obligatory, that they forget that the more they prove this, that he was a simple man and his teaching not divine, the farther will they be from the understanding of the question which interests them. They strain all their powers to prove that he was a simple man and that, therefore, his teaching was not divine. If we wish clearly to see this remarkable aberration, we need only think of Renan. Havet naïvely affirms that *Jésus Christ n'avait rien de chrétien.* And Souris proves with enthusiasm that Christ was a coarse and stupid fellow.

The question is not to prove that Jesus was not God, and that, therefore, his teaching is not divine, and not that he was not a Catholic, but to understand wherein the teaching consisted, which has been so elevated and so dear to men that men have recognized the preacher of this teaching to be God. It is this that I have tried to do, and have done, at least so far as I am concerned. And this I offer now to my brethren.

If the reader belongs to the immense majority of cultured men, educated in the faith of the church, who have rejected it on account of its incompatibility with sound reason and with conscience (whether he has still left love and respect for the spirit of the Christian teaching, or, according to the proverb, being furious at the fleas has chucked the fur coat into the stove, that is, considers all Christianity a dangerous superstition), I beg such a reader to remember that what repels him and presents itself as a superstition is not Christ's teaching; that Christ cannot be blamed for that monstrous tradition which has been foisted on his teaching and has been given out as Christianity. We must study only Christ's teaching, as it has reached us, that is, those words and actions which are ascribed to Jesus, and which have a didactic significance.

Such a reader, in perusing my exposition, will find that Christianity is not a mixture of what is profound with what is base, not a superstition, but, on the contrary, a very strict, pure, and complete metaphysical and esthetical teaching, above which human reason has not yet risen, and in whose circle, though not conscious of it, all human activity is moving, whether political, scientific, poetical, or philosophic.

If the reader belongs to that insignificant minority of cultured men who keep the church faith, confessing it, not for external reasons, but for the sake of inward peace, I beg such a reader, before reading this, to decide in his soul the question as to what is dearer to him, spiritual peace, or truth. If it is peace, I ask him not to read this, but if it is truth, I beg him to remember that Christ's teaching, as expounded here, in spite of the sameness of name, is an entirely different teaching, and that, therefore, the relation of him who confesses the church faith to this exposition is the same as the relation of a Mohammedan to the preaching of Christianity; that the question for him is not whether the proposed teaching is in accord with his faith, or not, but only what teaching is more in accord with his reason and his heart, his church teaching, or the one teaching of Christ. The question for him is whether he wants to accept the new teaching, or prefers to remain in his faith.

But if the reader belongs to those men who externally profess the church faith and who value it, not because they believe in its truth, but from external considerations, because they consider this profession and the preaching of it profitable for themselves, let him remember that, no matter how many brethren of the faith they may have, no matter how strong they may be, on what thrones they may seat themselves, by what high names they may call themselves, they are not the accusers, but the accused, and not through me, but through Christ. Such readers must remember that there is no need for them to prove anything; that they have long ago said what they had to say; that if even they proved what they want to prove, they prove only what all the hundreds of mutually excluding church creeds have proved long ago; that they must not prove, but justify themselves. They must justify themselves for their blasphemy, by which they have assimilated the teaching of Jesus the God to the teachings of Ezdra, of the councils, of a Theophilactes, and have allowed themselves to interpret God's words wrongly and to change them on the basis of men's words; to justify themselves for slandering God, by burdening Jesus the God with all the superstition in their hearts and giving it out as the teaching of Jesus; to justify themselves for their rascality, with which they concealed the teaching of God, who came to give the good to the world and substituted for it their own Holy Ghost faith, and by this substitution have deprived billions of people of the good which Christ brought to men, and, instead of the peace and love, brought to them, have introduced into the world sects, condemnations, and rascalities of every kind, covering them up with the name of Christ.

For these readers there are only two ways out: humble repentance and renunciation of their lie, or prosecution of those who accuse them for what they have been doing.

If they do not renounce the lie, there is but one thing left for them to do: to persecute me, for which I, finishing this writing, am prepared with joy and with fear for my weakness.

INTRODUCTION

THE ANNOUNCEMENT OF GOOD ACCORDING TO MATTHEW, MARK, LUKE, AND JOHN.

Mark i. 1. THE BEGINNING OF THE ANNOUNCEMENT OF GOOD OF JESUS CHRIST, THE SON OF GOD.

THE AIM OF THE BOOK

John xx. 31. THIS IS WRITTEN THAT MEN MIGHT BELIEVE THAT JESUS CHRIST IS THE SON OF GOD, AND THAT BELIEVING THEY RECEIVE LIFE THROUGH WHAT HE HAS BEEN.

Luke i. 1. SINCE MANY HAVE ALREADY BEGUN TO TELL CONNECTEDLY OF THE THINGS WHICH HAVE HAPPENED AMONG US,

2. AS THE EYEWITNESSES AND EXECUTORS OF THE TEACHING HAVE TRANS-MITTED TO US;

3. I, TOO, DECIDED, HAVING LEARNED EVERYTHING CORRECTLY FROM THE VERY FIRST, TO WRITE TO YOU, IN ORDER, THEOPHILUS,

4. THAT YOU MIGHT FIND OUT THE REAL TRUTH OF THOSE INJUNCTIONS WHICH YOU HAVE BEEN TAUGHT.

THE COMPREHENSION

John i. 1. THE COMPREHENSION OF LIFE BECAME THE BEGINNING OF ALL. AND THE COMPREHENSION OF LIFE STOOD FOR GOD. AND THE COMPREHENSION OF LIFE BECAME GOD.

2. IT GREW TO BE THE BEGINNING OF EVERYTHING FOR GOD.

3. EVERYTHING WAS BORN THROUGH THE COMPREHENSION, AND WITHOUT THE COMPREHENSION IS NOT ANYTHING BORN OF THAT WHICH IS ALIVE AND LIVES.

4. IN IT THERE GREW TO BE LIFE, THE SAME AS, THE LIGHT OF MEN GREW TO BE LIFE.

5. JUST AS THE LIGHT SHINES IN THE DARKNESS, AND THE DARKNESS DOES NOT SWALLOW IT.

6. A MAN WAS SENT FROM GOD, WHOSE NAME WAS JOHN.

7. HE CAME FOR THE SHOWING, TO SHOW THE LIGHT OF COMPREHENSION, THAT ALL MEN MIGHT BELIEVE IN THE LIGHT OF THE COMPREHENSION.

8. HE HIMSELF WAS NOT THE LIGHT, BUT CAME ONLY TO SHOW THE LIGHT OF COMPREHENSION.

9. IT BECAME THE TRUE LIGHT, SUCH AS LIGHTS UP EVERY MAN WHO COMES INTO THE WORLD.

10. IT APPEARED IN THE WORLD, AND THE WORLD WAS BORN THROUGH IT, AND THE WORLD DID NOT KNOW IT.

11. IT APPEARED IN SEPARATE PEOPLE, AND THE SEPARATE PEOPLE DID NOT RECEIVE IT WITHIN THEM.

12. BUT TO ALL THOSE WHO UNDERSTOOD IT, IT GAVE THE POSSIBILITY OF BECOMING SONS OF GOD, THROUGH FAITH IN ITS MEANING;

13. THEY WERE GENERATED NOT FROM BLOOD, NOR FROM THE LUST OF FLESH, NOR FROM THE LUST OF MAN, BUT FROM GOD.

14. AND THE COMPREHENSION BECAME FLESH AND TOOK ITS ABODE AMONG US, AND WE SAW ITS TEACHING, AS OF HIM WHO IS OF THE SAME ORIGIN WITH THE FATHER—THE PERFECT TEACHING OF GODLINESS IN FACT.

15. JOHN SHOWS ABOUT HIM, AND CRIES, AND SAYS, THIS IS HE WHOM I SPOKE, WHO COMES AFTER ME WAS BORN BEFORE ME, FOR HE WAS THE FIRST.

16. FOR FROM ITS FULFILLMENT DID WE ALL GET GODLINESS IN PLACE OF GODLINESS.

17. BECAUSE THE LAW WAS GIVEN BY MOSES. GODLINESS IN FACT TOOK PLACE THROUGH JESUS CHRIST.

WHEREIN THE UNDERSTANDING OF JESUS CHRIST CONSISTED

John i. 18. NO ONE HAS EVER COMPREHENDED OR WILL EVER COMPREHEND GOD; THE ONE-BORN, BEING IN THE HEART OF THE FATHER, HE HAS POINTED OUT THE PATH.

TOLSTOY'S COMMENTARY

This announcement is written in order that men might believe that Jesus Christ is a son of God and that, by the very faith in the same which he was, they might receive life. No one has ever understood or ever will understand God. All we know about God, we know because we have the understanding, and so the true beginning of everything is the understanding. (What we call God is the understanding. The understanding is the beginning of everything—it is the true God.)

Nothing can exist without the understanding. Everything has originated through the understanding. In the understanding is the force of life. Even as the whole diversity of things exists for us the whole understanding of life is the beginning of everything.

In the world, life does not embrace everything. In the world, life appears as the light amidst the darkness. The light shines so long as it shines, and the darkness does not retain the light and remains the darkness. Even thus in the world, life appears through death, and death does not retain life and remains death.

The source of life, the understanding, was in the whole world and in each living man. But the living men, living only because the understanding was in them, did not understand that they originated from the understanding.

They did not understand that the understanding gave them the possibility of blending with it, since they were not living from the flesh, but from the understanding. By understanding this and believing in their sonhood to the understanding, men could have the true life. But men did not understand that, and the life in the world was like the light in the darkness.

God, the beginning of all beginnings, no one has ever understood, or ever will understand, but the life in the understanding has pointed out the path to him.

And so Jesus Christ, living among us, has declared the understanding in the flesh, in as much as life originated from the understanding and is one birth with it, just as the son originates from the father and is of one birth with him.

And looking at his life, we understood the complete teaching of the godliness in fact, because, on account of his perfection, we understood the new godliness in the place of the old. The law was given by Moses, but the godliness in fact originated through Jesus Christ.

No one has ever seen, or ever can see, God, but the son of God in man has pointed out the path to him.

CHAPTER ONE

THE INCARNATION OF THE UNDERSTANDING. THE BIRTH AND CHILDHOOD OF JESUS CHRIST

BIRTH

Matt. i. 18. THE BIRTH OF JESUS CHRIST WAS LIKE THIS: WHEN HIS MOTHER WAS BETROTHED TO JOSEPH BEFORE THEY CAME TOGETHER, SHE WAS FOUND TO BE PREGNANT.

19. JOSEPH, HER HUSBAND, WAS JUST: HE DID NOT WISH TO ARRAIGN HER, AND INTENDED TO SEND HER AWAY WITHOUT PUBLIC ANNOUNCEMENT.

20. BUT WHILE HE WAS THINKING OF THIS, HE DREAMED THAT A MESSENGER FROM GOD HAD APPEARED TO HIM AND WAS SAYING, FEAR NOT TO RECEIVE MARY, THY WIFE, FOR WHAT WILL BE BORN OF HER WILL BE BORN OF THE HOLY GHOST.

21. AND SHE WILL BRING FORTH A SON AND WILL CALL HIM JESUS, WHICH MEANS THE SAVIOUR, FOR HE WILL SAVE PEOPLE FROM THEIR SINS.

24. WHEN JOSEPH AWOKE, HE DID AS THE ANGEL OF GOD HAD COMMANDED HIM TO DO, AND RECEIVED HER AS HIS WIFE.

25. AND HAD NOTHING TO DO WITH HER TILL SHE HAD BROUGHT FORTH HER FIRST SON, AND HE CALLED HIM JESUS.

CHILDHOOD

Luke ii. 40. THE BOY GREW AND BECAME MANLY IN SPIRIT, AND HIS REASON IMPROVED. AND THE LOVE OF GOD WAS UPON HIM.

41. HIS PARENTS WENT TO JERUSALEM EVERY YEAR FOR THE FEAST OF THE PASSOVER.

42. AND WHEN HE WAS TWELVE YEARS OLD, HIS PARENTS WENT TO ATTEND THE FEAST IN JERUSALEM, AS WAS THEIR CUSTOM.

43. WHEN THE FEAST WAS OVER AND THEY STARTED HOME, THE BOY JESUS TARRIED BEHIND IN JERUSALEM; AND JOSEPH AND HIS MOTHER DID NOT NOTICE IT.

44. THEY THOUGHT THAT HE WAS WITH HIS COMPANIONS, AND THEY WENT A DAY'S JOURNEY, AND THEY SOUGHT HIM AMONG THEIR KINSFOLK AND ACQUAINTANCES.

45. AND THEY DID NOT FIND HIM AND RETURNED TO JERUSALEM TO FIND HIM.

46. AND THEY FOUND HIM AFTER AWHILE IN THE TEMPLE: HE WAS SITTING AMIDST THE TEACHERS, ASKING THEM QUESTIONS, AND LISTENING TO THEM.

47. AND ALL THAT HEARD HIM WERE ASTONISHED AT HIS UNDERSTANDING AND AT HIS SPEECHES.

48. HIS PARENTS SAW HIM AND WERE SURPRISED, AND HIS MOTHER SAID TO HIM, SON, WHAT HAST THOU DONE TO US? THY FATHER AND I HAVE BEEN WORRYING AND LOOKING FOR THEE.

49. AND HE SAID TO THEM, WHY ARE YOU LOOKING FOR ME? DO YOU NOT KNOW THAT I MUST BE IN MY FATHER'S HOUSE?

50. BUT THEY DID NOT UNDERSTAND WHAT HE WAS SAYING TO THEM.

51. AND HE WENT UP TO THEM, AND WENT WITH THEM TO NAZARETH, AND OBEYED THEM. AND HIS MOTHER TOOK ALL HIS WORDS TO HEART.

52. AND JESUS INCREASED IN STATURE AND UNDERSTANDING, AND WAS IN FAVOUR WITH GOD AND MAN.

Luke iii. 23. AND JESUS WAS ABOUT THIRTY YEARS OF AGE, AND MEN THOUGHT THAT HE WAS JOSEPH'S SON.

JOHN THE BAPTIST

Mark i. 4. JOHN THE BAPTIST APPEARED IN THE PRAIRIE AND PREACHED BATHING AS A SIGN OF THE CHANGE OF LIFE, AS A SIGN OF THE LIBERATION FROM ERROR.

Matt. iii. 4. JOHN'S RAIMENT WAS OF CAMEL'S HAIR, AND HE WAS GIRDED WITH A LEATHERN GIRDLE. HE FED ON LOCUSTS AND HERBS.

Mark i. 1. THE BEGINNING OF THE ANNOUNCEMENT OF GOOD OF JESUS CHRIST THE SON OF GOD WAS:

2. AS IT IS WRITTEN IN THE PROPHETS, I SEND MY MESSENGER TO PREPARE MY WAY.

3. A VOICE CALLS TO YOU. IN THE WILDERNESS PREPARE YE THE WAY OF THE LORD, MAKE HIS PATHS EASY.

Luke iii. 5. SO THAT EVERY HOLLOW SHALL BE MADE EVEN, AND EVERY HILL AND MOUND SHALL BE BROUGHT LOW; SO THAT ALL THE CROOKED PLACES SHALL BE MADE STRAIGHT, AND THE MOUNDS SHALL BE MADE A SMOOTH ROAD.

6. AND THE WHOLE WORLD SHALL SEE THE SALVATION OF GOD.

Matt. iii. 2. JOHN SAID, COME TO YOUR SENSES, FOR THE KINGDOM OF HEAVEN IS HERE.

THE CONCOURSE OF PEOPLE TO BE BAPTIZED BY JOHN

Matt. iii. 5. AND TO JOHN CAME THE PEOPLE FROM JERUSALEM AND FROM THE VILLAGES ALONG THE JORDAN, AND FROM THE WHOLE COUNTRY OF JUDEA.

6. AND HE BATHED IN THE JORDAN ALL THOSE WHO CONFESSED THEIR ERRORS.

Luke iii. 7. AND HE SAID TO THE PEOPLE, O TRIBE OF VIPERS! WHO TAUGHT YOU TO FLEE FROM THE APPROACHING WILL OF GOD?

8. BRING FRUITS WHICH ARE IN CONFORMITY WITH THE CHANGE.

9. THE AXE IS ALREADY LAID UPON THE ROOT OF THE TREE, AND IF A TREE DOES NOT BRING FORTH GOOD FRUIT, IT IS CUT DOWN AND BURNT UP.

10. AND THE PEOPLE ASKED HIM, WHAT SHALL WE DO?

11. HE ANSWERED THEM, HE THAT HAS TWO COATS, LET HIM GIVE ONE TO HIM WHO HAS NONE; AND HE THAT HAS BREAD, LET HIM DO LIKEWISE.

12. THE TAX COLLECTORS CAME TO HIS BATHING, AND SAID TO HIM, TEACHER, WHAT SHALL WE DO?

13. JOHN SAID TO THEM, EXACT NO MORE THAN IS YOUR RIGHT.

14. AND THE SOLDIERS ASKED, WHAT SHALL WE DO? AND HE SAID, TROUBLE NO MAN, AND ACCUSE NONE FALSELY. BE CONTENT WITH YOUR CONDITION.

Luke iii. 18. AND, CALLING UP THE PEOPLE, HE ANNOUNCED MANY OTHER THINGS ABOUT THE TRUE GOOD.

Matt. iii. 11. AND HE CALLED OUT TO THE PEOPLE, AND SAID, I BATHE YOU IN WATER IN SIGN OF THE RENOVATION, BUT HE IS COMING WHO IS MIGHTIER THAN I AND OF WHOM I AM NOT WORTHY.

Mark i. 8. I WASH YOU IN WATER, BUT HE WILL PURIFY YOU BY THE SPIRIT (AND FIRE).

Matt. iii. 12. THE WHISK IS IN HIS HAND, AND HE WILL CLEAN HIS FLOOR. HE WILL GATHER THE WHEAT, AND WILL BURN THE CHAFF.

13. AND JESUS WAS PURIFIED BY JOHN.

CHRIST'S TEMPTATION IN THE WILDERNESS

Luke iv. 1. THEN JESUS BEING FULL OF THE SPIRIT WENT FROM THE JORDAN INTO THE WILDERNESS,

2. AND THERE THE TEMPTER TEMPTED HIM.

Mark i. 13. AND JESUS WAS IN THAT WILDERNESS FORTY DAYS, AND ATE NOTHING, AND GREW THIN.

Matt. iv. 3. AND THE TEMPTER CAME TO HIM, AND SAID, IF THOU ART A SON OF GOD, COMMAND THAT THESE STONES BE CHANGED INTO BREAD.

4. BUT JESUS ANSWERED, IT IS WRITTEN, MAN DOES NOT LIVE BY BREAD ALONE, BUT BY EVERYTHING WHICH PROCEEDS OUT OF THE MOUTH OF GOD (BY THE SPIRIT).

Luke iv. 9. THE TEMPTER BROUGHT JESUS CHRIST TO JERUSALEM, AND SET HIM ON THE ROOF OF A SYNAGOGUE, AND SAID TO HIM, IF THOU ART A SON OF GOD, CAST THYSELF DOWN FROM HERE:

10. FOR IT IS WRITTEN THAT HE WILL CHARGE HIS MESSENGERS IN REGARD TO THEE, TO KEEP THEE:

11. AND THEY SHALL CATCH THEE IN THEIR ARMS, SO THAT THY FOOT MAY NOT STRIKE AGAINST A STONE.

12. AND JESUS ANSWERED HIM, AND SAID, BECAUSE IT IS SAID, THOU SHALT NOT TEMPT THY GOD.

5. AND AGAIN THE TEMPTER TOOK HIM TO A HIGH MOUNTAIN, AND PRESENTED TO HIM ALL THE KINGDOMS OF THE EARTH IN A TWINKLING OF THE EYE.

6. AND SAID TO HIM, I WILL GIVE THEE ALL THIS POWER AND THEIR GLORY, FOR THEY ARE DELIVERED TO ME, AND TO WHOMSOEVER I WILL, I GIVE THEM.

7. IF THOU WILT WORSHIP ME, ALL SHALL BE THINE.

8. THEN JESUS ANSWERED, AND SAID, GO AWAY (EVIL) FOE! IT IS WRITTEN, THOU SHALT WORSHIP THE LORD, AND FOR HIM ALONE SHALT THOU WORK.

13. THEN THE TEMPTER DEPARTED FROM HIM FOR A TIME,

Matt. iv. 11. AND GOD'S POWER CAME AND SERVED HIM.

Luke iv. 14. AND JESUS RETURNED IN THE POWER OF THE SPIRIT TO GALILEE.

BEGINNING OF CHRIST'S PREACHING

Matt. iv. 17. FROM THAT TIME JESUS BEGAN TO PROCLAIM

Mark i. 14. THE KINGDOM OF GOD.

15. HE SAID, THE TIME HAS COME, THE KINGDOM OF GOD IS HERE. RENOVATE YOURSELVES AND BELIEVE IN THE ANNOUNCEMENT OF THE TRUE GOOD.

CHRIST'S FIRST DISCIPLES

John i. 36. AND JOHN AGAIN CAME TOGETHER WITH JESUS AND SAID ABOUT HIM, THIS IS THE LAMB OF GOD.

37. TWO OF JOHN'S DISCIPLES, HEARING THESE WORDS, FOLLOWED JESUS.

38. JESUS TURNED AROUND AND, SEEING THAT THEY FOLLOWED HIM, SAID TO THEM, WHAT ARE YOU LOOKING FOR? THEY SAID, RABBI (WHICH MEANS MASTER), WHERE DWELLEST THOU?

39. HE SAID TO THEM, COME AND SEE. THEY CAME AND SAW WHERE HE DWELT, AND THEY REMAINED WITH HIM A DAY.

40. ONE OF THESE TWO WAS ANDREW, SIMON PETER'S BROTHER.

41. HE LOOKED UP HIS BROTHER SIMON, AND SAID, WE HAVE FOUND THE MESSIAH, WHICH MEANS, THE CHOSEN ONE OF GOD.

42. AND HE WAS BROUGHT TO JESUS. JESUS LOOKED AT HIM, AND SAID, THOU ART SIMON THE SON OF JOHN. THOU SHALT BE CALLED PETER, WHICH MEANS, A ROCK.

Mark i. 19. AND WHEN HE WENT A DISTANCE AWAY FROM THERE, HE SAW JAMES THE SON OF ZEBEDEE, AND JOHN HIS BROTHER: THEY WERE IN A SHIP MENDING THEIR NETS.

20. AND HE CALLED THEM AT ONCE: AND THEY LEFT THEIR FATHER ZEBE-DEE IN THE SHIP WITH THE HIRED SERVANTS.

John i. 43. LATER, BEFORE GOING TO GALILEE, JESUS MET ALSO PHILIP, AND SAID TO HIM, COME WITH ME.

44. PHILIP WAS OF BETHSAIDA, OF THE SAME VILLAGE WITH PETER AND ANDREW.

45. PHILIP FOUND NATHANAEL, AND SAID TO HIM, WE HAVE FOUND THE ONE MOSES WROTE ABOUT IN THE LAW—IT IS JESUS OF NAZARETH.

46. AND NATHANAEL SAID TO HIM, CAN ANY GOOD THING COME OUT OF NAZARETH? PHILIP SAID TO HIM, GO AND SEE FOR THYSELF.

47. WHEN NATHANAEL CAME AND JESUS HAD A TALK WITH HIM, HE SAID TO HIM, NOW HERE IS A MAN IN WHOM THERE IS NO GUILE.

49. AND NATHANAEL SAID TO HIM, THOU ART A SON OF GOD; THOU ART THE KING OF ISRAEL.

51. AND HE SAID, THOU WILT FIND OUT SOMETHING MORE IMPORTANT THAN THAT, FOR I TELL YOU THE WHOLE TRUTH: YOU SHALL NOW FIND OUT THAT HEAVEN IS OPEN AND THE POWERS OF GOD WILL DESCEND TO THE SON OF MAN AND WILL ASCEND AGAIN TO HEAVEN.

JESUS CHRIST PREACHING IN NAZARETH

Luke iv. 16. AND JESUS CAME TO NAZARETH, WHERE HE HAD BEEN BROUGHT UP. AND, ACCORDING TO THE CUSTOM OF THE HOLIDAY, HE WENT INTO AN ASSEMBLY, AND BEGAN TO READ.

17. AND THEY GAVE HIM THE BOOK OF THE PROPHET ISAIAH. AND HE OPENED IT AT THE PLACE WHERE IT WAS WRITTEN,

18. THE SPIRIT OF THE ETERNAL ONE IS UPON ME: HE HAS ORDAINED ME TO ANNOUNCE THE GOOD TO THE UNFORTUNATE, THE BROKEN-HEARTED, TO PROCLAIM FREEDOM TO THOSE WHO ARE BOUND, AND LIGHT TO THE BLIND, AND SALVATION AND REST TO THOSE WHO ARE WEARY.

19. TO ANNOUNCE TO ALL THE TIME OF GOD'S MERCY.

20. AND CLOSING THE BOOK AND GIVING IT BACK TO THE SERVANT, HE SAT DOWN. AND THE EYES OF ALL WERE FASTENED ON HIM.

21. AND HE BEGAN TO SPEAK TO THEM, NOW IS THE SCRIPTURE FULFILLED IN YOUR EYES.

22. AND ALL WONDERED AT THE GRACIOUSNESS OF HIS WORDS, AND SAID, IS NOT THIS JOSEPH'S SON?

Mark vi. 3. IS NOT THIS THE CARPENTER?

Matt. xiii. 55. AND IS NOT THIS THE CARPENTER'S SON? IS NOT HIS MOTHER CALLED MARIAM? AND HIS BROTHERS JAMES, JOSES, SIMON, AND JUDAS?

Luke iv. 23. AND HE SAID TO THEM, OF COURSE, YOU SAY, PHYSICIAN, HEAL THYSELF.

Matt. xiii. 57. BECAUSE NO PROPHET IS UNDERSTOOD IN HIS OWN COUNTRY.

Matt. iv. 13. AND FROM NAZARETH HE WENT TO CAPERNAUM.

Mark i. 21. AND STRAIGHTWAY ON THE SABBATH HE WENT INTO THE ASSEMBLY AND BEGAN TO TEACH.

22. AND THEY WERE DELIGHTED WITH HIS TEACHING, FOR HE TAUGHT THEM FREELY, AND NOT AS THE SCRIBES.

TOLSTOY'S COMMENTARY

The understanding was made incarnate in Jesus Christ. Jesus Christ announced the true good to men. But the birth of Jesus Christ was as follows. His mother Mary was betrothed to Joseph; but before they began to live together as husband and wife, Mary turned out to be with child. Joseph was a good man and did not wish to disgrace her, so he accepted her as his wife. And he had no relations with her until she bore her first son, whom she called Jesus. And the boy grew and became manly and was intelligent above his years.

Here is what happened with him in his childhood. Jesus was twelve years old, when Mary went with Joseph to Jerusalem to celebrate a holiday, and they took the boy with them. The holiday was over, and they went home and forgot about the boy. Then they thought of him, and it occurred to them that he might have walked off with some children, and they asked about him along the road. The boy could not be found, and they returned to Jerusalem after him. Not until two days later did they find him in a synagogue, and he was sitting with the teachers and asking them questions and listening. And all marvelled at his intellect.

His mother saw him, and said, What hast thou done with us? Thy father and I have been worrying and looking for thee.

And he said to them, Where did you look for me? Do you not know that the son must be looked for in the house of his father?

And they did not understand his words. They did not understand that he, knowing that he had no carnal father, regarded God as his Father. After that Jesus lived with his mother and obeyed her in everything, and he increased in stature and understanding, and was in favour with God and man.

Thus he lived until he was thirty years of age. And all thought that Jesus was Joseph's son.

This is the way Jesus began to announce the good. The prophets had predicted that God was to come into the world. Prophet Malachi had said, My messenger will come before me to prepare the way for me.

Prophet Isaiah had said, A voice is calling to you: Prepare the way for the Lord in the wilderness, make his path even; let there be no hollows, nor mounds, nothing high, and nothing low. Then God will be among you and all will find their salvation.

In accordance with these words of the prophets, a new prophet, John, made his appearance in the time of Jesus Christ. John dwelt in the prairie of Judea on the Jordan. His raiment was of camel's hair, girded with a leathern girdle, and he fed on tree bark and on herbs. He called the people to a new life. And they confessed their errors to him, and he bathed them in the Jordan as a sign that their errors were corrected. He said to all, If you have observed that you shall not escape the will of God, be renovated. And if you wish to be renovated let it be seen from your works that you have changed. John said, Heretofore the prophets have said that God will come. I say to you that God has already come. He said, I purify you with water, but after me the one who is mightier than I will purify you with the spirit. When he comes he will purify you, as the master cleans his threshing-floor: the wheat he will gather, but the chaff he will burn. If a tree does not bring forth good fruit, it is cut down and burnt up. And the axe is already laid upon the root of the tree.

And the people asked him, What shall we do? He answered, He that has two coats, let him give one to him who has none; and he who has food, let him give it to him who has none.

Tax collectors came to him, and asked him, What shall we do? He said, Exact no more than is your right.

And the soldiers asked, What shall we do? He said, Offend no one. Do not cheat. Be satisfied with what is given you.

And many other things he proclaimed to the people about what is the present good.

Jesus was then thirty years old. He came to the Jordan to John, and heard his preaching about God's coming, about the necessity of being renovated, about people being purified by water, and about their future purification by the spirit, when God would come. Jesus did not know his carnal father and regarded God as his Father. He believed in John's preaching, and said to himself, If it is true that God is my Father, and I am a son of God, and if what John says is true, I need only to purify myself by the spirit that God may come to me.

And Jesus went into the wilderness to test the truth of his being a son of God, and of God's coming to him. He went into the wilderness and there lived for a long time without food and drink, and finally grew thin. And then doubt came over him, and he said to himself, Thou sayest that thou art a spirit, a son of God, and that God will come to thee, and yet thou art tormented because thou hast no bread, and God does not come to thee: consequently thou art no spirit, no son of God. But he said to himself, My flesh craves for bread, but not bread is needed for life: man lives not by bread, but by the spirit, by what is from God.

But hunger kept tormenting him. And he was overcome by another doubt, and he said to himself, Thou sayest that thou art a son of God, and that God will come to thee, and yet thou sufferest and canst not make an end to thy sufferings. And he imagined that he was standing on a roof of the temple, and the thought occurred to him, If I am a spirit, a son of God, I shall not be killed if I cast myself down from the temple, but an invisible power will preserve and sustain me, and will free me from all evil. Why should I not cast myself down, so as to cease suffering hunger? But he said to himself, Why should I tempt God whether he is with me or not? If I tempt him, I do not believe in him and he is not with me. God the spirit gives me life, and so in life, the spirit is always within me. And I cannot tempt him. I may stop eating, but I cannot kill myself, because I feel the spirit within me. But hunger continued to torment him. And it occurred to him, If I must not tempt God by casting myself down from the temple, I must not tempt him by starving when I want to eat. I must not deprive myself of all the appetites of the flesh. They are given to all men. And he imagined he saw all the kingdoms of earth and all men, as they lived and worked for the flesh, expecting a reward from it. And he thought, They work for the flesh, and the flesh gives them all which they have. If I shall work for it, the same will happen with me. But he said to himself, My God is not flesh, but spirit; by him I live, him I know always, him alone I worship, for him alone I work, and from him I expect my reward.

Then the temptation left him, and the spirit renovated him, and he knew that God had come to him and was always in him, and, having learned that, he returned to Galilee in the strength of the spirit. From that time on, having learned the power of the spirit, he began to announce the presence of God. He said, The time has come, renovate yourselves, believe in the announcement of the good.

From the wilderness Jesus went to John, and was with him.

When Jesus went away from John, John said of him, He is the true son of God (the chosen one). Two of John's disciples, hearing these words, left their old teacher and followed Jesus. Jesus saw that they were walking behind him, and so he stopped, and said, What do you want?

Teacher, we wish to be with thee and to learn thy teaching. He said, Come with me, and I will tell you everything. They went with him, and remained with him the whole day, staying until the tenth hour.

One of these disciples was called Andrew. And Andrew had a brother Simon. Having listened to Jesus, Andrew went to his brother Simon, and said to him, We have found the chosen one of God. Andrew took

Simon with him, and brought him to Jesus. This brother of Andrew Jesus called Peter, which means a stone. And these two brothers became the disciples of Jesus.

And Jesus walked on with his two disciples. After they had gone a distance, Jesus saw some fishermen in a ship. Those were Zebedee the father with hired servants and with two sons, James and John. They were sitting and mending their nets. Jesus began to speak with James and with John, and James and John left their father with the hired servants in the ship and went with Jesus and became his disciples.

Later, just before entering Galilee, Jesus met Philip, and he called him. Philip was of Bethsaida, of the same village with Peter and Andrew. When Philip recognized Jesus, he went to find his brother Nathanael, to whom he said, We have found the chosen one of God, of whom Moses has written, He is Jesus, the son of Joseph, of Nazareth. Nathanael was surprised to hear that the chosen one was from a neighboring village, and he said, Brother, it is queer that a messenger of God should come from Nazareth. Philip said, Come with me to him, and thou shalt see and hear for thyself. Nathanael agreed to it and went with his brother and met Jesus. When he heard him, he said to him, Yes, now I see that it is true that thou art the son of God and the King of Israel.

Jesus said to him, Thou wilt learn what is more important than this. Thou wilt learn that the kingdom of God has come, and so I tell you truly that the divine power will descend to all men, and from them will emanate the divine power. From now on God will no longer be separate from men, but men will blend with God.

And from the wilderness Jesus went to his home in Nazareth. And on a holiday he went, as usual, into an assembly and began to read. And they gave him the book of the prophet Isaiah. He unrolled it and began to read. In the book it was written, The spirit of the Lord is in me: he has chosen me to announce the good to the unfortunate and the broken-hearted, to proclaim freedom, light to the blind, and salvation and rest to the weary, to announce to all the time of the salvation, of God's mercy. He closed the book and gave it to the servant, and sat down, and all waited to hear what he would say. And he said, Now is the Scripture fulfilled in your eyes. God is in the world. The kingdom of God has come, and all the unfortunate, the broken-hearted, the blind, the weary—all shall receive salvation.

And many wondered at the goodness of his speech. And some said, But he is a carpenter and the son of a carpenter. And his mother is called

Mariam, and his brothers, James, Simon, Judas, and Joses, and we know them all: they are as poor as we are. And he said to them, No doubt you think that because I say that there are no longer any unfortunate and weary, and I have a poor father and mother and brothers, I am telling an untruth, and that I ought to make them happy. If you think so, you do not understand what I am saying. And thus, a prophet is never understood in his own country. And Jesus went to Capernaum, and on a Sabbath entered an assembly and began to teach. And all the people marvelled at his teaching, because his teaching was quite different from the teaching of the scribes. The scribes taught the law, which must be obeyed, and Jesus taught that all men were free.

CHAPTER TWO

GENERAL REMARK. THE NEW WORSHIP IN THE SPIRIT BY WORKS. THE REJECTION OF THE JEWISH GOD

THE ABOLITION OF THE LAW OF THE SABBATH

Luke vi. 1. HE HAPPENED ON A SABBATH TO CROSS THE CORN FIELDS; AND HIS DISCIPLES PLUCKED THE EARS OF CORN AND RUBBED THEM IN THEIR HANDS AND ATE THEM.

2. AND A FEW OF THE ORTHODOX SAW THAT AND SAID TO THEM, WHY DO YOU DO THAT WHICH OUGHT NOT TO BE DONE ON A SABBATH?

Matt. xii. 6. I TELL YOU, HERE IS SOMETHING WHICH IS MORE IMPORTANT THAN EXTERNAL HOLINESS.

7. IF YOU KNEW WHAT IT MEANS, I WILL HAVE LOVE FOR MEN, AND NOT SACRIFICES, YOU WOULD NOT BE CONDEMNING THE INNOCENT.

Mark ii. 27. AND HE SAID TO THEM, THE SABBATH WAS MADE FOR MAN, AND NOT MAN FOR THE SABBATH.

28. THEREFORE MAN IS LORD OF THE SABBATH.

Luke xiii. 10. JESUS HAPPENED TO BE TEACHING IN ONE OF THE ASSEMBLIES, AND IT WAS A SABBATH.

11. AND A WOMAN WAS THERE, AND A SPIRIT OF INFIRMITY HAD BEEN IN HER FOR EIGHTEEN YEARS.

12. JESUS SAW HER, AND CALLED HER, AND SAID, WOMAN, THOU ART FREED FROM THY INFIRMITY.

14. THE ELDER OF THE ASSEMBLY GREW ANGRY BECAUSE JESUS WAS PRAC-TICING ON THE SABBATH, AND SAID TO THE PEOPLE, THERE ARE SIX DAYS IN THE WEEK TO WORK IN, SO PRACTICE IN THOSE SIX DAYS, AND NOT ON THE SABBATH.

Luke xiv. 3. AND JESUS TURNED TO THE LEARNED ORTHODOX, AND ASKED, IS IT NOT LAWFUL TO HELP PEOPLE ON THE SABBATH?

4. AND THEY DID NOT KNOW WHAT TO SAY.

Luke xiii. 15. AND JESUS SAID TO THEM, HYPOCRITES! DOES NOT EACH ONE OF YOU ON THE SABBATH UNTIE HIS OX OR HIS ASS FROM THE STALL, AND LEAD HIM AWAY TO BE WATERED?

16. WHY, THEN, IS THIS WOMAN NOT TO BE HELPED?

Luke xiv. 6. AND THEY COULD NOT ANSWER HIM THIS.

Luke xiv. 5. AND AGAIN HE SAID, IF A SHEEP OF YOURS FALLS INTO A PIT, WILL YOU NOT PULL IT OUT AT ONCE, EVEN THOUGH IT BE A SABBATH?

Matt. xii. 12. BUT A MAN IS MUCH BETTER THAN A SHEEP. HE SAID, FOR THIS REASON IT IS NECESSARY TO DO WELL ON THE SABBATH.

THE CALLING OF MATTHEW

Matt. ix. 9. ONE TIME JESUS SAW A MAN SITTING ON THE ROAD AND COL-LECTING TAXES. THAT MAN'S NAME WAS MATTHEW, AND JESUS SAID TO HIM, FOLLOW ME. AND HE GOT UP, AND FOLLOWED HIM.

10. AND MATTHEW ENTERTAINED JESUS. AND IT HAPPENED THAT WHEN JESUS WAS SITTING IN HIS HOUSE, THERE CAME OTHER TAX COLLECTORS AND THOSE WHO HAD GONE ASTRAY, AND THEY SAT WITH JESUS AND HIS DISCIPLES.

THE DESTRUCTION OF THE RITES

Matt. ix. 11. AND THE LEARNED ORTHODOX SAW IT, AND SAID TO HIS DIS-
CIPLES, WHY DOES YOUR TEACHER EAT WITH TAX COLLECTORS AND WITH
THOSE WHO HAVE GONE ASTRAY?

Mark ii. 17. JESUS HEARD IT, AND SAID, NOT THOSE WHO ARE WELL, BUT
THOSE WHO ARE ILL NEED A PHYSICIAN. I DO NOT WISH TO CALL THE
ORTHODOX, BUT THOSE WHO HAVE GONE ASTRAY TO REPENTANCE.

Matt. ix. 13. GO AND LEARN WHAT IS MEANT BY, I WANT LOVE TOWARD
MEN, AND NOT SACRIFICES.

Mark vii. 1. AND THERE CAME TOGETHER AT HIS HOUSE ORTHODOX PEO-
PLE, AND SOME OF THEM WERE LEARNED, WHO CAME FROM JERUSALEM.

2. AND WHEN THEY SAW HIS DISCIPLES EAT BREAD WITH UNCLEAN, THAT
IS, WITH UNWASHED HANDS, THEY BEGAN TO CURSE.

3. FOR WITHOUT WASHING THEIR HANDS THEY DO NOT EAT WITH THE
HANDS, HOLDING THE TRADITION OF THE ELDERS.

4. NOR DO THEY EAT WHEN THEY COME FROM THE MARKET, UNLESS THEY
WASH THEIR HANDS. AND THEY KEEP MANY OTHER COMMANDMENTS,
SUCH AS THE WASHING OF DISHES, POTS, AND PANS.

5. FOR THAT REASON THE LEARNED ORTHODOX ASKED HIM, WHY DO NOT
THY DISCIPLES HOLD TO THE TRADITION OF THE FOREFATHERS, BUT EAT
BREAD WITH UNWASHED HANDS?

6. AND HE SAID TO THEM IN REPLY, WELL HAS ISAIAH SAID OF YOU HYPO-
CRITES, AS IT IS WRITTEN, THESE PEOPLE HONOR ME WITH THEIR MOUTHS,
BUT THEIR HEARTS ARE FAR FROM ME.

7. THEY WORSHIP ME BADLY, TEACHING DOCTRINES AND COMMANDMENTS
OF MEN.

8. YOU LAY ASIDE THE COMMANDMENT OF GOD, AND HOLD THE ENACT-
MENTS OF MEN, THE WASHING OF CUPS AND GLASSES, AND YOU DO MANY
OTHER SUCH THINGS.

9. AND JESUS SAID TO THEM, YOU HAVE READILY REJECTED THE COMMAND-MENT OF GOD, THAT YOU MAY KEEP YOUR OWN DECREE.

10. MOSES HAS TOLD YOU, HONOR THY FATHER AND THY MOTHER, AND, WHOSOEVER CURSES FATHER OR MOTHER, LET HIM DIE.

11. BUT YOU THINK THAT IF A MAN SAYS, CORBAN (WHICH MEANS, A GIFT TO GOD), THAT BY WHICH THOU MIGHTEST PROFIT BY ME,

12. HIM YOU NO LONGER PERMIT TO DO ANYTHING FOR HIS FATHER OR MOTHER.

13. YOU DESTROY THE WORD OF GOD BY THAT TRADITION OF YOURS, WHICH YOU HAVE DELIVERED. AND YOU DO MANY SUCH THINGS.

14. AND HE CALLED TOGETHER ALL THE PEOPLE, AND SAID, LISTEN TO ME EVERYONE OF YOU, AND UNDERSTAND.

15. THERE IS NOTHING WHICH, ENTERING MAN, CAN DEFILE HIM; BUT WHAT COMES OUT OF HIM WILL DEFILE A MAN.

16. IF YOU HAVE EARS TO HEAR, THEN UNDERSTAND!

17. WHEN HE WENT AWAY FROM THE PEOPLE INTO THE HOUSE, THE DIS-CIPLES ASKED HIM CONCERNING THE PARABLE.

18. AND HE SAID TO THEM, HAVE YOU NOT UNDERSTOOD IT? DO YOU NOT KNOW THAT NOTHING THAT ENTERS MAN FROM WITHOUT CAN DEFILE HIM?

19. BECAUSE IT ENTERS NOT HIS HEART, BUT HIS BELLY, AND GOES OUT THROUGH THE BACK, PURGING ALL FOOD.

20. BUT THAT WHICH COMES OUT OF MAN CANNOT HELP BUT DEFILE HIM.

21. FOR FROM THE HEART OF MEN PROCEED EVIL THOUGHTS, FORNICA-TION, LECHERY, MURDERS,

22. STEALING, SELFISHNESS, DECEPTION, IMPUDENCE, ENVIOUS EYES, CAL-UMNY, PRIDE, FOOLISHNESS.

23. ALL THESE EVIL THINGS COME FROM WITHIN, AND DEFILE THE MAN.

THE DESTRUCTION OF THE EXTERNAL TEMPLE

John ii. 13. AND THE JEWISH PASSOVER WAS AT HAND, AND JESUS WENT TO JERUSALEM.

14. AND HE SAW THEM SELL OXEN, SHEEP, AND DOVES IN THE TEMPLE, AND THE CHANGERS WERE SITTING THERE AND CHANGING MONEY.

15. AND HE PLAITED A WHIP OUT OF ROPES, AND DROVE OUT OF THE TEM-PLE THE SHEEP AND THE OXEN, AND SCATTERED THE CHANGERS' MONEY, AND THREW DOWN THE TABLES OF THE DOVE SELLERS.

16. AND HE SAID, TAKE THESE THINGS AWAY FROM HERE, AND DO NOT IMAGINE THAT A MARKET CAN BE A HOUSE OF MY FATHER

Mark xi. 16. AND HE DID NOT SUFFER ANY ARTICLES TO BE CARRIED THROUGH THE TEMPLE.

17. AND HE INSTRUCTED THEM, AND SAID, DO YOU NOT KNOW THAT IT IS WRITTEN, MY HOUSE OF PRAYER FOR ALL NATIONS? BUT YOU CONSIDER A DEN OF ROBBERS TO BE MY HOUSE.

John ii. 18. AND THE JEWS BEGAN TO SPEAK, AND THEY SAID TO HIM, WHAT RIGHT WILT THOU SHOW US FOR DOING THESE THINGS?

19. AND JESUS SAID TO THEM, DESTROY THIS TEMPLE, AND IN THREE DAYS I WILL RESTORE IT.

20. THE JEWS SAID, THIS TEMPLE WAS FORTY-SIX YEARS IN BUILDING, AND THOU WILT RESTORE IT IN THREE DAYS.

Matt. xii. 6. AND JESUS SAID TO THEM, I TELL YOU THAT MORE IMPORTANT THAN THE TEMPLE IS THIS,

7. THAT YOU SHOULD UNDERSTAND WHAT IS MEANT BY, I WANT COMPASSION TOWARD MEN, AND NOT CHURCH SERVICES.

John ii. 23. AND WHEN HE WAS IN JERUSALEM AT THE PASSOVER, MANY BELIEVED IN HIS TEACHING, COMPREHENDING THE PROOFS WHICH HE ADDUCED.

24. BUT JESUS HIMSELF DID NOT COMMIT HIMSELF TO THEIR FAITH, BECAUSE HE HIMSELF KNEW EVERYTHING,

25. AND SO HE DID NOT NEED TO HAVE ANYONE EXPLAIN ABOUT MAN TO HIM; FOR HE KNEW HIMSELF WHAT WAS IN MAN.

Mark xi. 18. AND THE SCRIBES AND THE ELDERS OF THE PRIESTS HEARD IT. AND THEY SOUGHT HOW THEY MIGHT DESTROY HIM: FOR THEY FEARED HIM, BECAUSE ALL THE PEOPLE MARVELED AT HIS TEACHING.

CHRIST'S DISCOURSE WITH A WOMAN OF SAMARIA

John iv. 3. AND JESUS WENT AWAY FROM JUDEA, AGAIN INTO GALILEE.

4. AND HE HAD TO GO THROUGH SAMARIA.

5. ONE DAY HE COMES TO A CITY OF SAMARIA, SYCHAR BY NAME, NEAR TO THE PLACE THAT JACOB GAVE TO HIS SON JOSEPH.

6. JACOB'S WELL WAS THERE. JESUS WAS WEARY OF HIS JOURNEY AND SAT DOWN NEAR THE WELL.

7. THERE COMES A WOMAN OF SAMARIA TO DRAW WATER, AND JESUS SAYS TO HER, WOMAN, GIVE ME TO DRINK.

8. FOR HIS DISCIPLES WERE GONE TO THE CITY TO BUY FOOD.

9. THEN THE WOMAN OF SAMARIA SAYS TO HIM, HOW IS IT THAT THOU, A JEW, ASKEST TO DRINK OF A SAMARITAN WOMAN? FOR THE JEWS HAVE NO DEALINGS WITH THE SAMARITANS?

10. BUT JESUS, ON THE CONTRARY, SAID TO HER, IF THOU KNEWEST THE GIFT OF GOD, AND WHO IT IS THAT SAYS, GIVE ME TO DRINK, THOU WOULDST HAVE ASKED OF HIM, AND HE WOULD HAVE GIVEN THEE SPRING WATER.

11. AND THE WOMAN SAID TO HIM, THOU HAST NO BUCKET, AND THE WELL IS DEEP, FROM WHERE, THEN, WILT THOU GET THAT SPRING WATER?

12. ART THOU GREATER THAN OUR FATHER JACOB? HE GAVE US THIS WELL. HE DRANK OF IT HIMSELF, AND HIS CHILDREN, AND HIS CATTLE.

13. AND JESUS SAID TO HER IN REPLY, WHOSOEVER DRINKS THIS WATER SHALL WANT TO DRINK AGAIN:

14. BUT WHOSOEVER DRINKS OF THE WATER THAT I SHALL GIVE, SHALL NEVER THIRST. BUT THE WATER THAT I SHALL GIVE HIM BRINGS FORTH IN HIM A SPRING OF WATER WHICH RUNS INTO EVERLASTING, NON-TEMPORAL LIFE.

John iv. 19. THE WOMAN SAYS TO HIM, SIR, I SEE THAT THOU ART A PROPHET.

20. OUR FATHERS WORSHIPPED GOD IN THIS MOUNTAIN, AND YOU SAY THAT IN JERUSALEM IS THE PLACE WHERE MEN OUGHT TO WORSHIP HIM.

21. AND JESUS SAID TO HER, WOMAN, BELIEVE ME, THE TIME IS NEAR WHEN YOU SHALL NEITHER IN THIS MOUNTAIN, NOR AT JERUSALEM, WORSHIP THE FATHER.

22. YOU WORSHIP YOU KNOW NOT WHOM, BUT WE WORSHIP WHOM WE KNOW.

23. BUT THE TIME IS COMING, AND IS ALREADY HERE, WHEN THE TRUE WORSHIPPERS SHALL WORSHIP THE FATHER IN THE SPIRIT AND IN DEEDS, FOR THE FATHER DEMANDS THAT OF THOSE WHO WORSHIP HIM.

24. GOD IS SPIRIT, AND HE OUGHT TO BE WORSHIPPED IN SPIRIT AND IN DEEDS.

25. AND THE WOMAN SAID TO HIM, I KNOW THAT MESSIAH WILL COME, WHO IS CALLED THE CHOSEN ONE OF GOD. WHEN HE IS COME, HE WILL TELL US ALL THINGS.

26. AND JESUS SAID TO HER, I THAT SPEAK TO THEE AM HE.

THE WITNESS OF JOHN CONCERNING CHRIST

John iii. 22. AFTER THAT JESUS AND HIS DISCIPLES CAME INTO THE LAND OF JUDEA, AND THERE LIVED WITH THEM, AND THOSE WHO WOULD WORSHIP GOD.

23. AND JOHN WAS PURIFYING IN ENON NEAR TO SALIM, BECAUSE THERE WAS MUCH WATER THERE, AND THEY CAME AND WERE PURIFIED.

24. FOR JOHN WAS NOT YET CAST INTO PRISON.

25. AND THERE AROSE A CONTENTION BETWEEN JOHN'S DISCIPLES WITH A JEW ABOUT THE PURIFYING.

26. AND THEY CAME TO JOHN, AND SAID TO HIM, SIR, HE WHO WAS WITH THEE AT THE JORDAN, AND TO WHOM THOU BOREST WITNESS, IS PURIFYING ALSO, AND ALL MEN COME TO HIM.

27. AND JOHN SAID, A MAN CANNOT TAKE UPON HIMSELF, IF HE IS NOT INSTRUCTED BY GOD.

31. HE WHO IS ABOVE IS HIGHER THAN ALL, AND HE WHO IS OF EARTH WILL BE OF EARTH, AND WILL SPEAK OF EARTH.

34. HE WHOM GOD HAS INSTRUCTED SPEAKS THE WORDS OF GOD.

32. AND WHAT HE HAS COMPREHENDED, THAT HE PROVES. NO MAN RECEIVES HIS PROOF.

33. HE WHO HAS RECEIVED HIS PROOF HAS CONFIRMED THAT GOD IS TRUE.

34. FOR IT IS IMPOSSIBLE TO MEASURE THE SPIRIT OF GOD.

35. FOR THE FATHER LOVES THE SON, AND HAS GIVEN ALL THINGS INTO HIS POWER.

36. HE WHO BELIEVES IN THE SON LIVES FOREVER, AND HE WHO DOES NOT BELIEVE IN THE SON IS AGAINST GOD.

JESUS DINING WITH SIMON. MARY MAGDALENE

Luke iv. 14. AND THERE WENT OUT NEWS OF HIM IN ALL THE SURROUNDING COUNTRY.

Luke xi. 37. AFTER THAT A CERTAIN ORTHODOX CAME TO HIM AND ASKED HIM TO LUNCH WITH HIM IN HIS HOUSE.

38. AND THE ORTHODOX, SEEING THAT JESUS DID NOT WASH BEFORE THE LUNCH, WAS SURPRISED.

39. AND JESUS SAID TO HIM, YOU ORTHODOX PEOPLE WASH THE OUTSIDE OF THE CUP AND THE PLATTER, BUT YOUR INSIDE IS FULL OF PLUNDER AND UNTRUTH.

40. FOOLS, HE WHO HAS MADE WHAT IS WITHOUT HAS ALSO MADE WHAT IS WITHIN.

41. BE MERCIFUL FROM WITHIN, AND THEN YOU SHALL SEE THAT EVERYTHING IS CLEAN.

Luke v. 32. FOR I HAVE COME HERE NOT TO CALL THE RIGHTEOUS TO THE RENOVATION, BUT THOSE WHO HAVE ERRED.

Luke vii. 37. AND A WOMAN OF THE CITY, WHO WAS AN INFIDEL, HEARING THAT JESUS WAS SITTING IN THE HOUSE OF AN ORTHODOX, WENT THERE AND BROUGHT A PITCHER OF OIL,

38. AND STANDING AT HIS FEET BEHIND, BEGAN TO WEEP AND TO WASH HIS FEET WITH HER TEARS, AND TO WIPE THEM WITH THE HAIR OF HER HEAD, AND TO ANOINT HIM WITH THE OIL.

39. WHEN THE ORTHODOX HOST SAW THIS, HE THOUGHT, IF HE WERE A REAL TEACHER, HE WOULD KNOW WHAT MANNER OF WOMAN THIS IS THAT IS TOUCHING HIM.

40. AND, TURNING AROUND, JESUS SAID TO HIM, SIMON, I WILL TELL THEE A FEW WORDS. AND HE SAID, MASTER, SPEAK!

41. A CERTAIN MASTER HAD TWO DEBTORS; THE ONE OWED FIVE HUNDRED PENCE, AND THE OTHER FIFTY.

42. AND NEITHER THE ONE NOR THE OTHER HAD ANYTHING TO PAY, AND THE MASTER FORGAVE THEM BOTH. TELL ME, WHICH OF THEM WILL BE MOST OBLIGED TO THE MASTER?

43. SIMON SAID, CERTAINLY HE TO WHOM HE FORGAVE MOST. AND JESUS SAID THOU HAST JUDGED RIGHTLY.

44. AND HE POINTED TO THE WOMAN, AND SAID TO SIMON, HERE I HAVE COME TO THY HOUSE, AND THOU GAVEST ME NO WATER TO WASH MY FEET WITH; BUT SHE WASHES MY FEET WITH TEARS, AND WIPES THEM WITH THE HAIR OF HER HEAD.

45. THOU DIDST NOT EMBRACE ME WHEN I ENTERED; BUT SHE HAS NOT CEASED KISSING MY FEET.

46. THOU DIDST NOT GIVE ME OIL TO ANOINT MY HEAD WITH; BUT SHE ANOINTS MY FEET WITH COSTLY OIL.

47. FOR THIS VERY REASON, I TELL THEE, SHE HAS BEEN DELIVERED FROM ERROR AND FROM GREAT ERROR, BECAUSE SHE LOVES MUCH. BUT HE TO WHOM LITTLE IS TO BE FORGIVEN LOVES LITTLE.

48. AND HE SAID TO HER, YES, ALL THY ERRORS ARE CORRECTED.

49. AND THOSE THAT WERE SITTING WITH HIM BEGAN TO SAY TO THEMSELVES, WHO IS HE THAT HE FREES FROM ERROR?

50. AND HE SAID TO THE WOMAN, THY FAITH HAS SAVED THEE; GO IN PEACE.

THE PARABLE OF THE PUBLICAN AND THE PHARISEE

Luke xviii. 10. AND JESUS SAID TO THEM, TWO MEN WENT INTO THE TEMPLE TO PRAY; THE ONE AN ORTHODOX, AND THE OTHER AN INFIDEL.

11. THE ORTHODOX THOUGHT MUCH OF HIMSELF, AND PRAYED AS FOLLOWS; I THANK THEE, O GOD, THAT I AM NOT AS OTHER MEN ARE, SELFISH, UNJUST, ADULTERERS, NOT AS THIS INFIDEL IS.

12. I FAST TWICE ON THE SABBATH, AND GIVE TITHES OF ALL I GET.

13. AND THE INFIDEL STOOD OFF AND COULD NOT LIFT UP HIS EYES TO HEAVEN, BUT STRUCK HIS BREAST AND KEPT SAYING, GOD LOOK AT ME ERRING ONE.

14. SO I TELL YOU, THE INFIDEL RETURNED MORE DELIVERED THAN THE ORTHODOX; FOR HE WHO EXALTS HIMSELF SHALL BE ABASED, AND HE WHO HUMBLES HIMSELF SHALL BE EXALTED.

Matt. ix. 14. THEN THE DISCIPLES OF JOHN WALKED UP TO HIM AND SAID, WHY DO WE AND THE ORTHODOX FAST OFT, BUT THY DISCIPLES DO NOT FAST?

15. AND JESUS SAID TO THEM, THE GUESTS CANNOT MOURN AT THE WEDDING, AS LONG AS THE BRIDEGROOM IS WITH THEM. WHEN THE BRIDE-GROOM IS NOT THERE, THEY MOURN.

THE PARABLE OF THE GARMENTS AND THE WINE

Luke v. 36. NO MAN TEARS A NEW GARMENT, IN ORDER TO PUT A NEW PATCH ON AN OLD GARMENT, FOR IT WILL TEAR THE NEW, AND THE OLD WILL BE OF NO USE.

37. AND NO MAN PUTS NEW WINE INTO OLD BOTTLES; ELSE THE BOTTLES WILL BURST, AND THE WINE WILL RUN OUT, AND THE BOTTLES WILL BE LOST.

38. BUT NEW WINE MUST BE PUT INTO NEW BOTTLES; AND BOTH ARE PRESERVED.

CHRIST'S PREACHING

Luke iv. 15. AND HE TAUGHT IN THE ASSEMBLIES AND WAS RESPECTED BY ALL.

42. THE PEOPLE HELD HIM BACK, THAT HE SHOULD NOT DEPART FROM THEM.

43. BUT HE SAID TO THEM, I MUST PREACH THE TRUE GOOD TO OTHERS ALSO, FOR I AM INTENDED FOR THAT.

Matt. iv. 14. AND THE WORD OF THE PROPHET ISAIAH WAS FULFILLED.

16. IN THE PAGAN COUNTRIES THE PEOPLE WALKED IN DARKNESS AND SAW A GREAT LIGHT; TO THEM WHO HAD LIVED IN THE DARKNESS OF DEATH, A NEW LIGHT SPRUNG UP.

Matt. xii. 17. SO THAT ALSO ANOTHER PROPHECY OF THE PROPHET ISAIAH WAS FULFILLED.

18. HERE IS MY CHILD WHOM I LOVE, MY BELOVED ONE, IN WHOM MY SOUL IS PLEASED. I HAVE PUT MY SPIRIT IN HIM, THAT HE MAY SHOW THE TRUTH TO THE NATIONS.

19. HE DOES NOT QUARREL, NOR CRY; AND HIS VOICE IS NOT HEARD IN THE STREETS.

20. HE WILL NOT BREAK A BRUISED REED, AND WILL NOT PUT OUT THE LIGHT WHEN IT GOES OUT, SO THAT THE TRUTH MAY VANQUISH THE LIE.

21. IN HIM IS ALL THE HOPE OF MEN.

Mark iii. 7. THEN JESUS WENT TO THE SEA.

8. AND A GREAT MULTITUDE FOLLOWED HIM FROM GALILEE, AND FROM JUDEA AND FROM IDUMEA, AND FROM JERUSALEM, AND FROM BEYOND THE JORDAN, AND THE PEOPLE FROM TYRE AND SIDON.

Matt. ix. 35. AND HE WENT ABOUT THE CITIES AND VILLAGES PROCLAIM-
ING IN THE ASSEMBLIES THE ANNOUNCEMENT ABOUT THE TRUE GOOD OF
THE KINGDOM OF HEAVEN.

TOLSTOY'S COMMENTARY

And Jesus allowed to all people that the former worship was a lie, and
that God ought to be served by works and by compassion toward men.

He happened on a Sabbath to walk with his disciples across a field.
On their way the disciples plucked some ears of corn, and rubbed them
in their hands, and ate them.

The Pharisees, the Orthodox, saw that, and said, It is not proper to
do that on a Sabbath. It is not lawful to work on a Sabbath, but you rub
the ears. Jesus heard that, and said to them, If you understood what is
meant by the words said by God to the prophet, I rejoice in the love of
men among themselves, and not in the sacrifices which they bring me,
you would not be condemning the innocent. The Sabbath has not been
established by God, but by man, consequently man is more important
than the Sabbath.

It happened another time on a Sabbath that, as Jesus was teaching in
an assembly, a sick woman went up to him and asked him to help her.

And Jesus began to treat her. Then a lawyer, an elder of the assembly,
grew angry at Jesus for it and said to the people, In the law of God it is
written, Six days in the week are for work, but on the Sabbath God has not
permitted men to work. Thereupon Jesus asked the lawyers and the Pharisees, Is it according to you not permitted to aid a man on a Sabbath?

And they did not know what to say.

Then Jesus said, Does not each one of you untie the cattle from the
stall and take them to drink on a Sabbath? Or if one of your sheep should
fall into a well, would you not run quickly to pull it out on a Sabbath? And
is not a man much better than a sheep? What, then, according to you, is a
man to do on a Sabbath, good or evil? To save the soul or to let it perish?
One must always do good, even on a Sabbath.

Pharisees and lawyers came to Jesus from Jerusalem. And they
saw that his disciples and he himself were eating bread together, with
unwashed hands. And the scribes began to condemn them, because they
themselves lived strictly as of old, washing their vessels, and without washing them they would not eat. Nor would they eat upon returning from
the market, unless they first washed their hands.

And the lawyers asked him, Why do you not live according to the old customs, and why do you take and eat bread with unwashed hands? And he said to them, Well has the prophet Isaiah said of you. God had said to him, Because these people cling to me only with words, and worship me only with their mouths, while their hearts are far from me, and because their fear of me is only a human command, which they have learned by heart, I will make a wonderful, unusual work over this people. The wisdom of their wise men shall disappear, and the reason of their thinking men shall be obscured. Woe to them who bestir themselves to conceal their desires from the Eternal One, and who do their works in the dark. Even so you omit that which is important in the law, that which is the commandment of God, and observe your own commandments, which is, to wash the cups. Moses said to you, Honor your father and your mother, and who will not honor his father or mother shall be put to death, but you have invented what anyone may say, I give to God what my parents have given, and fail to provide for your father or mother. Thus you destroy the commandments of God by human enactments. You do many such things.

And Jesus called all the people, and said, Listen all, and understand, There is nothing in the world which, going into man, can defile him, but that which comes out of him will defile a man. Let there be love and mercy in thy heart, and then all will be pure. Try to understand that.

And when he returned home, his disciples asked him what those words meant. And he said, Have you really not understood them? Do you not understand that nothing external and carnal can defile a man, because it enters not his soul, but his belly. It enters the belly, and with the excrements comes out of the back. Only that can defile a man which comes out of his soul, for from a man's soul come: fornication, lust, murder, theft, selfishness, malice, cheating, impudence, envy, pride, and every foolishness. All that evil comes out of the soul, and this alone can defile a man.

Jesus teaches the people that a new life has begun and that God is in the world upon earth, and this he tells everybody, and he tells his disciples that between man and God there is always a communion. This he teaches to all. And all are delighted with his teaching, because he teaches differently from the lawyers. The lawyers teach men that they must obey the laws of God, but he teaches them that they are free.

After that the passover came, and Jesus went to Jerusalem, where he entered the temple.

In the hall of the temple there were cattle, cows, oxen, and sheep, and baskets with doves, and behind counters sat changers with money. All that was necessary for the offerings to God. The animals were killed and sacrificed in the temple, and the money was offered there. In that consisted the prayers of the Jews.

Jesus entered the temple, plaited a whip, and drove all the cattle out of the hall, and let out all the doves, and scattered all the money.

And he commanded that no one should carry those things into the temple. He said, the prophet Isaiah has said, the house of God is not the temple in Jerusalem, but the whole world of God's people. And the prophet Jeremiah has also said to you, Do not believe the lying words that here is the house of the Eternal One, the house of the Eternal One, the house of the Eternal One. Do not believe that, but mend your life, do not judge falsely, do not oppress the stranger, the widow, and the orphan, do not spill innocent blood, and do not come into the house of the name of God, and do not say, Now we can calmly commit evil things. Do not make of my house a den of robbers.

And the Jews began to dispute, and they said to him, If thou prohibitest our prayer and our image of God, what kind of prayer wilt thou give?

And turning to them, Jesus said, Abandon this temple, and in three days I will call to life a new, a living temple to God.

And the Jews said, How canst thou make at once a new temple, since it took forty-six years to build this one?

And Jesus said, I am speaking to you about what is more important than the temple. You would not be speaking thus, if you understood the words of the prophet, I, God, do not rejoice in your sacrifices, but in your love among yourselves. The living temple is the whole world of the men of God, when they love each other.

And then many people in Jerusalem believed in what he spoke.

But he himself did not believe in anything external, because he knew everything which was in man.

He did not need to have any one to teach him about man, for he knew that the spirit of God was in man.

And the lawyers and the elders heard all that and sought how they might work his ruin, but they were afraid of him because all the people marvelled at his teaching.

And Jesus went again from Judea to Galilee. And it happened that he had to pass through Samaria. He was going past a Samaritan village, Sychar by name, near the place which Jacob had given to his son Joseph.

Jacob's well was there. Jesus was tired from his journey, and he sat down near the well; but his disciples went to the town to buy bread.

And there comes a woman from Sychar to fetch water. Jesus asks her to give him to drink.

She says to him, How is it thou askest me to give thee to drink? You Jews do not have dealings with us Samaritans.

And he says to her, If thou knewest me and knewest what it is I teach, thou wouldst not say that, but wouldst give me to drink, and I, too, would give thee living water. He who drinks of this water will want to drink again, but he who drinks of my water will be satisfied for ever, and this water of mine will lead him to life eternal.

The woman understood that he was speaking of divine things, and said to him, I saw that thou art a prophet and want to teach me; but how canst thou teach me divine things since thou art a Jew, and I a Samaritan? Our people pray to God in this mountain, and you Jews say that it is necessary to pray in Jerusalem. Thou canst not teach me divine things, because you have one God, and we another.

Then Jesus said to her, Believe me, woman, the time is near when neither in this mountain nor at Jerusalem will they pray to the Father. You pray to him whom you do not know, but we pray to the Father whom it is impossible not to know.

And the time has arrived and is already here when the true worshippers of God will worship the Father in the spirit and with deeds. The Father needs such worshippers. God is spirit, and he ought to be worshipped in spirit and with deeds.

The woman did not make out what he was telling her, and she said, I have heard that a messenger of God will come, the one who is called the anointed. He will tell everything.

And Jesus said to her, I who am talking with thee am he. Wait for nothing else.

After that Jesus came into the land of Judea, and there he lived with his disciples, and purified.

At that time John purified men near Salim in the river Enon, for John had not yet been cast into prison.

And there arose a dispute between the disciples of John and those of Jesus as to which was better, John's purification in water, or the teaching of Jesus.

And they came to John, and said to him, Now thou purifiest with water, but Jesus teaches only, and all men go to him. What dost thou say about it?

And John said, A man cannot teach of himself, if God does not instruct him. Whoever speaks of earth is earthly; and whoever speaks from God, is from God.

It is impossible to prove in anyway whether words that are spoken are from God or not from God. God is spirit. He cannot be measured nor proved. He who understands the words of God by that proves that he has understood God.

At one time Jesus saw a farmer of taxes collecting taxes. His name was Matthew. Jesus spoke with him, and Matthew understood him and liked his teaching and invited him to his house, and entertained him.

When Jesus came to Matthew, there came also Matthew's friends, tax collectors and corrupt people. Jesus did not loathe them, but sat down himself with his disciples. And the lawyers and Pharisees saw that and said to the disciples of Jesus, How is it your teacher is feasting with tax collectors and corrupt men? Jesus heard that, and said, He who boasts of being well does not need a physician, but he who is sick needs one. For this reason I do not wish to convert those who regard themselves as just, thinking that they are living in the truth, but teach those who think that they are living in sin.

While he was sitting in Matthew's house, there came a city woman, who was a prostitute. She had heard that Jesus was in Matthew's house, and came thither, and brought a vial with perfume. And she knelt down at his feet, and wept, and washed his feet with her tears, and wiped them with her hair, and poured the perfume out of the vial upon them.

Matthew saw that, and thought, He is hardly a prophet; if he were really a prophet, he would know what manner of woman is washing his feet; he would know that she is a whore, and would not permit her to touch him.

Jesus divined it, and turned around to Matthew, and said, Matthew, shall I tell thee what I think?

Tell me, he said.

And Jesus said, Listen. Two men considered themselves debtors of the same master: one to the amount of five hundred pence, and the other of fifty. And neither the one nor the other had any money to pay his debt. The master forgave both. Well, according to thy judgment, which of them will love the master and tend on him?

And Matthew said, of course, the one who owes most.

Jesus pointed to the woman, and said, Even thus it is with this woman. Thou considerest thyself a small debtor. I came to thy house, and thou didst not give me water with which to wash my feet, while she washes them with her tears and dries them with her hair.

Thou didst not kiss me, but she kisses my feet. Thou didst not give me oil with which to anoint my head, but she is rubbing costly ointments on my feet. He who thinks that he has nothing to be forgiven does not love. He who thinks that he is very guilty loves much. But for love everything is forgiven.

And he said to her, Thy sins are forgiven thee. And Jesus said, the whole thing is what each considers himself to be. He who considers himself to be good will not be good, and who considers himself bad is good.

Two men once came to the temple to pray, one of them a Pharisee, the other an infidel.

The Pharisee prayed like this, I thank thee, O Lord, that I am not as other men are, neither stingy, nor a cheat, nor a debauchee, nor such a worthless man as this tax collector. I fast twice a week, and of my possessions I give away a tithe.

But the infidel stood at a distance and did not dare to look up to heaven, and only struck his breast with his hands, and kept saying, O Lord, look down upon me, worthless man!

Well? The infidel was forgiven more than the Pharisee, because whoever exalts himself shall be humbled, and whoever humbles himself shall be exalted.

After that John's disciples came to Jesus, and said, Why do we and the lawyers fast much, while thou and thy disciples do not fast? And Jesus said to them, As long as the bridegroom is at the wedding no man mourns. Only when the bridegroom is not there do they mourn. If there is life there is no need of mourning.

And Jesus said also this, No one tears off a piece of a new garment to sew it on an old garment, for the new garment will be torn and the old one will not be mended. So we cannot accept your fasts. And we cannot pour new wine into old bottles, for the bottles will be torn, and the wine will run out. New wine has to be put in new bottles, and then both will be preserved.

And after that a Pharisee came to him, and called him to lunch at his house. He went in and sat down at the table. The Pharisee observed that he did not wash before lunch, and was surprised. Jesus said to him, Pharisees, you wash all the time from without, but are you clean from within? Be merciful to men, and everything will be clean.

And the fame spread about Jesus, and he was respected by all, so that the people kept him that he might not go away from them. But he said that he came to announce the good not only to one city, but to all men. And he went on to the sea. And a large multitude followed him from various cities. And he helped all. And he walked through cities and villages, everywhere announcing the kingdom of heaven and freeing men from all sufferings and vices.

Thus in Jesus Christ were fulfilled the prophecies of Isaiah, namely, that the people who had lived in darkness, in the darkness of death, saw the light; that he who received this light of truth will do no violence and no harm to men; that he is meek and humble; that, in order to bring truth to men in the world, he does not dispute and cry; that his loud voice is not heard; that he will not break a straw and will not blow out a night candle, and that the whole hope of men is in him.

CHAPTER THREE

THE KINGDOM OF GOD. CHRIST'S TESTIMONY CONCERNING JOHN

Matt. xi. 2. JOHN HEARD IN THE PRISON ABOUT THE WORKS OF JESUS, AND THROUGH HIS DISCIPLES HE SAID TO HIM,

3. ART THOU HE THAT SHOULD COME, OR SHALL WE LOOK FOR ANOTHER?

4. AND IN REPLY JESUS SAID TO THEM, GO AND TELL JOHN THOSE THINGS WHICH YOU HEAR AND SEE.

5. THE BLIND SEE, THE LAME WALK, THE DEAF HEAR, THE IMPURE ARE CLEANSED, THE DEAD WAKE UP, AND THE POOR LEARN OF THEIR GOOD.

6. AND HAPPY IS HE WHO WILL NOT RENOUNCE ME.

7. WHEN THEY WENT AWAY, JESUS BEGAN TO TALK TO THE MULTITUDES CONCERNING JOHN, WHAT DID YOU GO TO SEE IN THE WILDERNESS? A REED SHAKEN IN THE WIND?

8. OR WHAT ELSE DID YOU GO OUT TO SEE? A MAN CLOTHED IN RICH RAIMENT? HERE THEY ARE BEFORE YOU, THOSE WHO WEAR RICH RAIMENT AND LIVE IN EASE—THEY LIVE IN PALACES.

9. SO WHAT DID YOU GO OUT TO SEE? A PROPHET? VERILY, I SHALL TELL YOU ABOUT WHAT IS GREATER THAN A PROPHET.

10. THIS IS HE, OF WHOM IT IS WRITTEN, I SEND A MESSENGER BEFORE THY FACE; HE SHALL PREPARE THE WAY BEFORE THEE.

11. VERILY I TELL YOU, NO GREATER MAN HAS BEEN BORN OF A WOMAN THAN JOHN THE BAPTIST. THE LEAST HERE IS THERE, IN THE KINGDOM OF GOD, GREATER THAN ALL.

Luke xvi. 16. THE LAW AND THE PROPHETS WERE BEFORE JOHN. SINCE THAT TIME THE KINGDOM OF GOD HAS BEEN PREACHED AND EVERY MAN PASSES INTO IT ACCORDING TO HIS STRENGTH.

Matt. xi. 13. FOR ALL THE PROPHETS AND THE LAW BEFORE JOHN EXPRESSED THE WILL OF GOD.

14. IF YOU WILL, RECEIVE HIM AS ELIJAH, WHO WAS TO COME.

15. HE WHO WANTS TO UNDERSTAND WILL UNDERSTAND.

Luke vii. 29. AND ALL THE RABBLE HEARD HIM AND THE TAX COLLECTORS JUSTIFIED GOD, HAVING BEEN PURIFIED BY JOHN'S PURIFICATION.

30. BUT THE PHARISEES AND LAWYERS REJECTED THE COUNSEL OF GOD, NOT BEING PURIFIED BY JOHN.

31. AND JESUS SAID, TO WHOM ARE THE MEN OF THIS TRIBE TO BE LIKENED?

32. THEY ARE LIKE LITTLE CHILDREN. THE CHILDREN SIT IN THE STREET AND PRATTLE WITH ONE ANOTHER. THEY SAY, WE ARE PLAYING, AND YOU DO NOT DANCE; WE MOURN, AND YOU DO NOT WEEP.

33. JOHN CAME, AND HE DOES NOT EAT, NOR DRINK, AND YOU SAY, THE DEVIL IS IN HIM.

34. THE SON OF MAN COMES AND EATS AND DRINKS, AND YOU SAY, HE IS AN EATING MAN AND A DRUNKARD, A FRIEND OF TAX COLLECTORS AND OF PEOPLE WHO ERR.

35. AND WISDOM IS JUSTIFIED BY ITS WORKS.

THE COMING OF THE KINGDOM OF GOD

Luke xvii. 20. AND THE PHARISEES ASKED JESUS, WHEN AND HOW DOES THE KINGDOM OF GOD COME? AND HE ANSWERED THEM, THE KINGDOM OF GOD DOES NOT COME IN SUCH A WAY THAT IT CAN BE SEEN.

21. AND IT CANNOT BE SAID ABOUT IT, HERE IT IS, OR, THERE IT IS, FOR THE KINGDOM OF GOD IS WITHIN YOU.

23. AND THEY SHALL SAY TO YOU, HERE IT HAS COME, OR, HERE IT IS; DO NOT GO, DO NOT RUN AFTER IT.

24. FOR IT SHINES SUDDENLY, LIKE SHEET LIGHTNING IN THE SKY; AND SO SHALL ALSO BE THE SON OF MAN IN HIS TIME.

THE DISCOURSE WITH NICODEMUS

John iii. 1. THERE WAS A MAN, A PHARISEE, NAMED NICODEMUS, A JEWISH ELDER.

2. HE CAME TO JESUS AT NIGHT, AND SAID TO HIM, SIR, WE KNOW THAT THOU COMEST FROM GOD TO TEACH, FOR NO MAN WOULD BE ABLE TO PROVE IT IN SUCH A WAY, IF GOD WERE NOT WITH HIM.

3. AND JESUS REPLIED TO HIM, VERILY, I TELL THEE, ONLY HE WHO IS NOT BEGOTTEN BY GOD FROM ABOVE CAN FAIL TO UNDERSTAND WHAT THE KINGDOM OF GOD IS.

4. AND NICODEMUS SAID, HOW CAN A MAN BE BEGOTTEN WHEN HE IS OLD? HE CANNOT ENTER A SECOND TIME INTO HIS MOTHER'S WOMB, AND BE BORN.

5. AND JESUS ANSWERED HIM, VERILY, I TELL THEE, HE WHO IS NOT BY THE FLESH AND ALSO BY THE SPIRIT CANNOT ENTER THE KINGDOM OF GOD.

6. THAT WHICH IS BY THE FLESH IS FLESH, AND THAT WHICH IS BY THE SPIRIT IS SPIRIT.

8. THE SPIRIT BLOWS WHEREVER AND WHENEVER IT PLEASES, AND THOU UNDERSTANDEST ITS VOICE, BUT CANST NOT TELL WHENCE IT COMES, AND WHITHER IT GOES. SO IS EVERYONE THAT IS BORN BY THE SPIRIT.

7. AND SO DO NOT MARVEL, BECAUSE I HAVE TOLD THEE THAT WE MUST BE BEGOTTEN BY GOD.

9. AND NICODEMUS SAID IN REPLY, HOW CAN THAT BE?

10. AND JESUS ANSWERED HIM, THOU ART A TEACHER AND DOST NOT UNDERSTAND THESE THINGS.

11. VERILY, I TELL THEE, WE SPEAK OF WHAT WE KNOW, AND SHOW WHAT WE HAVE SEEN, BUT YOU DO NOT RECEIVE THE PROOFS OF OUR TESTIMONY.

12. I HAVE TOLD YOU OF WHAT IS UPON EARTH, AND YOU DO NOT BELIEVE; HOW, THEN, SHALL YOU BELIEVE, IF I TELL YOU OF WHAT IS IN HEAVEN?

13. FOR NO MAN HAS ASCENDED HEAVEN, BUT HE THAT CAME DOWN FROM HEAVEN, THE SON OF MAN, THE ONE WHO IS IN HEAVEN.

14. AND AS MOSES EXALTED THE SERPENT IN THE WILDERNESS (THAT MEN SHOULD NOT PERISH) EVEN SO THE SON OF MAN MUST BE EXALTED.

15. THAT WHOSOEVER BELIEVED IN HIM SHOULD NOT PERISH, BUT SHOULD HAVE LIFE OUTSIDE OF TIME.

16. FOR GOD SO LOVED THE WORLD OF MEN, AND GAVE HIS SON, JUST SUCH AS HE IS, THAT ALL RELYING ON HIM SHOULD NOT PERISH, BUT HAVE NON-TEMPORAL LIFE.

17. FOR GOD SENT HIS SON INTO THE WORLD NOT TO PUNISH THE WORLD, BUT THAT THE WORLD MIGHT LIVE THROUGH HIM.

18. HE WHO BELIEVES IN THE SON, WILL NOT BE PUNISHED; BUT HE WHO DOES NOT BELIEVE IS ALREADY PUNISHED, BECAUSE HE DOES NOT BELIEVE THAT THE SON IS JUST SUCH AS GOD.

19. AND THIS PUNISHMENT IS THAT THE LIGHT IS COME INTO THE WORLD, AND MEN PREFERRED DARKNESS TO LIGHT, BECAUSE THEIR DEEDS WERE EVIL.

20. FOR WHOEVER DOES EVIL SPURNS THE LIGHT SO THAT HIS DEEDS DO NOT APPEAR.

21. BUT WHO LIVES IN TRUTH GOES TOWARD THE LIGHT, SO THAT HIS DEEDS ARE MADE MANIFEST.

PARABLE OF THE SOWER

Matt. xiii. 1. JESUS WENT OUT OF THE HOUSE, AND SAT DOWN BY THE SEA.

2. AND SUCH A MULTITUDE GATHERED AROUND HIM THAT HE LEFT THE SHORE AND WENT INTO A SHIP; AND THE MULTITUDE STOOD ON THE SHORE.

3. AND HE SAID, A FARMER WENT OUT TO SOW.

4. AND SOME SEEDS FELL ON THE ROAD, AND THE BIRDS PICKED THEM UP.

5. AND OTHERS FELL ON A STONE, AND IMMEDIATELY SPRANG UP AND GREW.

6. AND WHEN THE SUN GREW WARM, THEY WILTED, FOR THERE WAS NO SOIL UNDER THEM TO TAKE ROOT IN, AND THEY WITHERED.

7. SOME FELL AMONG THORNS AND GREW UP, BUT THE THORNS CHOKED THEM (AND THEY YIELDED NO SEED).

8. AND STILL OTHERS FELL ON GOOD GROUND, AND THE EARS GREW OUT AND FILLED UP, AND THEY BROUGHT FORTH, SOME A HUNDRED, SOME FIFTY, AND SOME THIRTY.

9. HE WHO HAS UNDERSTANDING WILL UNDERSTAND.

Mark iv. 26. AND HE SAID, SO IS THE KINGDOM OF GOD, AS IF A FARMER CAST SEED INTO THE GROUND;

27. HE SLEEPS HIMSELF AT NIGHT AND GETS UP IN THE DAYTIME, AND THE SEED SPRINGS UP AND SWELLS, AND HE DOES NOT KNOW HOW.

28. THE EARTH BRINGS FORTH FRUIT OF ITSELF, FIRST THE BLADE, THEN THE EAR, AND THEN FILLS THE EAR WITH SEEDS.

29. BUT WHEN THE SEED DRIES UP, HE IMMEDIATELY SENDS THE REAPERS, BECAUSE THE TIME OF THE HARVEST HAS COME.

THE PARABLE OF THE LEAVEN

Matt. xiii. 33. THE KINGDOM OF HEAVEN IS LIKE A LEAVEN. A WOMAN TOOK IT AND PUT IT INTO A MEASURE OF FLOUR, TILL THE WHOLE WAS LEAVENED.

THE PARABLE OF THE WHEAT AND THE TARES

Matt. xiii. 24. AND JESUS SAID, THE KINGDOM OF HEAVEN MAY BE LIKENED TO THIS: A FARMER SOWED GOOD SEED IN HIS FIELD:

25. IN THE NIGHT HIS ENEMY CAME AND SOWED TARES AMONG THE WHEAT, AND WENT AWAY.

26. WHEN THE WHEAT WAS IN THE EAR AND BEGAN TO FILL UP, THEN ALSO APPEARED THE TARES.

27. THE SERVANTS CAME TO THE MASTER AND SAID, DIDST THOU SOW IMPURE SEED IN THEY FIELD? THERE ARE MANY TARES THERE.

28. THE MASTER SAID, NOT I, BUT ANOTHER MAN, HAS DONE THAT. THE SERVANTS SAID, COMMAND US, AND WE WILL WEED OUT THE TARES.

29. BUT THE MASTER SAID, IT IS NOT NECESSARY TO WEED THEM OUT, FOR WHEN YOU WEED OUT THE TARES YOU WILL RUIN THE WHEAT.

30. LET THE WHEAT GROW WITH THE TARES UNTIL HARVEST TIME; AND IN THE TIME OF HARVEST I WILL TELL THE REAPERS TO PICK OUT THE TARES AND BURN THEM, AND THEN I WILL HARVEST THE WHEAT AND TAKE IT TO THE BARN.

Matt. xiii. 36. AND THE DISCIPLES BEGAN TO ASK JESUS, EXPLAIN TO US THE PARABLE ABOUT THE TARES OF THE FIELD.

37. AND JESUS SAID TO THEM, THE FARMER WHO IS SOWING THE GOOD SEED IS THE SON OF MAN.

38. THE FIELD IS THE WORLD OF MEN; THE GOOD SEED ARE THE CHILDREN OF THE KINGDOM OF GOD; THE TARES ARE THE EVIL MEN.

39. THE STRANGER IS TEMPTATION. THE HARVEST IS THE END OF THE LIFE ON EARTH; AND THE REAPERS ARE THE POWER OF GOD.

40. AS THE TARES ARE GATHERED AND BURNED, SO WILL IT BE AT THE END OF THE LIFE UPON EARTH.

41. THE SON OF MAN WILL SEND HIS SERVANTS, AND THEY WILL TAKE AWAY FROM AMONG THE PEOPLE OF HIS KINGDOM ALL THE DECEPTIONS AND ALL THOSE WHO DO WRONG.

42. AND WILL CAST THEM INTO THE FIRE, AND THERE WILL BE WAILING AND GNASHING OF TEETH.

43. THEN WILL THE RIGHTEOUS SHINE AS THE SUN IN THE KINGDOM OF THEIR FATHER. HE WHO HAS REASON WILL UNDERSTAND.

THE PARABLE OF THE DRAWNET

Matt. xiii. 47. AGAIN, THE KINGDOM OF GOD IS LIKE A DRAWNET: IT WAS CAST INTO THE SEA AND GATHERED FISH OF EVERY KIND.

48. THE NET WAS FULL; THEY DREW IT OUT TO THE SHORE AND SAT DOWN, AND GATHERED THE GOOD FISH INTO PAILS, AND THE WORTHLESS WERE THROWN AWAY.

EXPLANATION OF THE PARABLE OF THE SOWER

Matt. xiii. 10. AND HIS DISCIPLES CAME TO HIM AND SAID,

Luke viii. 9. WHY DOST THOU SPEAK IN PARABLES?

Matt. xiii. 11. HE REPLIED TO THEM BECAUSE IT IS GIVEN TO YOU TO KNOW THE INWARD MEANING OF THE KINGDOM OF GOD.

Mark iv. 11. BUT THOSE WHO ARE WITHOUT RECEIVE IT IN PARABLES.

Matt. xiii. 13. FOR THIS REASON I SPEAK TO THEM IN PARABLES.

Matt. xiii. 9. HE WHO HAS REASON WILL UNDERSTAND.

14. AND IN THEM IS FULFILLED THE PROPHECY OF ISAIAH. BY HEARING YOU WILL HEAR, AND WILL NOT UNDERSTAND; AND YOU WILL LOOK WITH YOUR EYES, AND WILL NOT SEE.

15. FOR THE PEOPLE'S HEART HAS GROWN FAT AND THEY HAVE CLOSED THEIR EYES SO THAT THEY DO NOT SEE, AND WITH THEIR EARS THEY DO NOT HEAR; AND INTO THEIR HEART THEY DO NOT RECEIVE, LEST THEY BE CONVERTED AND I HEAL THEM.

16. BUT YOUR EYES ARE BLESSED, FOR THEY SEE; AND YOUR EARS, FOR THEY HEAR.

17. VERILY I TELL YOU THAT THE PROPHETS AND SAINTS HAVE DESIRED TO SEE WHAT YOU SEE, AND COULD NOT PERCEIVE AND HEAR WHAT YOU HAVE COMPREHENDED.

18. NOW YOU WILL UNDERSTAND THE PARABLE OF THE SOWER.

Luke viii. 11. THE SEED IS THE COMPREHENSION OF GOD.

Matt. xiii. 19. WHEN ANYONE HEARS THE TEACHING ABOUT THE KINGDOM OF GOD AND DOES NOT TAKE IT TO HIS HEART, THERE COMES THE ENEMY AND TAKES AWAY WHAT WAS SOWN IN HIS HEART. THAT IS THE SEED WHICH IS SOWN BY THE WAYSIDE.

20. WHAT IS SOWN ON THE STONE IS HE WHO HEARS THE TEACHING OF THE KINGDOM OF GOD AND UNDERSTANDS THE TEACHING, AND THEN RECEIVES IT WITH JOY IN HIS HEART;

21. AND DOES NOT HOLD THE ROOT IN HIMSELF, BUT FOR A WHILE ONLY. AND WHEN PRESSURE AND PERSECUTION FOR THE TEACHING COMES, HE AT ONCE SUBMITS TO DECEPTION.

22. AND WHAT IS SOWN AMONG THE THORNS IS HE WHO UNDERSTANDS THE TEACHING; AND WORLDLY CARES AND LOVE OF RICHES CHOKE THE TEACHING, AND IT BRINGS NO FRUIT.

23. BUT WHAT HAS FALLEN ON GOOD GROUND IS HE WHO HAS UNDERSTOOD THE TEACHING AND RECEIVES IT INTO HIS HEART; THAT BEARS SOME A HUNDREDFOLD, SOME FIFTY, AND SOME THIRTY.

Luke viii. 18. SEE TO IT HOW YOU UNDERSTAND. HE WHO HOLDS ON GETS IT, AND HE WHO DOES NOT HOLD ON HAS EVEN THAT TAKEN FROM HIM WHICH HE THINKS HE HAS.

PARABLE OF THE HIDDEN TREASURE

Matt. xiii. 44. THE KINGDOM OF GOD IS LIKE A TREASURE HIDDEN IN A FIELD. A MAN HAS FOUND THE TREASURE AND HAS HIDDEN IT (AGAIN). AND FOR THE JOY OF HAVING FOUND IT HE GOES AND SELLS ALL THAT HE HAS, AND BUYS THAT FIELD.

45. AGAIN, THE KINGDOM OF HEAVEN IS AS WHEN A MERCHANT IS BUYING UP PRECIOUS STONES;

46. AND HAVING FOUND A PRECIOUS STONE, HE GOES AND SELLS ALL (THE FORMER) THAT HE HAD, AND BUYS THAT ONE.

PARABLE OF THE MUSTARD SEED

Matt. xiii. 31. THE KINGDOM OF HEAVEN IS LIKE A BIRCH SEED, WHICH A MAN TOOK, AND SOWED IN HIS FIELD.

32. THOUGH IT IS THE LEAST OF ALL SEEDS, IT WILL BE GREATER THAN ANY GRASS WHEN IT IS GROWN, AND WILL BECOME A TREE, AND THE FEATHERED BIRDS WILL MAKE NESTS IN ITS BRANCHES.

TOLSTOY'S COMMENTARY

Jesus announces that the kingdom of God has come, and yet no visible change has taken place. He announces to his disciples that from now on heaven is open, and between heaven and men there is a constant communion. He announces that it is not necessary to separate ourselves from corrupt people, that they are not guilty, and that those only are guilty who think that they are good because they execute the law of God.

He announces that no external purification is needed, that only that which comes from within can defile, and that only the spirit purifies.

He announces that it is not necessary to observe the Sabbath, that this observance is foolish and false, and that the Sabbath is a human institution.

He announces that not only are fasts useless, but that all the old external rites are harmful for his teaching.

Finally, he announces that it is not right to serve God with sacrifices. We do not need oxen, nor sheep, nor doves, nor money, not even the temple itself; that there is a spirit; that the spirit does not want sacrifices, but love; and that the spirit is to be served—by all, always, at all times—in the spirit and with deeds.

When the Pharisees saw and heard all that, they came to Jesus and began to ask him how he preached the kingdom of God, since he rejected God. And he answered them, The kingdom of God, as I preach it, is not the same as what the former prophets preached about. They said that God will come with all kinds of manifestations, but I say that the kingdom of God is such that its coming cannot be seen.

And if you are told that it has come or is coming, or that it is here, you do not believe. The kingdom of God is not in time and not in any place; it is like lightning—here and there and everywhere, and it has no time and no place, because here it is, within you.

After that a Pharisee, a Jewish elder, Nicodemus, came to Jesus in secret, and said to him, Thou teachest that the kingdom of God has come, and that it is within us, and yet thou dost not order men to fast and to offer sacrifices, but destroyest the temple; so what kind of a kingdom of God is yours, and where is it?

And Jesus answered him, Thou must understand that if a man is begotten by God the Father, he sees the kingdom of God. Nicodemus did not understand what Jesus told him, that every man was already begotten by God, and said, How can a man, if he is begotten from the flesh of the father and has grown old, again creep into the womb of his mother and again be begotten by the flesh by God?

And Jesus answered him, Understand what I say, I say that man, besides the flesh, is begotten by the spirit, and so each man is of flesh and of the spirit, and so each man can enter the kingdom of God. Of the flesh is flesh. Of the flesh can not the spirit be born; only of the spirit can there be the spirit. The spirit is that which lives in thee, and it lives freely and rationally, and it is that for which thou knowest neither beginning nor end. And every man feels it in himself. And so why dost thou wonder when I tell thee that we must be begotten from heaven by God, by the spirit?

Nicodemus said, Still I do not believe that that could be possible.

Then Jesus said to him, What teacher art thou if thou dost not understand that? Thou must understand that I am not talking of any recondite things; I am talking of what we all know; I assure men of what we all see. How wilt thou believe in what is in heaven, if thou dost not believe in what is on earth, in thyself? No one has been in heaven, but there is on earth in man the son of God, the spirit, the one which is God.

The very son of God in man must be worshipped, as you worshipped God, when Moses in the wilderness exalted not the flesh of the serpent, but its image, and that image became the salvation of men. Even so we must exalt the son of God in man, not the flesh of man, but the son of God in man, in order that men, relying upon it, may not know death, but shall have non-temporal life in the kingdom of God.

Not for the ruin, but for the good of the world has God given his son, who is like himself. He gave him for this, that every man, relying upon him, might not perish, but might have non-temporal life. He did not bring his son, life, into the world of men, in order to destroy men, but that the world of men might live by it and be in the kingdom of God.

And he who relies on God is in the kingdom of God, in the power of God; and he who does not depend on him destroys himself, by not relying on that which is life. Destruction consists in this, that life came into the world, but men themselves walk away from life. Life is the light of men. The light came into the world, but men prefer darkness to light, and do not walk toward the light. The light is the understanding, and so he who does evil evades the light, the understanding, that his deeds may not be seen, and remains in the power of God.

In his remarks to the Pharisees and discourse with Nicodemus Jesus explains what he means by the kingdom of God and by God.

God and the kingdom of God are in men. God is the non-carnal principle which gives life to man. This non-carnal principle he calls the son of God in man, the son of man. The son of man is the understanding. It has to be exalted and deified, and by it we must live. He who lives in the understanding lives non-temporally; he who does not live in it does not live—he perishes.

What, then, is this God the Father, who is not the creator of everything and not separate from the world, as the Jews understood him to be? How are we to understand this Father, whose son is in man, and how are we to understand his relation to men?

To this Jesus replies in parables.

The kingdom of God is not to be understood as you think, namely, that for all men the kingdom of God will come in some one place and at some certain time, but that in the whole world there are always some people who rely upon God, who become the sons of the kingdom, and others, who do not rely upon him, who are destroyed.

God the spirit, the Father of that spirit which is in man, is God and the Father of those only who recognize themselves as his sons. And so only those exist for God who have retained within them what he has given them.

And Jesus began to talk to them about the kingdom of God, and he explained it by examples. He said, God the Father sows in the world the life of the understanding, just as the farmer sows his seeds in his field. He sows in the whole field, without paying any attention to where each seed will fall.

And some seeds fall by the wayside and the birds come and pick them. And other seeds fall on the stones, where they grow indeed, but soon wither, because they cannot take root. And others again fall into the thorns, and the thorns choke the wheat, and the ears will grow, but will not fill up. And others again fall in good ground, and these spring up and make up for the lost seeds and grow full in the ears, and some ears give a hundredfold, and some sixty and some thirty.

Just so God has scattered the understanding among men. In some it is lost, and in others it bears a hundredfold, and they form the kingdom of God.

Thus the kingdom of God is not such as you imagine it to be, namely, that God is ruling over you. God is only the understanding, and the kingdom of God will be in those who will take it. But God does not govern men.

As the farmer casts the seeds into the ground and does not think of them, but the seeds swell and sprout themselves, and grow into blades and ears, and fill up, and the master sends the reapers to cut them down, when they are ripe; so also has God given his son, the understanding, to the world, and the understanding grows of itself in the world, and the sons of the understanding form the kingdom of God.

As a woman puts the leaven into the trough and mixes it with the flour, and does not mix it anymore, but waits for it to leaven of itself and rise; so God does not enter into the life of men, as long as they live. God gave the understanding to the world, and the understanding lives itself among men and forms the kingdom of God. God the spirit is the God of life and good, and so there are no death and no evil for him. Death and evil are for men, and not for God.

The kingdom of heaven may be compared with this: a farmer has sowed good seed in his field. The farmer is the spirit of God; the field is the world; and the seeds are the sons of the kingdom of God.

The farmer lies down to sleep, and the enemy comes and sows tares. The enemy is temptation; the tares are the sons of the temptation. And now the servants come to the farmer and say, Hast thou sowed bad seed? Many tares have sprung up in thy field. Send us to weed them out. But the farmer says, It is not necessary, for when you weed out the tares you will tramp down the wheat. Let them grow together; when the harvest comes, I will tell the reapers to pick out the tares and will have them burned, and the wheat I will gather in my barn.

The harvest is the end of human life, and the reapers are the power of God. And as the tares will be burned and the wheat will be cleaned and garnered, even so at the end of life everything will perish which was the deception of time, and there will be left only the true life in the spirit. For God there is no evil. God preserves that which he needs, which is his own; and what is not his does not exist for him.

The kingdom of heaven is like a drawnet. The net is cast out in the sea and brings up all kinds of fish. Then, when the drawnet is pulled out, the spoiled fish are taken out and cast into the sea. Even so it will be at the end of time. The power of God will pick out the good, and the bad will be rejected.

And when he finished speaking, his disciples began to ask him how these parables were to be understood.

And he said to them, These parables have to be understood in two ways. All these parables I speak because there are some, like you, my disciples, who understand what the kingdom of God consists in, who understand that the kingdom of God is within us, and who know how to enter it, but others do not understand that. Others look and do not see, and listen and do not understand, because their hearts have grown fat.

And so I speak in parables for two purposes; I speak to both. To some I say what the kingdom is to God, and I tell them that some enter the kingdom, and others do not, and they can understand me. But to you I tell how to enter the kingdom of God. And look and understand the parable of the sower as is proper. For you the parable means this:

Every man who hears the teaching of the kingdom of God, but does not take it to his heart, is overcome by deceit, and he destroys the teaching in his heart—it is the seed sown by the wayside. What is sown on the stones is he who hears the teaching and accepts it with joy. But there is no root in him, and he receives it only for a while, and when pressure is brought to bear and offence is offered him for his teaching, he himself takes offence. What is sown among the wormwood is he who hears the teaching, but the cares of the world and his eagerness for wealth chokes the teaching and it gives forth no fruit. And what is sown on the good ground is he who hears the teaching and understands and brings forth fruit, some a hundredfold, and some sixty, and some thirty.

For he who holds on will get much, and he who does not hold will be deprived of the last.

And so see to it how you understand the parables. Understand them in such a way that you do not submit to deception, offences, cares, but bring forth fruit a hundredfold and enter the kingdom of God.

The kingdom of God grows large in the soul from nothing, but gives everything. It is like a birch seed, which is the smallest of seeds; when it grows up it is greater than all the trees, and the birds of heaven make their nests in it.

After that there came the disciples of John to ask Jesus whether he was the one of whom he had said that he opened the kingdom of God and renovated men by the spirit.

Jesus replied, and said, Look and listen, and tell John whether the kingdom of God has come and whether men are renovated by the spirit. Tell him how I preach the kingdom of God. In the prophecies it says that when the kingdom of God comes, all men will be blessed; tell him, then, that my kingdom of God is such that the poor are blessed, and that every man who hears me becomes blessed.

Having dismissed the disciples of John, Jesus began to explain to the people what kingdom of God John had announced.

He said, When you went to be baptized by John in the wilderness, what did you go to see? If you wanted to see a man dressed in rich raiment, such men live here in palaces. What, then, is it that you saw in the wilderness? Do you think that you went because John was a prophet? Do not think so. John was not a prophet, but the one of whom the prophets have written. He is the one who has announced the coming of the kingdom of God.

Verily I tell you, No greater man has been born than John. He was in the kingdom of God, and so he was greater than all.

The law and the prophets were needed before John; but since John, and even now, the kingdom of God upon earth is announced, and he who makes an effort enters into it.

The lawyers and the Pharisees did not understand what it was John was announcing, and they had no regard for him. This tribe, the lawyers and the Pharisees, regard as truth only what they themselves invent. They learn their law by rote and listen to each other. But what John has said and what I say they do not hear, nor understand. Of all that John has said they understood only so much, that he fasted in the wilderness, and they say, The devil is in him. Of what I say they have understood only this much, that I do not fast, and they say, He eats and drinks with the tax collectors, and is a friend of corrupt people.

They are like children in the street, who prattle with one another and wonder why no one listens to them. Their wisdom is seen by their works.

Everything which I teach men to do is easy and simple, for the kingdom of God is announced as bliss.

CHAPTER FOUR

THE LAW (THE SERMON ON THE MOUNT). THE RICH AND THE POOR

Matt. ix. 35. AND JESUS WENT ABOUT ALL THE CITIES AND VILLAGES, TEACHING IN THE ASSEMBLIES, AND, PREACHING, ANNOUNCED THE PRESENCE OF GOD.

36. LOOKING AT THE MULTITUDES, JESUS WAS MOVED WITH COMPASSION FORM THEM, FOR THEY WERE LIKE MANGY SHEEP WITHOUT A SHEPHERD.

Matt. v. 1. AND SEEING THE MULTITUDES, JESUS WENT UP INTO A MOUNTAIN AND SAT DOWN THERE, AND HIS DISCIPLES CAME TO HIM.

Luke vi. 20. AND LIFTING HIS EYES TO HIS DISCIPLES HE SAID, BLESSED ARE YOU MENDICANTS, FOR YOURS IS THE KINGDOM OF GOD.

21. BLESSED ARE THOSE OF YOU WHO HUNGER NOW, FOR YOU SHALL BE FILLED.

Luke vi. 21. HAPPY ARE THOSE WHO WEEP NOW, FOR YOU WILL LAUGH.

22. HAPPY ARE YOU, WHEN MEN WILL ACCOUNT YOU FOR NOTHING AND WILL RENOUNCE YOU, AND REPROACH YOU, AND CONDEMN YOUR WORK, AND CALL IT BAD FOR THE SAKE OF THE SON OF MAN.

23. REJOICE THEN AND DANCE, FOR YOUR REWARD IS GREAT WITH GOD. THEIR FATHERS DID THE SAME WITH PROPHETS.

24. BUT PITIFUL ARE YOU WHO ARE RICH! YOU ARE PITIFUL, BECAUSE YOU REMOVE CONSOLATION FROM YOURSELVES.

25. PITIFUL ARE YOU THAT ARE FULL! FOR YOU WILL BE SUFFERING. PITIFUL ARE YOU WHO LAUGH NOW! FOR YOU WILL MOURN AND WEEP.

26. PITIFUL YOU ARE, WHEN ALL MEN PRAISE YOU! FOR SO DID THEIR FATHERS PRAISE THE FALSE PROPHETS.

THE SALT OF THE EARTH, THE LIGHT OF THE WORLD

Matt. v. 13. YOU ARE THE SALT OF THE WORLD. IF THE SALT IS NOT SALTED, WITH WHAT SHALL WE SALT? IT IS NOT GOOD FOR ANYTHING, BUT TO BE THROWN UNDER PEOPLE'S FEET.

14. A CITY THAT IS SET ON A HILL CANNOT BE HID.

15. AND HE WHO LIGHTS A CANDLE DOES NOT PUT IT UNDER A BUSHEL, BUT ON A CANDLESTICK, THAT IT MAY LIGHT ALL IN THE ROOM.

16. LET YOUR LIGHT SO SHINE BEFORE MEN, THAT THEY MAY SEE YOUR GOOD WORKS AND UNDERSTAND GOD YOUR FATHER.

THE ETERNAL LAW

Matt. v. 17. DO NOT THINK THAT I AM TEACHING HOW TO DESTROY THE LAW. I AM NOT TEACHING TO DESTROY, BUT TO FULFILL.

18. VERILY I TELL YOU, AS LONG AS HEAVEN AND EARTH STAND, SO LONG WILL EVERY STATUTE OF THE LAW STAND BEFORE YOU, UNTIL IT IS FULFILLED.

19. SO THAT IF ANYONE WILL REGARD AS UNNECESSARY EVEN ONE OF THESE FEW RULES AND WILL TEACH MEN SO, HE WILL BE THE LEAST IN THE KINGDOM OF GOD. BUT HE WHO WILL DO AND TEACH WILL BE THE GREATEST IN THE KINGDOM OF GOD.

20. I TELL YOU IN ADVANCE THAT IF YOUR FULFILLMENT WILL BE SUCH AS IS THE FULFILLMENT OF THE SCRIBES AND THE PHARISEES, YOU WILL IN NO CASE ENTER INTO THE KINGDOM OF GOD.

FIRST COMMANDMENT: THOU SHALT NOT BE ANGRY

Matt. v. 21. YOU HAVE HEARD THAT IT WAS SAID TO THOSE OF OLD TIME, THOU SHALT NOT KILL; HE WHO KILLS IS SUBJECT TO JUDGMENT.

22. BUT I TELL YOU, HE WHO IS ANGRY WITH HIS BROTHER IS ALREADY SUBJECT TO JUDGMENT. AND HE WHO SAYS TO HIS BROTHER, RASCAL, IS SUBJECT TO CRIMINAL PROSECUTION. AND HE WHO SAYS TO HIS BROTHER, CRAZY, IS SUBJECT TO FIRE.

23. SO THAT IF THOU BRINGEST THY GIFT TO THE ALTAR, AND THERE REMEMBEREST AND THAT HE HAS SOMETHING AGAINST THEE;

24. LEAVE THERE THY GIFT BEFORE THE ALTAR, AND GO, FIRST MAKE THY PEACE WITH THY BROTHER, AND THEN COME AND OFFER THE GIFT.

25. SHOW THY GOOD-WILL TO THY ADVERSARY, WHILE HE IS STILL ON THE WAY WITH THEE; LEST HE DELIVER THEE TO THE JUDGE, AND THE JUDGE DELIVER THEE TO THE OFFICER, AND THOU FIND THY WAY INTO PRISON.

26. THEN, THOU KNOWEST THYSELF, THOU WILT NOT GET OUT OF IT UNTIL THOU HAST PAID THE LAST CENT.

SECOND COMMANDMENT: THOU SHALT NOT COMMIT ADULTERY

Matt. v. 27. YOU HAVE HEARD THAT IT IS SAID, THOU SHALT NOT COMMIT ADULTERY.

31. AND IT IS SAID, WHOEVER WILL SEPARATE FROM HIS WIFE, LET HIM GIVE HER A DISCHARGE.

32. BUT I TELL YOU, THAT WHOEVER SEPARATES FROM HIS WIFE, NOT ONLY COMMITS DEBAUCHERY, BUT ALSO CAUSES HER TO COMMIT ADULTERY. AND HE WHO MARRIES A DIVORCED WOMAN ALSO COMMITS ADULTERY.

28. AND WHOEVER LOOKS ON A WOMAN TO LUST AFTER HER IS REALLY COMMITTING ADULTERY.

29. IF THY EYE CATCHES THEE, PLUCK IT OUT, AND CAST IT AWAY FROM THEE, FOR IT IS MORE PROFITABLE FOR THEE THAT ONE EYE SHOULD PERISH, THAN THAT THY WHOLE BODY SHOULD BURN.

30. IF THY RIGHT HAND CATCHES THEE, CUT IT OFF, AND CAST IT FROM THEE. IT IS MORE PROFITABLE FOR THEE THAT ONE OF THY HANDS SHOULD PERISH, THAN THAT THE WHOLE BODY SHOULD BURN.

THIRD COMMANDMENT: THOU SHALT NOT SWEAR

Matt. v. 33. YOU HAVE ALSO HEARD THAT IT HAS BEEN SAID TO THOSE OF OLD TIME, KEEP THY OATH, PERFORM WHAT THOU HAST SWORN BEFORE GOD;

34. BUT I TELL YOU, DO NOT SWEAR AT ALL; DO NOT SWEAR BY HEAVEN— GOD IS THERE;

35. NOR BY THE EARTH—IT IS GOD'S; NOR BY THE CHURCH—IT IS ALSO GOD'S.

36. NOR SWEAR BY THY HEAD, BECAUSE THOU CANST NOT MAKE ONE HAIR OF THY HEAD WHITE OR BLACK.

37. AND SO LET YOUR WORDS BE, YES, YES; NO, NO; AND WHAT IS SUPERFLUOUS IN RESPECT TO THESE WORDS IS BEGOTTEN BY THE DEVIL (DECEPTION).

FOURTH COMMANDMENT: RESIST NOT ABUSE

Matt. v. 38. YOU HAVE HEARD THAT IT HAS BEEN SAID, AN EYE FOR AN EYE, AND A TOOTH FOR A TOOTH:

39. BUT I SAY, DO NOT STRUGGLE AGAINST ABUSE; IF ONE STRIKE THEE ON THY RIGHT CHEEK, TURN TO HIM THE LEFT ALSO.

41. AND IF ONE COMPELS THEE TO WALK A MILE WITH HIM, WALK TWO.

42. GIVE TO EACH MAN WHO ASKS THEE. DO NOT RUN AWAY FROM HIM WHO WANTS TO BORROW FROM THEE, AND DO NOT ASK BACK THY OWN, WHICH ANOTHER HAS TAKEN FROM THEE.

40. AND SO, IF A MAN WANTS TO SUE THEE TO TAKE THY COAT AWAY, GIVE HIM ALSO THY CLOAK.

Luke vi. 37. AND DO NOT SUE, THAT YOU MAY NOT BE SUED, AND DO NOT JUDGE ANY ONE, THAT YOU MAY NOT BE JUDGED: FORGIVE, AND YOU SHALL BE FORGIVEN.

Matt. vii. 2. FOR IN WHAT WAY YOU JUDGE, YOU SHALL BE JUDGED; AND WITH WHAT MEASURE YOU MEASURE, IT SHALL BE MEASURED TO YOU.

3. WHY DOST THOU LOOK FOR THE MOTE IN THY BROTHER'S EYE? THOU DOST NOT SEE THAT THERE IS A WHOLE CHIP IN THY OWN EYE.

4. HOW WILT THOU SAY TO THY BROTHER, BROTHER, I WILL TAKE THE MOTE OUT OF THY EYE, SINCE THOU DOST NOT FEEL THE CHIP IN THY OWN EYE?

5. DECEIVER! FIRST PULL THE CHIP OUT OF THY OWN EYE, THEN THOU WILT SEE HOW TO TAKE THE MOTE OUT OF THY BROTHER'S EYE.

Luke vi. 39. CAN THE BLIND LEAD THE BLIND? THEY WILL BOTH FALL INTO A DITCH.

40. THE DISCIPLE IS NOT ABOVE HIS TEACHER. EVEN IF HE HAS LEARNED EVERYTHING HE WILL BE AS HIS TEACHER.

43. FOR NO BAD FRUIT CAN COME FROM A GOOD TREE; NO GOOD TREE BRINGS FORTH BAD FRUIT.

44. EVERY TREE IS KNOWN BY ITS FRUIT.

Matt. xii. 35. A GOOD MAN OUT OF THE GOOD TREASURE IN HIS HEART BRINGS FORTH GOOD THINGS; AND AN EVIL MAN OUT OF THE EVIL TREASURE IN HIS HEART BRINGS FORTH EVIL THINGS.

Matt. vii. 6. DO NOT GIVE WHAT IS HOLY TO THE DOGS, AND DO NOT CAST WHAT IS MOST PRECIOUS BEFORE THE SWINE, LEST THEY TRAMPLE THEM UNDER THEIR FEET, AND THEN TURN AGAINST YOU AND TEAR YOU UP.

15. KEEP AWAY FROM THE FALSE TEACHERS, WHO COME TO YOU IN SHEEP'S CLOTHING, BUT INWARDLY ARE RAVENING WOLVES.

Matt. xii. **34.** BROOD OF MONSTERS! HOW CAN YOU SPEAK GOOD THINGS, SINCE YOU ARE EVIL?

36. I TELL YOU THAT EVERY IDLE WORD THAT MEN SPEAK THEY WILL PAY FOR WHEN THE ACCOUNTING COMES.

37. FOR BY WORDS THOU SHALT BE JUSTIFIED, AND BY WORDS THOU SHALT BE CONDEMNED.

FIFTH COMMANDMENT: WAGE NO WAR

Matt. v. **43.** YOU HAVE HEARD THAT IT HAS BEEN SAID, DO GOOD TO THY NEIGHBOR, AND COUNT THY ENEMY AS NOTHING.

44. BUT I TELL YOU, DO GOOD TO YOUR ENEMIES, DO GOOD TO THOSE WHO ACCOUNT YOU AS NOTHING; DO GOOD TO THOSE WHO THREATEN YOU, AND PRAY FOR THOSE WHO ATTACK YOU;

45. THAT YOU MAY BECOME THE EQUAL CHILDREN OF YOUR FATHER IN HEAVEN. HE MAKES THE SUN RISE ON THE EVIL AND ON THE GOOD, AND SENDS THE RAIN ON THE JUST AND ON THE UNJUST.

Luke vi. **33.** AND IF YOU DO GOOD TO THOSE WHO DO GOOD TO YOU, WHAT DESSERT IS THERE IN THAT? FOR ALL NATIONS DO THE SAME.

32. AND IF YOU DO GOOD TO YOUR BROTHERS ONLY, WHAT ADDITIONAL THING DO YOU DO TOWARD THE OTHER NATIONS? EVERY NATION DOES THE SAME.

Matt. v. **48.** BE THEREFORE GOOD TO ALL MEN, AS YOUR FATHER IN HEAVEN IS GOOD TO ALL.

Matt. vii. **12.** THEREFORE ALL THINGS WHICH YOU WOULD THAT MEN SHOULD DO TO YOU, DO YOU TO THEM; FOR THIS IS THE LAW AND THE PROPHETS.

OF ALMS, FASTING, AND PRAYER

Matt. vi. 1. TAKE HEED THAT YOU DO NOT DO WHAT IS RIGHTEOUS FOR MEN, TO BE SEEN OF THEM. IF YOU DO SO, THERE IS NO DESERT IN YOUR RIGHTEOUSNESS BEFORE YOUR FATHER IN HEAVEN.

2. SO WHEN THOU ART COMPASSIONATE TO MEN, DO NOT SOUND A TRUMPET BEFORE THEE, AS THE COMEDIANS DO IN THE GATHERINGS, IN THE STREETS, THAT MEN MAY PRAISE THEM. YOU SEE YOURSELVES THAT THEY HAVE RECEIVED THEIR REWARD.

3. BUT WHEN THOU ART COMPASSIONATE, DO IT SO AS NOT TO KNOW WHETHER IT IS THY RIGHT HAND, OR THY LEFT, WHICH IS DOING IT,

4. SO THAT THY PITY FOR MEN MAY BE IN THE SECRET OF THY HEART; THY FATHER SEES IN THE SECRET OF THY HEART AND WILL REPAY THEE.

16. WHEN THOU DEPRIVEST THYSELF OF ANYTHING, BE NOT MOROSE, LIKE COMEDIANS, FOR THEY PURPOSELY SADDEN THEIR FACES THAT MEN MAY SEE THAT THEY FAST. THOU KNOWEST THYSELF, THEY RECEIVE THEIR REWARD FOR IT.

17. WHEN THOU RESTRAINEST THYSELF FROM ANYTHING, PERFUME THY HEAD AND WASH THY FACE;

18. THAT MEN MAY NOT SEE THAT THOU ART FASTING, BUT THAT THY FATHER MAY SEE IN THY HEART. AND THY FATHER, SEEING IN THY HEART, WILL REWARD THEE.

5. AND WHEN THOU PRAYEST, BE NOT AS THE LIARS: THEY ALWAYS PRAY IN THE ASSEMBLIES, STOPPING IN THE CORNERS OF THE STREETS, THAT THEY MAY BE SEEN BY MEN. THOU SEEST THYSELF, THEY RECEIVE THEIR REWARD.

6. BUT THOU, WHEN THOU PRAYEST, ENTER INTO THY CLOSET, SHUT THE DOOR, AND PRAY TO THY FATHER. AND THY FATHER WILL SEE IN THY SOUL AND WILL REPAY THEE.

7. WHEN YOU PRAY, DO NOT WAG YOUR TONGUES, AS THE COMEDIANS DO. THEY THINK THAT THEIR PRATTING WILL BE HEARD.

8. BE NOT LIKE THEM, FOR YOUR FATHER KNOWS WHAT YOU NEED, BEFORE YOU OPEN YOUR MOUTHS.

9. PRAY LIKE THIS: FATHER!

10. LET THY KINGDOM BE. LET THY WILL BE IN THEE AND IN ME.

11. GIVE US OUR DAILY FOOD WHICH WE NEED.

12. AND FORGIVE US OUR GUILT, BECAUSE WE FORGIVE ALL WHO ARE GUILTY TOWARD US.

Mark xi. 25. WHEN YOU BEGIN TO PRAY, FORGIVE, IF YOU HAVE ANY-THING AGAINST ANY, SO THAT YOUR FATHER IN HEAVEN MAY FORGIVE YOU YOUR TRESPASSES.

26. IF YOU DO NOT FORGIVE, YOUR FATHER IN HEAVEN WILL NOT FOR-GIVE YOUR TRESPASSES.

OF LAYING UP TREASURE

Matt. vi. 19. AND DO NOT INCREASE YOUR LIVINGS UPON EARTH; HERE MOTHS AND RUST CORRUPT ALL, AND THIEVES DIG UNDER AND STEAL.

20. BUT LAY UP FOR YOURSELVES LIVINGS IN HEAVEN; THERE MOTHS AND RUST DO NOT CORRUPT THINGS, AND THIEVES DO NOT DIG UNDER AND STEAL.

21. FOR WHERE YOUR LIVING IS, THERE WILL ALSO YOUR HEART BE.

22. THE EYES ARE THE LIGHT OF THE BODY. IF THY EYES ARE NOT DIM, THE WHOLE BODY WILL BE FULL OF LIGHT.

23. BUT IF THY EYES ARE DIM, THY WHOLE BODY WILL BE FULL OF DARKNESS. IF THEREFORE THY LIGHT IS DARKNESS, HOW GREAT IS THAT DARKNESS!

24. NO MAN CAN WORK FOR TWO MASTERS, FOR HE WILL ESTEEM ONE LITTLE, AND WILL RESPECT THE OTHER; HE WILL DO ONE'S WILL, AND WILL FORGET THE OTHER. YOU CANNOT WORK FOR GOD AND FOR MAMMON.

Luke xii. 15. TAKE HEED, AND BEWARE OF EVERY SELFISHNESS, FOR A MAN'S LIFE DOES NOT CONSIST IN HAVING MORE THAN HE NEEDS.

Matt. xvi. 26. WHAT PROFIT IS IT TO A MAN, IF HE GAINS THE WHOLE WORLD, AND LOSES HIS SOUL? YOU CANNOT REDEEM THE SOUL WITH RICHES.

Matt. vi. 25. THEREFORE I TELL YOU, DO NOT TROUBLE YOURSELVES ABOUT WHAT YOU ARE GOING TO EAT AND DRINK; NOR TROUBLE YOUR-SELVES ABOUT YOUR BODY, WHAT YOU WILL PUT ON. IS NOT THE LIFE MORE THAN FOOD, AND THE BODY MORE THAN RAIMENT?

26. LOOK AT THE BIRDS OF THE AIR: THEY DO NOT SOW, NOR REAP, NOR GATHER INTO BARNS; BUT THE FATHER FEEDS THEM. IS NOT MAN MORE PRECIOUS THAN THE BIRDS?

27. TRY AS YOU MAY, YOU CANNOT ADD THE LEAST BIT TO YOUR LIFE.

28. AND WHY DO YOU TROUBLE YOURSELVES ABOUT RAIMENT? LOOK AT THE FLOWERS OF THE FIELD, HOW THEY BLOOM; THEY DO NOT WORK, NOR SPIN.

29. AND SOLOMON IN ALL HIS GLORY WAS NOT BETTER DRESSED THAN ONE OF THE FLOWERS OF THE FIELD.

30. IF GOD CAN CLOTHE SO THE GRASS OF THE FIELD, WHICH LIVES TODAY, AND TOMORROW IS BURNED UP, WHY SHOULD HE NOT CLOTHE YOU? YOU DO NOT BELIEVE WELL!

31. THEREFORE DO NOT TROUBLE YOURSELVES; DO NOT CONSIDER WHAT YOU ARE GOING TO EAT AND WHAT TO DRINK, AND HOW YOU WILL BE CLOTHED.

32. ALL THESE THINGS ALL THE NATIONS NEED, AND YOUR FATHER IN HEAVEN KNOWS THAT YOU NEED ALL THAT.

34. SO DO NOT TROUBLE YOURSELVES ABOUT WHAT WILL BE TOMORROW. TOMORROW WILL HAVE ITS OWN CARE. SUFFICIENT ARE THE CARES FOR ONE DAY.

33. FIRST OF ALL SEEK TO BE IN THE WILL OF GOD AND TO ENTRUST YOURSELVES TO THE WILL OF GOD; ASK FOR THE CHIEF THING, AND THE INSIGNIFICANT WILL COME ITSELF.

Matt. vii. 7. ASK, AND IT SHALL BE GIVEN YOU; SEEK, AND YOU SHALL FIND; KNOCK, AND IT SHALL BE OPENED TO YOU.

8. FOR EVERY ONE WHO WISHES RECEIVES; AND HE WHO SEEKS FINDS; AND TO HIM WHO KNOCKS IT SHALL BE OPENED.

9. IS THERE A MAN AMONG YOU WHO, IF HIS SON ASKS BREAD, WILL GIVE HIM A STONE?

10. OR, IF HIS SON ASKS HIM FOR A FISH, WILL GIVE HIM A SNAKE?

11. IF YOU, EVIL PEOPLE, KNOW WHAT IS GOOD AND GIVE IT TO YOUR CHILDREN, HOW THEN WILL YOUR FATHER IN HEAVEN NOT GIVE THE GOOD SPIRIT TO HIM WHO ASKS HIM FOR IT?

THE NARROW WAY

Matt. vii. 13. ENTER BY THE NARROW ENTRANCE, FOR A LEVEL ENTRANCE AND A BROAD WAY LEAD TO DESTRUCTION, AND MANY ENTER THAT WAY.

14. AND A NARROW ENTRANCE AND A NARROW WAY LEAD INTO LIFE, AND NOT MANY FIND IT.

Luke xii. 32. FEAR NOT, LITTLE FLOCK, FOR THE FATHER HAS WISHED TO TEACH US HIS WILL.

PARABLE OF THE HOUSE BUILT UPON A ROCK

Matt. vii. 22. MANY WILL TELL ME ON THAT DAY, LORD, LORD, HAVE WE NOT TAUGHT AND DRIVEN OUT THE EVIL FOR THY SAKE? AND HAVE WE NOT ESTABLISHED THE POWER FOR THY SAKE?

23. AND THEN WILL I TELL THEM, I NEVER KNEW YOU: GO AWAY FROM ME, YOU THAT HAVE COMMITTED LAWLESSNESS.

24. THEREFORE WHOSOEVER HEARS THESE WORDS AND FULFILLS THEM IS LIKE A WISE MAN WHO BUILT HIS HOUSE UPON A ROCK.

25. AND THE RAIN CAME DOWN, AND THE BROOKS BEGAN TO FLOW, AND THE WINDS BLEW, AND PRESSED AGAINST THE HOUSE, AND IT DID NOT FALL: FOR IT WAS FOUNDED ON A ROCK.

26. AND EVERY ONE THAT UNDERSTANDS THESE WORDS AND DOES NOT DO WHAT I TELL HIM IS LIKE A FOOLISH MAN WHO BUILT HIS HOUSE UPON THE SAND.

27. AND THE RAIN CAME, AND THE BROOKS BEGAN TO FLOW, AND THE WIND BLEW AND STRUCK THE HOUSE, AND IT FELL, AND THERE WAS A GREAT NOISE;

28. AND IT HAPPENED THAT WHEN JESUS FINISHED HIS DISCOURSE, THE PEOPLE WERE DELIGHTED WITH HIS TEACHING:

29. FOR HE TAUGHT THEM AS A FREE MAN, AND NOT AS THE SCRIBES TAUGHT.

THE CHOOSING OF THE TWELVE APOSTLES

Luke vi. 12. AT THAT TIME JESUS WENT INTO THE MOUNTAINS TO PRAY, AND HE PRAYED ALL NIGHT TO GOD.

13. AND WHEN IT WAS DAY, HE CALLED HIS DISCIPLES, AND CHOSE OF THEM TWELVE AND CALLED THEM HIS MESSENGERS:

14. SIMON (WHOM HE HAD NAMED A ROCK), AND ANDREW HIS BROTHER, AND JAMES, AND JOHN, PHILIP AND BARTHOLOMEW,

15. MATTHEW AND THOMAS, JAMES THE SON OF ALPHEUS, AND SIMON CALLED ZELOTES,

16. AND JUDAS THE BROTHER OF JAMES, AND JUDAS ISCARIOT, THE ONE WHO BECAME THE TRAITOR.

17. AND HE CAME DOWN WITH THEM, AND STOPPED IN THE PLAIN; AND HIS DISCIPLES AND A GREAT MULTITUDE FROM JUDEA AND FROM JERUSALEM, AND FROM THE SEA COAST OF TYRE AND SIDON. THEY ALL CAME TO HEAR HIM.

TOLSTOY'S COMMENTARY

John announced the coming of God into the world. He said that men must be purified in the spirit in order that they may know the kingdom of God.

Jesus, who did not know his carnal father and who recognized God as his Father, heard John's sermon and asked himself what this God was, how he came into the world, and where he was. And, departing into the wilderness, Jesus learned that the life of man was in the spirit, and having convinced himself of this, that man always lives through God, that God is always in men, and that the kingdom of God has always been and is always, and that men need only recognize that, Jesus left the wilderness and began to prophesy to men that God has always been and is always in the world, and that to know him we need be purified or regenerated in the spirit.

He announced that God wants no prayers, sacrifices, or temples, but that what he wants is serving him in the spirit, doing good; he announced that the kingdom of God must not be understood in this way, that God will come at some particular time and in some particular place, but that in the whole world and at all times all men, having purified themselves in the spirit, may live in the power of God. He announced that the kingdom of God does not come in a visible manner, but that it is within men. To be a participant in the kingdom one must be purified in the spirit, that is, exalt the spirit within oneself, and serve it. He who exalts his spirit enters the kingdom of God and receives non-temporal life. The possibility of exalting the spirit and becoming a participant in the kingdom of God lies in every man, and ever since John announced the kingdom of God, the Jewish law has become unnecessary. Every man who understands the kingdom of God, by his own efforts, having exalted the spirit in himself and working for God, enters into the power of God.

To work for God and live in the kingdom, that is, to submit to him and fulfill his will, it is necessary to know the law of this kingdom. And so Jesus announces wherein the exaltation of the spirit and the work for God must consist, what is the law of the kingdom of God.

Jesus prays all night long, and choosing twelve men, who understand him completely, goes out to the people with them, and tells them what the exaltation of the spirit and the service of God consists in, what the law of the kingdom of God is.

The law of God's power consists above all in this, that the whole man should give himself over into the power of God, and Jesus, casting a glance at the people and pointing to the disciples, says:

Happy are you, vagrants, you are in the power of God. You are happy. What of it if you are hungry now? After you have been hungry, you will eat. You are happy. Even though you are mourning and weeping now, you will have your consolation later. You are happy. Let men esteem you little and drive you away from everywhere. Be glad of it, for thus did they drive all those men who announced the will of God.

But unfortunate are you, rich men, for you have received everything which you have wished for, and shall receive nothing more. If you are filled now, you will be hungry. If you are merry now, you shall be sad. Unfortunate you are, if all praise you, for all men praise only liars.

Happy are you, vagrants, for you are in the power of God; you are happy only when you are vagrants not only in appearance, but with your soul; just as the salt is good only when it is salt not merely in appearance, but is salty in itself. You know yourselves that true happiness lies in being a vagrant. But if you are vagrants only in appearance, you are like unsalted salt, and are good for nothing. If you understand this, then show by your deeds that you want to be vagrants, and be not like others.

If you are the light of men, show your light, and do not hide it, so that men may see indeed that you know the truth, and, looking at your deeds, may understand that you are the children of the Father your God.

Do not think that being a vagrant means being lawless. I do not teach in order to loosen your hands from the divine law; on the contrary, I teach you to fulfill the divine law. As long as there are men under heaven, the law as to what may be done, and what not, exists for men. There will be no law when men will naturally do everything according to the law. Here I give you some rules for the fulfillment of the law.

If a man shall not fulfill a single one of them and shall teach you that it may be left unfulfilled, he will be farthest away from God; but he who fulfills them all and teaches you to do so will be nearest to God. For, if in the fulfillment of the law by you there will not be more truth than in the fulfillment of the law of the Pharisees and the scribes, you will not unite with God.

Here are the rules:

First rule: The justice of the scribes and the Pharisees consists in this, that if a man kills another, he must be tried and sentenced to punishment.

But my rule is that it is as bad to grow angry with your brother as it is to kill. I forbid anger against a brother with the same threat with which the Pharisees and scribes forbid murder. Still more severely and with a greater threat do I forbid you cursing a brother, and still more severely and with a still greater threat do I forbid your insulting a brother.

I forbid this, because you consider it necessary to go to the temple, to offer sacrifices, and you go and offer sacrifices and regard the sacrifices as important; still more important are peace, concord, and love among yourselves for the sake of God, and you cannot pray or think of God if there is even one man with whom you are not at peace.

Second rule:

The Pharisees and scribes say, If thou committest adultery, thou and the woman are to be killed together, and if thou wantest to commit adultery, give thy wife a writ of divorcement.

But I say, If thou leavest thy wife, thou art not only a debauchee, thou also causest her to commit debauchery, and him also who takes her up. If thou livest with thy wife and takest it into thy head to fall in love with another woman, thou art already an adulterer, and art worthy of having that done to thee which is done with an adulterer. And I forbid this with the same threat with which the Pharisees and scribes forbid committing fornication with another woman, because every debauchery causes the soul to perish, and it is better for thee to renounce carnal pleasure than to cause the ruin of thy life.

And so the second rule is: Satisfy thy lust with thy wife and do not think that love of woman is good.

The third rule is this:

The Pharisees and scribes say, Do not pronounce in vain the name of the Lord thy God, for God will not let go unpunished the man who uses his name in vain, that is, Do not invoke God in a lie, and again, Do not swear in my name in a lie, and do not dishonor the name of thy God. I am the Lord (your God), that is, do not swear by me in untruth, so as to defile your God.

But I say that every oath is a defilement of God, and so do not swear at all. Thou canst not promise anything, for thou art entirely in the power of God. Thou canst not make a single gray hair black, how then canst thou swear in advance that thou wilt do so and so, and how canst thou swear by God? Every oath of thine is a defilement of God, for if thou hast to carry out an oath which is contrary to the will of God, it will turn out that thou hast promised to act against his will, and so every oath is an evil. Besides, an oath is foolish and meaningless.

So here is the third rule: Never swear to any one about anything. Say, Yes, when it is, Yes, and, No, when it is, No, and know that if thou art required to swear, it is evil.

Fourth rule:

You have heard that it has been said of old time, An eye for an eye, and a tooth for a tooth. The Pharisees and scribes teach you to do every-thing which is written in the old books as to how you are to punish for all kinds of crimes. It says there that he who destroys life must give his life, an eye for an eye, a tooth for a tooth, a hand for a hand, an ox for an ox, a slave for a slave, and so forth.

But I tell you, Do not struggle against evil with evil, and not only do not demand an ox for an ox, a slave for a slave, life for life, but do not even resist evil. If a man wants to get thy ox by a lawsuit, give him two; if a man wants to get thy coat away, give him also thy cloak; if a man knocks a tooth out of one jaw, offer him also the other jaw. If they compel thee to do a certain amount of work, work twice as much. If they take thy property from thee, give it to them. If they do not return thy money to thee, do not ask for it, and so, do not judge and do not litigate, and do not punish, and you will not be judged and punished. Forgive everybody and you will be forgiven, for if you are going to judge men, they will judge you. Besides, you must not judge, because all of us men are blind and do not see the truth. How can I with dust-filled eyes see the dust in my brother's eye? First I must clean my own eyes, and whose eyes are clean? If we judge, we are ourselves blind. If we are going to judge others and punish them, we are like the blind guiding the blind.

Besides, says Jesus, What do we teach? We punish by force, with wounds, maiming, and death, that is, with malice, precisely what is for-bidden in the commandment, Thou shalt not kill. And what comes of it? We want to teach men, and we corrupt them. What else can there be but that the pupil will learn from the teacher and be exactly like him? What will he do after he has learned everything? The same that the teacher does: he will commit violence, and will kill.

And do not think that you will find justice in the courts. To turn the love of justice over to the courts is the same as throwing precious pearls before the swine, for they will tread them underfoot and will break them.

And so the fourth rule is: No matter how much they may offend thee, do not put out the evil by evil, do not sit in judgment or go to court, do not punish, and do not complain.

Fifth rule:

The Pharisees and scribes say, Make no war on thy brother in thy heart; arraign thy neighbor, and thou wilt not bear his sins; kill all the men, and take all the wives and the cattle from thy enemy, that is, Respect thy countrymen and have no regard for strangers.

But I tell you, Do good not only to thy countrymen, but also to strangers. Let strangers esteem you little, let them attack and offend you, respect them, and do them good. Only then will you be true children of your Father. To him all are alike. If you are good to your countrymen alone, you are doing what all nations are doing, and that leads to wars. But be the same to all nations, and you will be the children of God. All men are his children, consequently all are your brothers.

And so the fifth rule is: Observe toward foreign nations what I have told you to observe among yourselves. There are no hostile nations, no different kingdoms and kings. All are brothers, all are children of the same Father. Make no distinction among people according to nations and kingdoms.

So: (1) Do not be angry; (2) do not amuse yourself with the lust of fornication; (3) do not swear to any one about anything; (4) do not sit in judgment and do not litigate; and (5) make no distinction between the different nations; know no kings and no kingdoms.

And here is another instruction, which includes all these rules: *Everything which you wish that men should do to you, do you to them.* When you will execute this, it is clear that your life will be changed. You will have no property, and that is not necessary. Do not build up your life upon earth, but build it in God. The life on earth will perish, and the life in God will not perish. And do not think of the life upon earth, for if you will think of it, you will not be able to think of the life in God. Where the soul is, there is the heart also.

And if there is no light in your eyes, you are all in darkness. So if you wish and look for the darkness, you will enter the darkness. It is impossible to look with one eye upon heaven and with the other upon earth; it is impossible to repose your heart in an earthly life and to think of God. You will work either for the earthly life, or for God. And so: Beware of every selfishness. Man's life is not from what he has, but from God, so that if a man should take the whole world, there would be no profit to his soul from it. And foolishly will act the man who will cause his life to perish in order to obtain as many possessions as possible.

Consequently, do not trouble yourselves as to what you are going to eat and drink, and how you are going to clothe yourselves. Life is more important than food and raiment, and God has given it to you.

Look at God's creatures, at the birds. They do not sow, nor reap, nor collect the grain, but God feeds them. And is not man as much as the birds before God? If God has given life to man, he will be able to feed him also. And you know yourselves that no matter how much you trouble yourselves, you are not able to do anything for yourselves. You cannot lengthen your life for one little hour. (The thought is beyond the mountains, but death is behind the shoulders.)

And do not trouble yourselves so much about your raiment. The flowers of the field do not work, nor spin, and yet they are adorned as Solomon never adorned himself. If God has so adorned the grass, which grows today and tomorrow will be mowed down, will he not clothe you?

Do not have any care and trouble yourselves; do not say that you must think of what you are going to eat and what you will wear. All men need that, and God knows the need of every one.

Even so do not trouble yourselves as to what will be, as to the future. Live for the present day. Take heed that you are in the will of God. Desire only the one thing which is important, and the rest will come to you itself. Try only to be in the will of God, and you will be in it. He who knocks, to him it will be opened; who asks, to him it will be given. If you will ask for what is present, what you need, it will be given to you.

Is there a father who would give his son a stone instead of bread, or a snake instead of a fish? How, then, will your Father refuse to give you what you really need, if you ask him for it? But what you really need is the life of the spirit, so ask for that alone.

To pray does not mean to do what the hypocrites are doing in the churches, or in the sight of men. They do so for men, and from them they receive their praise, and not from God. But if thou wishest to enter into the will of thy Father, go there where no one can see thee and pray to thy Father the spirit, and the Father will see what there is in thy soul, and will give thee the true spirit. And do not uselessly wag thy tongue, as the hypocrites do. Thy father knows what thou needest, before thou openest thy mouth.

This is the way you ought to pray: Our Father! Let me be in thy kingdom, that is, let thy will be in me. Give me such food as I need. And forgive me my faults, as I forgive them in others.

If you ask God for the spirit, find no fault with men, and God will forgive you your faults. And if you do not forgive men, God will not forgive you.

Do nothing to be praised by men. If you do so for men, you will receive your reward from men.

So if thou art compassionate toward men, do not sound thy trumpet about it before men, for the hypocrites do so, that men may praise them. They receive what they wish. But thou, if thou art compassionate to men, do good in such a way that no one may see it. And thy Father will see it, and will give thee what thou needest.

And if thou sufferest oppression for the sake of God, do not weep and complain before men, as the hypocrites do, that men may see and praise them, for they receive what they want. But do differently: if thou sufferest for the sake of God, go about with a happy face, that men may not see, but thy Father will see, and will give thee what thou needest.

Such is the entrance into the kingdom of God. There is but one entrance to the will of God, and it is narrow. There is always but one entrance, and all around is a large and broad field, and if you walk over it you will not come to the haven. Only a narrow path leads into life, and only a few walk over it.

Do not lose your courage, though a little flock you be. You will enter into it, because the Father will teach you his will.

CHAPTER FIVE

The Fulfillment of the Law Gives the True Life. The New Teaching about God

Matt. ix. 36. JESUS WAS SORRY FOR THE PEOPLE, BECAUSE THEY DID NOT UNDERSTAND WHAT THE TRUE LIFE CONSISTED IN, AND WERE TORMENTED WITHOUT KNOWING WHY, LIKE SHEEP WITHOUT A SHEPHERD.

Matt. xi. 28. AND HE SAID, GIVE YOURSELVES TO ME, ALL YOU WHO ARE IN LABOR, WHO ARE LADEN ABOVE YOUR STRENGTH, AND I WILL GIVE YOU REST.

29. TAKE MY YOKE UPON YOU, AND LEARN OF ME; FOR I AM MEEK AND LOWLY IN HEART, AND YOU WILL FIND REST IN LIFE.

30. FOR MY YOKE IS EASY, AND MY WAGON IS LIGHT.

JESUS CHOOSES THE DISCIPLES AND DISCOURSES TO THEM

Luke x. 1. AFTER THAT JESUS APPOINTED OTHER SEVENTY MEN, AND SENT THEM TWO AND TWO IN HIS PLACE INTO EVERY CITY AND PLACE, WHERE HE HIMSELF HAD TO BE.

2. AND HE SAID TO THEM, THE FIELD IS GREAT, BUT THE LABORERS ARE FEW. THE MASTER MUST SEND THE LABORERS INTO THE FIELD.

Matt. x. 7. GO AND PROCLAIM, SAYING, THE KINGDOM OF GOD HAS COME.

Mark vi. 8. AND COMMANDED THEM THAT THEY SHOULD TAKE NOTH-
ING ON THEIR JOURNEY, SAVE A STAFF; NO SCRIP, NO BREAD, NO MONEY IN
THEIR PURSE.

9. AND PUT ON HEMP SHOES AND ONE COAT,

Matt. x. 10. FOR HE WHO WORKS IS WORTHY OF HIS COAT.

Mark vi. 10. AND WHATEVER HOUSE YOU ENTER, STAY THERE TILL YOU
LEAVE THAT LOCATION.

12. WHEN YOU ENTER A HOUSE, GREET THE HOST, SAYING, PEACE BE TO
YOUR HOUSE.

13. IF THE HOSTS AGREE, PEACE WILL BE IN THAT HOUSE, AND IF THEY DO
NOT AGREE, YOUR PEACE WILL REMAIN WITH YOU.

Mark vi. 11. AND IF THEY DO NOT RECEIVE YOU, NOR LISTEN TO YOU, GO
AWAY FROM THERE, SHAKE OFF THE DUST UNDER YOUR FEET AS A SIGN
THAT YOU DO NOT WANT ANYTHING FROM THEM.

Matt. x. 22. AND THEY WILL HATE YOU FOR MY TEACHING, BUT HE WHO
WILL BE FIRM TO THE END WILL BE SAFE.

23. AND IF THEY ATTACK YOU IN ONE CITY, FLEE TO ANOTHER.

16. AND SO I SEND YOU LIKE SHEEP INTO THE MIDST OF WOLVES: BE THERE-
FORE AS WISE AS SERPENTS, AND SIMPLE AS DOVES.

Mark xiii. 9. BUT TAKE HEED: FOR THEY WILL DELIVER YOU TO THE
COURTS; AND THEY WILL FLOG YOU IN THE ASSEMBLIES, AND WILL BRING
YOU TO THE RULERS AND KINGS FOR MY SAKE, TO SHOW BEFORE THEM.

Matt. x. 19. BUT WHEN THEY DELIVER YOU TO THE COURTS, TAKE NO
THOUGHT HOW AND WHAT YOU WILL SPEAK; FOR YOU WILL BE TAUGHT AT
THAT HOUR WHAT YOU SHALL SPEAK.

20. NOT YOU YOURSELVES WILL SPEAK, BUT THE SPIRIT OF THE FATHER
WILL SPEAK IN YOU.

23. YOU WILL NOT HAVE GONE OVER THE CITIES OF JUDEA, WHEN THE SON OF MAN WILL APPEAR.

26. THEREFORE DO NOT FEAR THEM.

Mark iv. 22. FOR IN THE SOUL IS HID WHAT WILL BE MANIFESTED; EVERY-THING WHICH IS KEPT, IS KEPT IN ORDER THAT IT MAY BECOME MANIFEST IN THE WORLD.

Luke xii. 3. AND EVERYTHING WHICH YOU HAVE SPOKEN IN SECRET WILL BE HEARD IN THE LIGHT; WHAT YOU HAVE SPOKEN IN THE EAR IN CLOSETS WILL BE PROCLAIMED FROM THE HOUSETOPS.

4. I TELL YOU, MY FRIENDS, BE NOT AFRAID OF THOSE WHO KILL THE BODY, AND BEYOND THAT CAN DO NOTHING TO YOU.

5. I WILL SHOW YOU WHOM YOU SHALL FEAR. FEAR HIM WHO KILLS AND DESTROYS THE SOUL. VERILY I TELL YOU, FEAR HIM.

6. ARE NOT FIVE SPARROWS SOLD FOR A CENT? AND THEY ARE NOT FOR-GOTTEN BY GOD, AND NOT ONE WILL DIE WITHOUT YOUR FATHER.

7. EVEN THE HAIRS OF YOUR HEAD ARE ALL NUMBERED. THEREFORE BE NOT AFRAID: YOU ARE OF MORE VALUE THAN SPARROWS.

8. I TELL YOU, WHOEVER WILL BE WITH ME BEFORE MEN, WITH HIM THE SON OF MAN WILL BE BEFORE THE POWERS OF GOD.

Matt. x. 34. DO NOT THINK THAT I HAVE BROUGHT PEACE UPON EARTH: I HAVE NOT BROUGHT PEACE, BUT DISCORD.

Luke xii. 49. I HAVE COME TO SEND FIRE ON EARTH; HOW ANXIOUS I AM THAT IT SHOULD BURN UP!

50. THERE IS A REGENERATION THROUGH WHICH I MUST PASS, AND I LANGUISH TILL IT BE ACCOMPLISHED.

9. AND WHOEVER WILL DENY ME BEFORE MEN WILL BE DENIED BEFORE THE POWERS OF GOD.

51. OR DO YOU THINK THAT I TEACH PEACE UPON EARTH? NO, NOT PEACE, BUT DISCORD:

52. FOR FROM NOW ON FIVE IN ONE HOUSE WILL BE DIVIDED, THREE FROM TWO, AND TWO FROM THREE.

53. THE FATHER WILL BE DIVIDED FROM HIS SON, AND THE SON FROM HIS FATHER: AND THE MOTHER FROM THE DAUGHTER, AND THE DAUGHTER FROM THE MOTHER; AND THE MOTHER-IN-LAW, AND THE DAUGHTER-IN-LAW FROM THE MOTHER-IN-LAW.

Matt. x. 36. AND A MAN'S FOES WILL BE HIS OWN HOUSEHOLD.

21. AND THE BROTHER WILL DELIVER THE BROTHER UP TO DEATH, AND THE FATHER THE CHILD; AND THE CHILDREN WILL RISE UP AGAINST THEIR PARENTS, AND WILL DELIVER THEM UP TO DEATH.

Luke xiv. 26. IF A MAN WANTS TO BE WITH ME, AND WILL NOT ESTEEM LITTLE HIS FATHER, AND MOTHER, AND WIFE, AND CHILDREN, AND BROTHERS, AND SISTERS, AND HIS OWN LIFE, HE CANNOT BE MY DISCIPLE.

Matt. x. 37. HE WHO LOVES HIS FATHER AND MOTHER MORE THAN ME DOES NOT AGREE WITH ME; AND HE WHO LOVES HIS SON OR DAUGHTER MORE THAN ME DOES NOT AGREE WITH ME.

Luke ix. 23. AND HE SAID TO ALL, IF ANY MAN WANTS TO BE MY DISCIPLE, LET HIM DENY HIS DESIRES, AND LET HIM AT ANY HOUR BE READY FOR THE GALLOWS, AND THEN ONLY WILL HE BE MY DISCIPLE.

Matt. x. 39. HE WHO TAKES CARE OF HIS LIFE WILL CAUSE HIS LIFE TO PERISH, AND HE WHO RUINS HIS LIFE FOR MY SAKE WILL SAVE IT.

Luke x. 17. AND THE SEVENTY WHOM HE SENT OUT RETURNED WITH JOY, AND SAID, SIR, THE EVIL IS VANQUISHED BY US THROUGH THY POWER.

18. AND HE SAID TO THEM,

20. BUT DO NOT REJOICE THAT THE EVIL IS VANQUISHED BY YOU; RATHER REJOICE, BECAUSE YOU ARE IN THE KINGDOM OF HEAVEN.

21. THEN JESUS REJOICED IN HIS SPIRIT, AND SAID, I RECOGNIZE THEE, MY FATHER, LORD OF HEAVEN AND EARTH, BECAUSE THOU HAST HID THIS FROM THE WISE AND PRUDENT, AND HAST REVEALED IT TO CHILDREN. THOU ART TRULY THE FATHER! IN THIS HAS THY LOVE BEEN EXPRESSED.

Matt. xi. 27. EVERYTHING HAS BEEN DELIVERED TO ME BY MY FATHER, AND NO MAN RECOGNIZES THE SON, BUT THE FATHER; NEITHER DOES A MAN KNOW WHO THE FATHER IS, BUT THE SON, AND HE TO WHOM THE SON WILL REVEAL HIM.

EVIL IS NOT DESTROYED BY EVIL

Mark iii. 20. AND THEY CAME HOME, AND AGAIN THERE WAS GATHERED A MULTITUDE, SO THAT THEY COULD NOT DINE.

21. AND WHEN HIS HOUSEHOLD HEARD OF IT, THEY WENT TO SEIZE HIM, FOR THEY SAID, HE IS BESIDE HIMSELF.

22. AND THE SCRIBES CAME FROM JERUSALEM AND SAID THAT HE WAS AN EVIL SPIRIT, AND THAT HE DESTROYED EVIL BY EVIL.

23. AND CALLING THEM UP, HE SAID TO THEM IN PARABLES, HOW CAN EVIL BE CAST OUT BY EVIL?

24. AND IF A POWER RISES AGAINST ITSELF, THAT POWER CANNOT STAND.

26. AND IF EVIL WILL GO AGAINST ITSELF, IT CANNOT STAND, BUT HAS AN END.

Luke xi. 19. IF I CAST OUT EVIL WITH EVIL, HOW DO YOU CAST IT OUT? BE THEREFORE YOUR OWN JUDGES.

20. BUT IF I CAST OUT THE EVIL WITH THE SPIRIT OF GOD, THEN THE KINGDOM OF GOD WAS BEFORE.

Matt. xii. 29. OR ELSE, HOW CAN ONE ENTER INTO A STRONG MAN'S HOUSE AND RUIN HIM? FIRST THE STRONG MAN HAS TO BE BOUND AND THEN ONLY CAN HIS HOUSE BE RUINED.

30. HE WHO IS NOT WITH ME IS AGAINST ME. HE WHO DOES NOT GATHER, SCATTERS.

31. THEREFORE I TELL YOU, EVERY ERROR, EVERY FALSE WORD IS LEFT TO MEN;

32. AND IF A MAN SAYS A FALSE WORD AGAINST THE SON OF MAN, IT WILL BE FORGIVEN HIM: BUT IF A MAN SAYS SOMETHING AGAINST THE SPIRIT OF GOD, IT WILL NOT BE FORGIVEN HIM, NEITHER IN THIS WORLD, NOR IN THE WORLD TO COME.

33. EITHER MAKE THE TREE GOOD, THEN ITS FRUIT WILL BE GOOD: OR MAKE THE TREE BAD, AND THEN THE FRUIT WILL BE BAD: FOR THE TREE IS KNOWN BY ITS FRUIT.

34. TRIBE OF VIPERS, YOU CANNOT SPEAK GOOD THINGS, BECAUSE YOU ARE EVIL. THE MOUTH SPEAKS WHAT THE HEART WANTS TO UTTER.

35. A GOOD MAN LETS OUT OF HIS HEART WHATEVER GOOD HE HAS TREASURED IN IT; AND AN EVIL MAN LETS OUT WHATEVER EVIL HE HAS GATHERED IN HIS HEART.

36. AND I TELL YOU, EVERY IDLE WORD WHICH A MAN SPEAKS WILL BE LOOKED INTO, TO SEE WHY IT HAS BEEN SAID, IN THE DAY OF THE ACCOUNTING.

Luke ix. 49. AND JOHN SAID TO HIM, TEACHER, WE SAW A MAN CASTING OUT EVIL LIKE THEE, AND WE FORBADE HIM, BECAUSE HE DOES NOT GO WITH US.

50. JESUS SAID TO THEM, DO NOT FORBID HIM: HE WHO IS NOT AGAINST US IS WITH US.

THE INFIRM MAN HEALED

John v. 1. AFTER THIS THERE WAS A FEAST OF THE JEWS; AND JESUS WENT TO JERUSALEM.

2. THERE IS IN JERUSALEM AT THE SHEEP MARKET A POOL, WHICH IS CALLED IN HEBREW "BETHESDA," WITH FIVE PORCHES.

3. ON THESE LAY A GREAT MULTITUDE OF SICK PEOPLE: OF BLIND, INFIRM, AND LAME. THEY WERE ALL WAITING FOR THE MOTION OF THE WATER.

4. FOR THEY SUPPOSED THAT AN ANGEL WENT DOWN AT CERTAIN TIMES INTO THE POOL, AND STIRRED THE WATER, AND THAT IF ONE WAS THE FIRST AFTER THE STIRRING OF THE WATER TO ENTER THE POOL, HE WOULD BE MADE WELL, NO MATTER WHAT DISEASE HE HAD.

5. AND THERE WAS THERE A CERTAIN MAN, WHO HAD BEEN INFIRM FOR THIRTY-EIGHT YEARS.

6. JESUS SAW HIM LIE, AND LEARNED THAT HE HAD BEEN SO FOR A LONG TIME, AND SAID TO HIM, DOST THOU WISH TO BE MADE WELL?

7. THE FEEBLE MAN SAID, WHY SHOULD I NOT WANT IT, SIR? BUT I HAVE NO MAN, WHEN THE WATER IS STIRRED, TO PUT ME IN THE POOL; I AM ALWAYS TOO LATE. WHEN I RUSH IN, ANOTHER HAS LEAPED IN BEFORE ME.

8. AND JESUS SAID TO HIM, WAKE UP, TAKE THY BED, AND WALK.

9. AND THE MAN AWOKE IMMEDIATELY, AND TOOK UP HIS BED, AND WALKED.

John v. 9. THAT HAPPENED ON A SABBATH.

10. AND JEWS SAID TO THE MAN, TODAY IS THE SABBATH: THOU SHOULDST NOT TAKE UP THY BED.

11. AND HE ANSWERED THEM, THE MAN WHO RAISED ME TOLD ME, TAKE UP THY BED, AND WALK.

12. AND THEY ASKED HIM, WHAT MAN IS IT WHO TOLD THEE, TAKE UP THY BED, AND WALK?

13. AND THE WEAK MAN DID NOT KNOW WHO HE WAS, FOR JESUS HAD SECRETLY MINGLED WITH THE PEOPLE.

14. AFTERWARD JESUS MET HIM IN THE TEMPLE, AND SAID TO HIM, NOW THOU ART WELL; SEE TO IT THAT THOU MAKEST NO NEW MISTAKES, OR THOU WILT FARE WORSE.

15. AND THE MAN WENT AND TOLD THE JEWS THAT IT WAS JESUS WHO HAD RAISED HIM.

16. AND THE JEWS ATTACKED JESUS, FOR THAT HE HAD DONE ON THE SABBATH.

17. JESUS ANSWERED THEM, MY FATHER WORKS WITHOUT CESSATION, AND SO DO I.

18. AND THE JEWS TRIED THE MORE TO KILL HIM, BECAUSE HE NOT ONLY HAD BROKEN THE SABBATH, BUT ALSO CALLED GOD HIS FATHER, AND MADE HIMSELF EQUAL WITH GOD.

19. AND JESUS SAID, DO YOU NOT UNDERSTAND THAT THE SON OF MAN CAN DO NOTHING OF HIMSELF, IF HE DID NOT KNOW WHAT THE FATHER IS DOING? WHAT THE FATHER IS DOING, THE SON DOES ALSO.

20. THE FATHER LOVES THE SON, AND HAS SHOWN HIM EVERYTHING. AND HE WILL SHOW HIM GREATER THINGS, SO THAT YOU WILL MARVEL.

21. FOR AS THE FATHER ROUSES THE MORTALS AND VIVIFIES THEM, EVEN SO THE SON VIVIFIES WHOM HE WILL.

22. FOR THE FATHER DOES NOT CHOOSE, BUT HAS COMMITTED THE CHOICE TO THE SON.

23. THAT ALL MEN SHOULD HONOR THE SON, AS THEY HONOR THE FATHER. HE WHO DOES NOT HONOR THE SON DOES NOT HONOR THE FATHER, WHO HAS SENT HIM.

24. YOU UNDERSTAND THAT HE WHO UNDERSTANDS MY COMPREHENSION AND RELIES UPON HIM WHO HAS SENT ME HAS NON-TEMPORAL LIFE, AND FOR HIM THERE IS NO DEATH, BUT HE HAS ALREADY PASSED FROM DEATH TO LIFE.

25. TRULY I TELL YOU, THE HOUR HAS COME, WHEN THE MORTALS WILL UNDERSTAND THE VOICE OF THE SON OF GOD, AND, HAVING UNDERSTOOD, WILL LIVE.

26. FOR AS THE FATHER LIVES IN HIMSELF, SO HAS HE GIVEN TO THE SON LIFE IN HIM;

27. AND HAS GIVEN HIM FREEDOM TO MAKE A CHOICE, AND EVEN BY THIS HE IS A MAN.

28. DO NOT MARVEL AT THIS: FOR THE HOUR HAS COME, WHEN ALL THE MORTALS WILL UNDERSTAND THE VOICE OF THE SON OF GOD

29. AND THOSE WHO HAVE DONE GOOD WILL ENTER INTO THE AWAKENING OF LIFE; AND THOSE WHO HAVE DONE EVIL WILL ENTER INTO THE EXILE OF DEATH.

30. I CAN DO NOTHING OF MY OWN SELF: AS I UNDERSTAND, SO I CHOOSE. MY CHOICE IS CORRECT, FOR I DO NOT SEEK MY WILL, BUT THE WILL OF THE FATHER WHO HAS SENT ME.

31. IF I WERE THE ONLY ONE TO GIVE ASSURANCE OF MYSELF, MY ASSURANCE WOULD BE FALSE;

32. BUT THERE IS ANOTHER WHO ASSURES CONCERNING ME THAT I AM DOING THE TRUTH. AND YOU KNOW THAT HIS ASSURANCE IS CORRECT AS TO MY DOING THE TRUTH.

36. FOR THE WORKS WHICH MY FATHER HAS TAUGHT ME TO FULFILL, THE SAME WORKS THAT I DO WITNESS OF ME THAT THE FATHER HAS SENT ME.

37. AND THE FATHER WHO HAS SENT ME, HE SHOWS AND HAS SHOWN CONCERNING ME. BUT YOU HAVE IN NO WAY UNDERSTOOD HIS VOICE, AND YOU HAVE NOT KNOWN WHO HE IS.

38. AND YOU HAVE NOT WITHIN YOU THE COMPREHENSION, SUCH AS WOULD ABIDE IN YOU, FOR YOU DO NOT BELIEVE HIM WHOM HE HAS SENT.

39. READ CAREFULLY THE SCRIPTURES: BY THEM YOU THINK YOU HAVE ETERNAL LIFE; AND THEY ASSURE CONCERNING ME.

40. YOU WILL NOT BELIEVE ME THAT YOU WILL HAVE LIFE.

41. HUMAN JUDGMENTS I DO NOT RECEIVE.

42. BUT I HAVE LEARNED THAT IN YOU THERE IS NO TRUTH AND NO LOVE OF GOD.

43. I TEACH YOU IN THE NAME OF MY FATHER, AND YOU DO NOT RECEIVE MY TEACHING. AND IF ANOTHER WILL TEACH YOU IN HIS OWN NAME, HIS TEACHING YOU WILL RECEIVE.

44. WHAT CAN YOU RELY UPON, SINCE YOU RECEIVE YOUR TEACHING FROM MEN, AND DO NOT SEEK THE TEACHING THAT COMES FROM THE ONLY SON, WHO IS OF THE SAME BIRTH WITH THE FATHER.

45. I DO NOT ACCUSE YOU BEFORE THE FATHER, BUT MOSES, IN WHOM YOU TRUST, ACCUSES YOU.

46. IF YOU HAD BELIEVED MOSES, YOU WOULD BELIEVE ME TOO, FOR HE WROTE OF ME.

47. IF YOU DO NOT BELIEVE HIS WRITINGS, HOW CAN YOU BELIEVE MY WORDS?

THE PARABLE OF THE INHERITANCE (THE TALENTS)

Luke xix. 11. WHEN THEY HEARD THIS, JESUS ADDED AND SPOKE A PARABLE, THAT THEY MIGHT NOT THINK THAT THE KINGDOM OF GOD WOULD COME WITHOUT AN EFFORT.

12. HE SAID, A CERTAIN NOBLEMAN RECEIVED AN INHERITANCE AND HAD TO GO TO A DISTANT KINGDOM TO GET IT, AND TO RETURN.

13. SO HE CALLED HIS TEN SERVANTS, AND GAVE THEM HIS PROPERTY.

Matt. xxv. 15. TO ONE HE GAVE FIVE TALENTS, TO ANOTHER TWO, AND TO ANOTHER ONE; TO EVERY MAN ACCORDING TO HIS ABILITY.

Luke xix. 13. AND SAID TO THEM, TURN IT TO ACCOUNT.

Matt. xxv. 15. AND HIMSELF WENT AWAY.

16. THEN THE MAN WHO HAD RECEIVED THE FIVE TALENTS WENT AND TRADED WITH THEM, AND MADE OTHER FIVE TALENTS.

17. AND LIKEWISE DID HE WHO HAD TWO TALENTS.

Luke xix. 14. BUT THE COUNTRYMEN OF THE MAN HAD NO USE FOR HIM, AND ANNOUNCED TO HIM, WE WILL NOT HAVE THEE AS A KING.

15. AND IT CAME TO PASS, THAT THAT MAN RECEIVED THE KINGDOM AND RETURNED HOME AND SENT FOR THE SERVANTS, TO WHOM HE HAD GIVEN THE MONEY, THAT HE MIGHT KNOW HOW MUCH EACH HAD GAINED.

Matt. xxv. 19. AND HE ASKED FOR THEIR ACCOUNTS.

20. AND HE WHO HAD RECEIVED FIVE TALENTS CAME AND BROUGHT OTHER FIVE TALENTS, AND SAID, MASTER, THOU GAVEST ME FIVE TALENTS: I HAVE GAINED FIVE TALENTS MORE WITH THEM.

21. AND HIS MASTER SAID TO HIM, WELL DONE! THOU ART A GOOD AND FAITHFUL SERVANT: THOU HAST BEEN FAITHFUL IN LITTLE THINGS, I WILL PUT THEE IN CHARGE OF GREATER THINGS. REJOICE WITH THY MASTER.

22. THEN CAME ANOTHER, TO WHOM TWO TALENTS HAD BEEN GIVEN, AND SAID, MASTER, THOU GAVEST ME TWO TALENTS, AND I HAVE GAINED TWO MORE WITH THEM.

Luke xix. 17. AND THE MASTER SAID TO BOTH, WELL DONE! YOU ARE GOOD AND FAITHFUL SERVANTS. YOU HAVE BEEN FAITHFUL IN SMALL THINGS, AND SO I WILL PUT YOU IN CHARGE OF GREATER THINGS: REJOICE WITH THE MASTER.

Matt. xxv. 24. AND HE TO WHOM ONE TALENT HAD BEEN GIVEN, CAME, AND SAID, MASTER, HERE IS THY TALENT. I KNEW THAT THOU ART A HARD

MAN, TAKING WHERE THOU HAST NOT PLACED, AND REAPING WHERE THOU HAST NOT SOWN.

25. AND I WAS AFRAID OF THEE, AND WRAPPED IT IN A CLOTH, AND HID IT IN THE EARTH. HERE IT IS, TAKE IT.

26. AND HIS MASTER SAID TO HIM, THOU ART A BAD AND LAZY SERVANT. ACCORDING TO THY SPEECH WILL I JUDGE THEE. THOU KNEWEST THAT I AM A HARD MAN, TAKING WHERE I DO NOT PLACE, AND REAPING WHERE I DO NOT SOW:

Luke xix. 23. WHY, THEN, DIDST THOU NOT TURN MY MONEY TO ACCOUNT? THEN I SHOULD HAVE RECEIVED IT WITH INTEREST AT MY COMING.

24. AND THE MASTER SAID TO HIS SERVANTS, TAKE FROM HIM THE TALENT, AND GIVE IT TO HIM WHO HAS TEN.

25. AND THEY SAID, MASTER, HE HAS ALREADY TEN.

26. I TELL YOU, A SURPLUS WILL BE GIVEN TO HIM WHO SAVES; AND FROM HIM WHO DOES NOT SAVE, EVEN WHAT HE HAS WILL BE TAKEN FROM HIM.

Matt. xxv. 30. AND I TAKE THE USELESS SERVANT AND THROW HIM OUT.

Luke xix. 27. BUT MY ENEMIES, WHO DID NOT WANT ME TO BE THEIR KING, SHALL NOT EXIST FOR ME.

OF THE BREAD OF LIFE

John iv. 31. ONCE HIS DISCIPLES ASKED HIM, TEACHER, HAST THOU EATEN?

32. AND HE SAID TO THEM, I HAVE FOOD THAT YOU KNOW NOT OF.

33. AND THE DISCIPLES SAID TO ONE ANOTHER, HAS ANY ONE BROUGHT HIM SOMETHING TO EAT?

34. AND JESUS SAID TO THEM, MY FOOD IS THIS, THAT I DO THE WILL OF HIM WHO HAS SENT ME, AND FULFILL HIS WORKS.

35. DO NOT SAY, THERE ARE FOUR MONTHS YET, AND THEN COMES THE HARVEST. I TELL YOU, LIFT UP YOUR EYES AND LOOK ON THE FIELDS: THEY ARE RIPE ALREADY FOR THE HARVEST.

36. AND HE WHO REAPS IS PAID, AND HE GATHERS FRUIT FOR THE NON-TEMPORAL LIFE, SO THAT HE WHO HAS SOWED REJOICES WITH HIM WHO REAPS.

37. FOR THE PROVERB IS TRUE, ONE SOWS, AND ANOTHER REAPS.

38. I TEACH YOU TO REAP WHERE YOU DID NOT LABOR. OTHERS LABORED, BUT YOU PARTICIPATE IN THE LABOR OF OTHERS.

John vi. 27. AND JESUS SAID TO THE MULTITUDE, YOU ARE CARING FOR YOUR EARTHLY FOOD, BUT I TELL YOU, EARN NOT THE PERISHABLE FOOD, BUT THE ONE WHICH WILL ENDURE INTO EVERLASTING LIFE, WHICH THE SON OF MAN WILL GIVE YOU: ON HIM IS GOD'S SEAL.

28. AND THEY SAID TO HIM, WHAT MUST WE DO THAT WE MAY DO THE WORKS OF GOD?

29. AND JESUS REPLIED TO THEM, THIS IS THE WORK OF GOD, THAT YOU TRUST HIM WHOM HE HAS SENT.

30. WHAT EXAMPLE WILL THOU GIVE US THAT WE MAY BELIEVE THEE? WHAT ART THOU DOING?

31. OUR FATHERS ATE MANNA IN THE DESERT, AS IT IS WRITTEN, HE GAVE THEM BREAD FROM HEAVEN TO EAT.

32. AND JESUS SAID TO THEM, YOU KNOW YOURSELVES THAT IT WAS NOT MOSES WHO GAVE YOU THIS BREAD FROM HEAVEN, BUT MY FATHER GIVES YOU TRUE BREAD FROM HEAVEN.

33. FOR THE BREAD OF GOD IS THAT WHICH COMES DOWN FROM HEAVEN, AND GIVES LIFE TO THE WORLD.

34. AND THEY SAID TO HIM, THEN GIVE US THAT BREAD.

35. AND JESUS SAID TO THEM, I AM THE BREAD OF LIFE: HE WHO GIVES HIMSELF TO ME WILL NEVER BE HUNGRY; AND HE WHO WILL BELIEVE ME, WILL NEVER THIRST.

36. BUT I HAVE TOLD YOU THIS ALREADY, AND YOU HAVE SEEN AND DO NOT BELIEVE.

37. EVERYTHING WHICH THE FATHER GIVES ME WILL COME TO ME; AND HIM WHO GIVES HIMSELF TO ME I WILL NOT CAUSE TO PERISH.

38. BECAUSE I HAVE COME DOWN FROM HEAVEN, NOT TO DO MY WILL, BUT THE WILL OF THE FATHER WHO SENT ME.

39. AND THE WILL OF MY FATHER WHO HAS SENT ME IS THIS, THAT I SHOULD NOT CAUSE TO PERISH ANYTHING HE HAS GIVEN ME, BUT SHOULD KEEP IT ALIVE TO THE LAST DAY.

40. FOR THIS IS THE WILL OF HIM WHO HAS SENT ME. SO THAT EVERYONE WHO HAS COME TO KNOW THE SON OF MAN AND BELIEVES IN HIM HAS NON-TEMPORAL LIFE. AND I WILL AWAKE HIM AT THE LAST DAY.

41. AND THE JEWS BEGAN TO DISPUTE, BECAUSE HE SAID, I AM THE BREAD WHO CAME DOWN FROM HEAVEN.

42. AND SAID, IS NOT THIS JESUS, THE SON OF JOSEPH? WE KNOW HIS FATHER AND HIS MOTHER. HOW THEN DOES HE SAY THAT HE CAME DOWN FROM HEAVEN?

43. AND JESUS ANSWERED AND SAID TO THEM, DO NOT DISPUTE AMONG YOURSELVES.

44. NO MAN CAN BELIEVE ME, IF THE FATHER WHO HAS SENT ME DOES NOT DRAW HIM. AND I WILL AWAKE HIM AT THE LAST DAY.

45. IT IS WRITTEN IN THE PROPHETS, AND YOU WILL BE ALL TAUGHT ABOUT GOD. HE WHO KNOWS ABOUT THE FATHER AND HAS LEARNED THE TRUTH WILL GIVE HIMSELF TO ME.

46. NOT THAT ANY MAN HAS SEEN THE FATHER; BUT HE WHO IS IN GOD, HE HAS SEEN THE FATHER.

47. VERILY I TELL YOU, HE WHO BELIEVES HAS NON-TEMPORAL LIFE.

48. I AM THE BREAD OF LIFE.

49. YOUR FATHERS ATE MANNA IN THE WILDERNESS AND DIED.

50. I AM THE BREAD FROM HEAVEN, AND HE WHO EATS OF IT DOES NOT DIE.

51. I AM THE BREAD OF LIFE WHICH CAME DOWN FROM HEAVEN. IF ANY MAN EATS OF THIS BREAD, HE WILL LIVE FOREVER: AND THE BREAD WHICH I WILL GIVE IS MY CARNAL LIFE; I HAVE GIVEN IT IN PLACE OF THE LIFE OF THE WORLD.

52. AND THE JEWS BEGAN TO MURMUR AMONG THEMSELVES, AND SAID, HOW CAN HE GIVE US MEAT TO EAT?

53. AND JESUS SAID TO THEM, VERILY, I TELL YOU, IF YOU DO NOT EAT THE FLESH OF THE SON OF THE MAN, AND DRINK HIS BLOOD, THERE WILL BE NO LIFE IN YOU.

54. HE WHO EATS HIS FLESH AND DRINKS HIS BLOOD HAS NON-TEMPORAL LIFE.

55. FOR MY FLESH IS FOOD INDEED, AND MY BLOOD IS TRUE DRINK.

56. HE WHO EATS MY FLESH AND DRINKS MY BLOOD IS IN ME, AND I AM IN HIM.

57. AND AS THE LIVING FATHER HAS SENT ME, AND I LIVE BY THE FATHER; SO TOO HE WHO EATS ME IN SPIRIT, HE WILL LIVE ONLY BY MY WILL.

58. SUCH IS THE BREAD WHICH CAME DOWN FROM HEAVEN; NOT AS YOUR FATHERS ATE THE MANNA, AND DIED. HE WHO WILL CHEW THIS BREAD, WILL LIVE A NON-TEMPORAL LIFE.

John xii. 24. YOU KNOW YOURSELVES THAT IF A KERNEL OF WHEAT FALLS INTO THE GROUND AND DOES NOT DIE, IT REMAINS. BUT IF IT DIES, IT BRINGS FORTH A GREAT INCREASE.

25. HE WHO LOVES HIS SOUL WILL CAUSE IT TO PERISH; AND HE WHO DOES NOT LOVE HIS SOUL IN THIS WORLD WILL KEEP IT FOR EVER.

John vi. 59. HE SPOKE THESE THINGS, AS HE TAUGHT IN AN ASSEMBLY IN CAPERNAUM.

60. MANY OF HIS DISCIPLES HEARD IT, AND SAID, THIS IS A HARD SAYING. WHO CAN UNDERSTAND IT?

61. AND JESUS DIVINED THAT HIS DISCIPLES WERE MURMURING ABOUT IT, AND HE SAID TO THEM, YOU ARE DISTURBED,

62. BECAUSE YOU SEE THAT THE SON OF MAN IS BECOMING WHAT HE WAS BEFORE.

63. THE SPIRIT LIVES, BUT THE BODY IS NOT GOOD FOR ANYTHING. THE WORDS WHICH I TOLD YOU ARE THAT THERE IS SPIRIT, AND SO THERE IS NON-TEMPORAL LIFE.

TOLSTOY'S COMMENTARY

And Jesus was sorry for men, because they perished not knowing wherein the true life was, and suffered and were harassed, themselves not knowing why, like abandoned sheep without a shepherd. And Jesus says to the people, You worry about the life of the flesh: you are hitched to a wagon which you cannot pull, and have put on a yoke which was not made for you. Understand my teaching and follow it, and you will know rest and joy in life. I give you another yoke and another wagon—spiritual life. Hitch yourselves to it, and you will learn of rest and bliss from me.

You must be meek and humble, and then you will find bliss in your life, for my teaching is a yoke which is made for you, and the execution of my teaching is a light wagon, made according to your strength.

And Jesus went through cities and villages, and taught all the blessedness of life according to the will of God. Then he chose seventy men from among those who were near to him, and sent them to those places where he wanted himself to be. He said to them, Many men do not know the good of the true life—I am sorry for all of them and wish to teach all, but as the master is not able to attend to the harvest of the whole field, so I cannot attend to it. Go to different cities, and in all places announce the coming of God and the law of God. Say that to be blessed one must be a vagrant, and that the law is all in five rules against evil: (1) not to be angry; (2) not to commit debauchery; (3) not to swear, to make no promises whatever; (4) not to resist evil, not to go to court; and (5) not to make any distinction between men, and to disregard kings and kingdoms.

And so execute these rules yourselves. First of all, be mendicants, vagrants. Take nothing with you, neither scrip, nor bread, nor money. All you must have is raiment on your body, and footgear. Announce the blessedness of the mendicants, and so, above all, be an example of mendicancy. Choose no hosts to stop with, but stay in whatever house you enter first. When you come into the house, greet the hosts. If they receive you, all is well; and if not, go to another house. You will be hated for what you will say, and they will attack and drive you away. And if they drive you away, go to another village; and if they drive you from it, go to another still. They will drive you, as wolves drive the sheep, but do not lose your courage and do not weaken to the last hour. And they will take you into court and will judge you, and flog you, and take you before the officers, that you may justify yourselves before them. And when they will take you to court, do not lose your courage, and do not think what you are going to say. The spirit of God will tell you what to say. Before you will have gone through all the cities, men will understand your teaching, and will turn to you.

Be not afraid. What is hidden in the souls of men will come out. What you will tell to two or three will be scattered among thousands. Above all, do not fear those who may kill your body. What of it if they kill your body? They can do nothing to your soul. So do not fear them. Fear this, that your body and soul may not perish, if you depart from the law. This is what you want to fear.

For one cent you can buy five sparrows, and even they do not die without the will of God. And a hair of the head will not fall without the will of God, so what are you to fear, if you are in the will of God? God will be with him who before men will be one with the will of God; but who before men will renounce the will of God, him God will renounce also. Not all will believe in my teaching, that it is necessary to be a mendicant, a vagrant, not to be angry, not to commit debauchery, not to swear, not to judge or go to court, not to wage war. And those who will not believe will hate it, because it deprives them of what they like, and there will be dissension.

My teaching will, like a fire, burn up the world. And so there must be dissension in the world. There will be dissension in every house. Father will be against son, mother against daughter, and the housefolk will be haters of those who will understand my teaching. And they will kill them. For he who will understand my teaching will see no meaning in his father, or mother, or wife, or children, or all his property. He who thinks more of his father or mother than of my teaching has not understood my teaching. He who is not at all times ready for all kinds of sufferings of the flesh is not my disciple. He who will care for this carnal life will cause the true life to perish, and he who will cause this carnal life to perish according to my teaching will save his life.

The seventy disciples went out over the cities and villages, and did what Jesus had commanded. When they returned, they told Jesus with joy, The devilish teaching about anger, adultery, oaths, judgments, and wars is everywhere giving way before us.

And Jesus said to them, Do not rejoice because the evil is yielding to you, but because you are in the will of God.

And then Jesus rejoiced on account of the power of the spirit, and said, From the fact that my disciples have understood me and that the evil is vanquished by them, I see that thou art the highest spirit—the beginning of everything, truly the Father of men—because what the wise and learned men could not understand with all their learning, the unreasoning have understood by recognizing themselves to be the children of the Father. And thou, as the Father, hast disclosed everything to them, through the love which is between a father and his son. Everything which a man needs to know is disclosed to him through the love of the Father for the son and of the son for the Father. Only him who recognizes himself as the son does the Father recognize.

And the people of his house came and wanted to bind him, for they thought that he was mad.

And the Pharisees and the lawyers came from Jerusalem, and said, He is mad: he wants to mend a lesser evil with a greater evil. That there may be no mendicants, he wants to make all men mendicants, and he wants nobody to be punished, and the robbers to kill everybody, and to have no wars, though then the enemies will kill everybody.

And he said, You say that my teaching is evil, and at the same time you say that I destroy the evil. That cannot be, for evil cannot be destroyed by evil. If I destroy evil, my teaching cannot be evil, for evil cannot go against itself. If evil went against itself, there would be no evil. You cast out the evil according to your law. How do you cast out the evil? By the law of Moses, and this law is from God. But I cast out the evil with the spirit of God, which has always been in you. It is only for this reason that I can expel the evil. And the fact that I expel evil is a proof to you that my teaching is true, and that the spirit of God is in men and is stronger than the carnal lusts. If that did not exist, it would not be possible to vanquish the lust of evil, as it is impossible to enter the house of a strong man and rob it. To rob the house of a strong man, it is necessary first to bind the man. And thus are men bound by the spirit of God.

He who is not with me is against me. He who does not harvest in the field only loses the corn, for he who is not with me is not with the spirit of God—he is an adversary of the spirit.

And so I tell you that every human mistake and every false interpretation will be forgiven, but the false interpretation about the spirit of God will not be forgiven. If a man says a word against another, that will pass; but if he will say a word against what is holy in man—against the spirit of God, that will not pass unnoticed; scold me as much as you please, but do not call evil the good which I am doing. Man will not be forgiven for calling the good evil, that is, the works which I do. One has to be with the spirit of God, or against it.

Either consider the tree good, and its fruit good, or consider it bad, and its fruit bad, for by its fruit is the tree esteemed. You see me expel evil, consequently my teaching is good. Every man who expels evil, no matter what his teaching may be, cannot be against us, but is with us, for one can expel evil only with the spirit of God.

After that Jesus came for the holiday to Jerusalem. And there was then a pool in Jerusalem. And they said about this pool that an angel stepped into it, and that caused the water of the pool to well up, and if one leaped into the water immediately after it began to well up, he was cured from whatever disease he may have had.

And there were porches built around this pool. And on these porches lay all kinds of sick people, waiting for the water in the pool to well up, in order to leap into it.

Jesus came to the pool, and saw a man lying on a porch. Jesus asked who he was. The man told him that he had been ailing for thirty-eight years, and that he had been waiting for a long time to be the first to leap into the pool, after the water had begun to well up, but that he could never succeed, for others got in before him.

Jesus looked at him, and said, In vain dost thou wait here for a miracle from the angel. There are no miracles. There is one miracle, and that is, that God has given life to men, and it is necessary to live with all one's powers. Do not wait for anything at this pool, but take thy bed, and live according to the divine law, according to the strength which God will give thee.

The sick man obeyed him, and got up and went away.

Jesus said to him, Thou seest thyself that thou hast the strength. See to it that thou wilt not believe again in all this deception. Do not make this error again, but live according to the power which God gives thee.

And the man went and told everybody what had happened to him. And all those who had been working the deception of the pool and were making a living thereby grew angry, and they did not know how to wreak their vengeance and to annoy the sick man and Jesus for having disclosed their deception. They found a pretext for doing so in its being a Sabbath, for on the Sabbath it was not permitted, according to their law, to work. At first they attacked the sick man, and said, How didst thou dare take up thy bed on the Sabbath? It is not lawful to work on the Sabbath.

The sick man said to them, He who raised me up told me to take up the bed.

They said, Who ordered thee to do so?

He said, I do not know. A man came up to me and went away again.

The Pharisees made their way to Jesus, and, finding him, they said, How couldst thou order the man to rise and take up his bed on a Sabbath?

To this Jesus said to them, My Father never stops working, and so I will never stop working, whether it be a weekday or a Sabbath. The Sabbath did not make man, but man made the Sabbath.

Then the people grew angrier still, because he dared to call God his Father. And they attacked him, and Jesus replied to them, A man could not do anything of himself, if God the Father—the spirit of God in man—did not point out to him what to do. God, the Father of man, lives and works always, and man lives and works always. God the Father gave men reason for their own good, and showed them what is good and what bad.

Just as God gives life, so also the spirit of God gives life. God the Father does not choose and decide anything himself, but, having taught men what is good and what bad, he leaves everything to man to do, so that men may honor the spirit of God and obey it within themselves, as they honor and obey God. He who does not honor the spirit of God in himself does not honor God. You must understand that he who has completely abandoned himself to my teaching has exalted the spirit in himself, and in it reposes his life, he has non-temporal life and is already freed from death. It is clear that now the dead, having understood the meaning of their life, that they are the sons of God, will live. For as God is alive in himself, so is the SON alive in himself. The freedom of the choice is the same as that the spirit of God is in man—it is the whole man.

Do not marvel at this teaching; the time has come when all mortals will be divided. Some, who do good, will find life, and those who do evil will be destroyed.

I cannot choose anything of myself. What I have understood from the Father, that I choose. My choice is correct, if I do not hold to my own wish, but to the meaning which I have understood from the Father. If I were the only one to assure you that I am right, because I want it to be so, you might not have believed me. But there is another who gives the assurance about me—that I am doing right. That is the spirit of God, and you know that this assurance is true.

You see by my works that the Father has sent me. God the Father has shown concerning me in your souls and in the Scriptures. You have not understood his voice, and you have not known him. You have not his firm understanding within you, for you do not believe that which he has sent—the spirit of God in your souls.

Try to understand it: you expect to find life in your souls, and you will find there within you the spirit of God.

But you will not believe me that you will have life.

I esteem little your praying in your temples, and your observing the fasts and the Sabbaths according to human laws; the true love of the true God is not in you.

I teach you in the name of my Father and of yours, but you do not understand me. If a man will teach you in his own name, you will believe him. What can you rely upon, since you receive your sayings from one another, and do not seek the teaching as to the Father of the son. I am not the only one who shows you that you are wrong before your Father. That same Moses, in whom you trust, shows you that you are wrong and do not understand him. If you relied on what Moses said, you would rely also on what I tell you. If you do not rely on his writings, you will not believe my teaching, either.

And that they might understand it, that they might understand that it is possible to enter into the will of God without an effort, he told them a parable: A king received an inheritance. In order to receive this inheritance, the king had for a time to depart from his kingdom. And so the king went away.

But before his departure he distributed his possessions among his subjects, giving to each according to his ability: to one five talents, to another two, to a third one, and he commanded them to work without him and to gain by these talents as much as each could.

When the king went away, each man did with his property whatever he could. Some worked, and he who had five talents earned other five talents; another with his one talent gained ten more; others with their two talents gained two, or with their one gained five more or only one more; and others again did not work with the money given to them by their master, but hid the money away in the ground. Those who had taken five talents had the five talents left; those who had taken two had two, and those who had taken one had one left. And others again, who did not work with the master's money, did not want to appear before the king, but sent word to him that they did not wish to be under his power.

When the time came, the king returned into his kingdom, and he called all his subjects to give accounts of themselves, what each had done with what had been given him.

And one servant came, the one to whom five talents had been given, and he said, With the five talents I have gained five more. And another came, to whom one talent had been given, and he said, Here, with the one talent I have gained ten more. And then came he who had received two talents, and he brought two more, and the one who had received one brought five more. And still another to whom one talent had been given brought one more.

And the master praised them all alike and rewarded them alike. He said to all alike, I see that you are good and faithful servants: you have worked over my possessions, and so I receive you as equal participants in what is mine. We shall rule together.

After that came those subjects who had not worked over the master's possessions. And one of them said, Master, thou gavest me a talent at thy departure. I know that thou art a hard man and wantest to take from us what thou hast not given us, and so I was afraid of thee and from fear hid away thy talent. Here it is in full. What thou hast given me I return to thee. And others who had received five talents, and those who had received ten talents, brought back the master's talents, and they said the same to him.

Then the master said to them, Foolish people! You say that out of fear of me you hid your talents in the ground and did not work with them. If you knew that I was a hard man and will take what I have not given, why did you not try to do what I commanded?

If you had worked with my talent, your possessions would have been increased, and you would have done my will, and I might have had mercy on you, and you would not have fared worse. But now you have not got away from my power anyway.

And the master took the talents away from those who had not worked with them, and told his servants to give them to those who had gained more.

And the servants said, Master, they have enough as it is. But the king said, Give to those who have earned for me, for to him who looks after his own it shall be added, and from him who does not look after his own even the last shall be taken from him.

But drive away these foolish and lazy servants. Let them not be here. And drive away those also who sent word to me that they did not want to be in my power, and let them not be here.

This king is the beginning of life—the spirit. The world is the kingdom, but he does not himself govern the kingdom, but, like a peasant, he casts out the seed and leaves it alone. And the field brings forth blades, ears, and kernels of its own accord. The talent is the understanding in every man. God the spirit has put the understanding in every man, and leaves men to live according to their will.

God himself decides nothing, but having instructed man in everything, leaves it to every man to decide for himself. Not all have the same talent, but each receives according to his ability. Not to all is the same understanding given, but it is given, and for God there is no greater and no lesser. All God needs is work over the understanding. Some work with the talent of their master; others do not work for their master; others again do not work and do not acknowledge the master. Some men live by the understanding; others do not live by it; and others again do not acknowledge it. The master comes back and asks for an account. That is the temporal death and accounting of life. Some come and say that they have worked with the talent, and they enter into the life of the master.

And the master does not count who has worked more, and who less. All become alike participants in the life of the master. He who accepts the understanding has life.

He who has the understanding and relies on him who has sent it has non-temporal life and knows no death: he has passed into life. Others come and say that they have not worked with the talent; they do not refuse the talent; they only say that there is no sense in working, for, whether they work or not, they will meet with punishment. They know the severity of the master. Other men have the understanding, but do not rely on it. They say to themselves, Whether I work or not, I shall die, and nothing will be left, and so there is no sense doing anything with it. To this the king says, If thou knowest that I am severe, thou oughtest so much the more to have done my will. Why did you not try to do it? If men know that temporal death is inevitable, why should they not try to live by the doing of the will of God—by the understanding? And the king says, Take the talent from them, and give it to those who have. It makes no difference to the king where the talents are, so long as they are, just as it makes no difference to the peasant what kernel will bring forth ears, so long as he has a harvest. If the understanding gives life to men according to their will, then those who do not hold it cannot live and stand outside of life. And after the temporal death nothing will be left of them. And of the men who do not acknowledge the king's power, the king says, Throw those men out. These other men not only fail to work with the understanding and life, but even despise the Father of the spirit who has given it to them—they, too, cannot live, and are also destroyed with death.

CHAPTER SIX

THE FOOD OF LIFE. MAN LIVES NOT BY BREAD ALONE. OF THE CARNAL AND THE SPIRITUAL KINSHIP

Matt. xii. 46. AND WHILE HE TALKED, HIS MOTHER AND HIS BROTHERS CAME UP AND STOOD AT A DISTANCE, WISHING TO SPEAK WITH HIM.

47. A MAN SAW THEM, AND SAID TO HIM, THY MOTHER AND THY BROTHERS ARE STANDING A LITTLE WAY OFF: THEY WANT TO SPEAK WITH THEE.

48. AND HE SAID, WHO IS MY MOTHER? AND WHO ARE MY BROTHERS?

49. AND HE POINTED WITH HIS HAND TO HIS DISCIPLES AND SAID, HERE ARE MY MOTHER AND MY BROTHERS.

50. FOR HE WHO DOES THE WILL OF GOD MY FATHER IS MY BROTHER, AND MY SISTER, AND MY MOTHER.

Luke xi. 27. AND IT HAPPENED, AS HE SAID THIS, A WOMAN FROM AMONG THE PEOPLE LIFTED UP HER VOICE, AND SAID TO HIM, BLESSED IS THE WOMB THAT BORE THEE, AND THE TEATS WHICH THOU HAST SUCKED.

28. BUT HE SAID, BLESSED IS HE, WHO UNDERSTANDS THE COMPREHENSION OF GOD AND KEEPS IT.

Luke ix. 57. AND ON THE WAY A MAN SAID TO JESUS, I WILL FOLLOW THEE EVERYWHERE, MY MASTER.

58. AND JESUS SAID TO HIM, FOXES HAVE HOLES, AND BIRDS HAVE NESTS; BUT THE SON OF MAN HAS NO ABIDING PLACE.

THE STORM ON THE LAKE

Luke viii. 22. AND ONE DAY HE HAPPENED TO GO INTO A SHIP WITH HIS DISCIPLES, AND HE SAID TO THEM, LET US SAIL TO OTHER SIDE OF THE LAKE, AND THEY SAILED AWAY.

23. AND AS THEY SAILED, THERE ROSE A GREAT STORM, AND CAME OVER THE LAKE; AND THEY WERE DRENCHED, AND THEY WERE ENDANGERED; BUT HE SLEPT IN THE STERN.

24. AND HIS DISCIPLES CAME TO HIM AND AWOKE HIM, SAYING, TEACHER, TEACHER, WE PERISH. THEN HE ROSE,

25. AND SAID TO THEM, WHERE IS YOUR FAITH?

Matt. viii. 26. AND HE SAID TO THEM, WHY DO YOU LOSE YOUR COURAGE, YOU OF LITTLE FAITH? AND HE REBUKED THE WIND AND THE SEA; AND THE WINDS DIED DOWN, AND THERE WAS A CALM.

Matt. vi. 34. DO NOT TROUBLE YOURSELVES ABOUT THE FUTURE. THERE IS ENOUGH EVIL FOR THE PRESENT.

Luke ix. 59. AND TO ANOTHER JESUS SAID, FOLLOW ME. AND THAT MAN SAID, ALLOW ME FIRST TO GO AND BURY MY FATHER.

60. AND JESUS SAID TO HIM, LET THE DEAD BURY THE DEAD, BUT YOU FOLLOW ME, AND ANNOUNCE THE GOSPEL OF THE LORD.

61. AND ANOTHER MAN SAID, I WILL FOLLOW THEE, BUT LET ME FIRST ATTEND TO MY HOUSE.

62. AND JESUS SAID TO HIM, HE WHO HAS TAKEN HOLD OF THE PLOUGH AND LOOKS BACK IS NOT FIT FOR THE KINGDOM OF GOD.

JESUS AT THE HOUSE OF MARTHA AND MARY

Luke xii. 31. SEEK ONLY TO BE IN THE WILL OF GOD, AND EVERYTHING ELSE WILL BE GIVEN YOU.

Luke x. 38. JESUS HAPPENED ONE DAY TO BE WALKING WITH HIS DISCIPLES, AND THEY ENTERED A VILLAGE. A WOMAN NAMED MARTHA INVITED THEM TO THEIR HOUSE.

39. AND SHE HAD A SISTER NAMED MARY. MARY SAT DOWN AT JESUS' FEET, AND LISTENED TO HIS TEACHING.

40. BUT MARTHA WAS BUSY PREPARING A GOOD RECEPTION FOR THEM, AND SHE WENT UP TO JESUS, AND SAID, EVIDENTLY THOU DOST NOT CARE THAT MY SISTER HAS LEFT ME TO SERVE ALONE. TELL HER TO HELP ME.

41. BUT JESUS SAID TO HER IN REPLY, OH, MARTHA, MARTHA, THOU ART TROUBLING THYSELF ABOUT MANY THINGS,

42. BUT ONE THING IS NEEDED, AND MARY HAS CHOSEN WHAT IS THE BEST. WHAT SHE HAS CHOSEN WILL NOT BE TAKEN FROM HER.

Luke ix. 23. AND HE SAID TO THEM ALL, IF YOU WISH TO FOLLOW ME, RENOUNCE YOURSELVES AND BE PREPARED FOR EVERYTHING AT ANY TIME, AND THEN FOLLOW ME.

24. HE WHO WANTS TO SAVE HIS LIFE, WILL LOSE IT. AND HE WHO CAUSES HIS LIFE TO PERISH FOR MY SAKE, WILL SAVE IT.

25. WHAT PROFIT IS IT TO A MAN, IF HE SHOULD GAIN THE WHOLE WORLD, AND THEREBY CAUSE HIS RUIN OR HIS HARM?

26. HE WHO IS ASHAMED OF MY WORDS, OF HIM THE SON OF MAN WILL BE ASHAMED, WHEN HE APPEARS IN THE PRESENCE OF THE FATHER AND BEFORE THE POWERS OF GOD.

PARABLE OF THE RICH MAN

Luke xii. 15. AND HE SAID TO THEM, TAKE CARE, AND BEWARE OF EVERY ABUNDANCE, FOR THERE CAN BE NO LIFE IN WHAT HE POSSESSES.

16. AND HE TOLD THEM A PARABLE, THERE WAS A RICH MAN, WHOSE LAND BROUGHT FORTH GOOD HARVESTS,

17. AND HE THOUGHT, WHAT SHALL I DO? I HAVE NO ROOM TO PUT MY FRUITS AWAY.

18. AND HE SAID, THIS IS WHAT WILL I DO: I WILL PULL DOWN MY BARNS, AND BUILD NEW ONES; AND I WILL TAKE ALL MY CORN AND ALL MY POSSESSIONS THERE.

19. AND I WILL SAY TO MY SOUL, SOUL, THOU HAST LARGE POSSESSIONS TO LAST FOR MANY YEAR. SLEEP, EAT, DRINK, AND BE MERRY.

20. AND GOD SAID TO HIM, THOU FOOL, THIS NIGHT THY SOUL WILL BE TAKEN FROM THEE, SO OF WHAT GOOD ARE THY PROVISIONS?

21. SO IT HAPPENS WITH HIM WHO LAYS UP FOR HIMSELF, AND DOES NOT GROW RICH IN GOD.

THE PARABLE OF THE FIG TREE

Luke xiii. 1. THERE WERE SOME PRESENT, AND THEY TOLD HIM OF THE GALILEANS, WHOM PILATE HAD KILLED.

2. AND JESUS SAID TO THEM IN REPLY, DO YOU IMAGINE THAT THIS GALI-LEANS WERE MORE SINFUL THAN THE REST, THAT THIS HAPPENED TO THEM?

3. NOT AT ALL. BUT IF YOU DO NOT COME TO YOUR SENSES, YOU WILL ALL PERISH IN THE SAME WAY.

4. OR THOSE EIGHTEEN, WHO WERE KILLED BY THE TOWER FALLING UPON THEM, DO YOU THINK THAT THEY DESERVED THAT MORE THAN ALL THE OTHER INHABITANTS OF JERUSALEM?

5. NOT AT ALL. BUT IF YOU DO NOT COME TO YOUR SENSES, YOU WILL ALL PERISH IN THE SAME WAY.

6. AND HE TOLD THEM THIS PARABLE: A MAN HAD AN APPLE TREE GROW-ING IN HIS GARDEN, AND HE CAME TO SEE WHETHER THERE WAS ANY FRUIT ON IT, AND HE FOUND NONE.

7. AND HE SAID TO THE GARDENER, THREE YEARS I HAVE BEEN COMING HERE AND LOOKING FOR FRUIT ON THIS APPLE TREE, AND THERE IS NONE. CUT IT DOWN; WHY SHOULD IT SPOIL THE GROUND?

8. BUT THE GARDENER SAID, MASTER, LET IT ALONE FOR ANOTHER SUMMER, AND I WILL DIG ABOUT IT, AND MANURE IT,

9. PERHAPS IT WILL BEAR FRUIT; AND IF IT DOES NOT BEAR THEN, CUT IT DOWN.

Luke xiii. 54. AND HE SAID TO THE PEOPLE, WHEN YOU SEE A CLOUD FROM THE WEST, YOU SAY AT ONCE, THERE COMES A SHOWER, AND SO IT IS.

55. AND WHEN IT BLOWS FROM THE SOUTH, YOU SAY, IT WILL BE HOT; AND SO IT HAPPENS.

56. YOU CAN GUESS BY THE LOOKS OF THE EARTH AND THE SKY; HOW THEN DO YOU GUESS IN REGARD TO YOUR PRESENT CONDITION?

57. WHY DO YOU NOT SEE IN YOURSELVES WHAT IS RIGHT?

Luke xiv. 25. AND A GREAT MULTITUDE WENT WITH HIM; AND HE TURNED, AND SAID TO THEM,

26. HE WHO COMES TO ME, AND DOES NOT FORSAKE HIS FATHER, AND MOTHER, AND WIFE, AND CHILDREN, AND BROTHERS, AND SISTERS, AND HIS CARNAL LIFE ALSO CANNOT BE INSTRUCTED BY ME.

27. AND HE WHO DOES NOT DRAG HIS CROSS AND DO THE SAME AS I DO, CANNOT BE INSTRUCTED.

28. FOR EACH OF YOU, WISHING TO BUILD A HOUSE, WILL FIRST SIT DOWN AND FIGURE OUT HIS EXPENSES, TO SEE WHETHER HE CAN FINISH IT.

29. LEST, HAVING BEGUN WITHOUT FINISHING IT, MEN MIGHT MOCK HIM,

30. HERE IS A MAN WHO HAS BEGUN TO BUILD AND WAS NOT ABLE TO FINISH.

31. OR A KING, GOING TO WAGE WAR AGAINST ANOTHER KING, SITS DOWN FIRST AND THINKS WHETHER HE IS ABLE WITH TEN THOUSAND TO FIGHT AGAINST TWENTY THOUSAND.

32. OR ELSE, HE WILL SEND AMBASSADORS FROM A DISTANCE, TO MAKE PEACE.

33. SO NONE OF YOU CAN BE TAUGHT BY ME, UNLESS YOU HAVE FIRST MADE YOUR ACCOUNTS.

34. SALT IS GOOD; BUT IF IT HAS LOST ITS FLAVOR, IT CANNOT BE USEFUL.

35. IT IS NEITHER DIRT, NOR DUNG, AND HAS TO BE THROWN OUT. HE WHO HAS SENSE WILL UNDERSTAND.

THE PARABLE OF THE SUPPER

Luke xiv. 15. WHEN ONE OF THOSE WHO WERE WITH HIM HEARD IT, HE SAID TO HIM, BLESSED IS HE WHO EATS BREAD IN THE KINGDOM OF GOD.

16. AND JESUS SAID, A MAN PREPARED GREAT FEAST, AND INVITED MANY.

17. AND SENT HIS SERVANTS TO TELL THE GUESTS, IT IS TIME FOR THE SUPPER. GO, IT IS READY NOW.

18. AND THEY BEGAN ONE AFTER ANOTHER TO EXCUSE THEMSELVES. THE FIRST SAID, I HAVE BOUGHT A PIECE OF GROUND, AND I MUST GO AND SEE IT.

19. ANOTHER SAID, I HAVE BOUGHT FIVE YOKE OF OXEN, AND I GO TO TRY THEM: PRAY, HAVE ME EXCUSED.

20. A THIRD SAID, I HAVE JUST MARRIED, AND THEREFORE I CANNOT COME.

21. AND THE SERVANT CAME AND TOLD EVERYTHING TO HIS MASTER. THE MASTER GREW ANGRY, AND SAID TO HIS SERVANTS, GO OUT AT ONCE INTO THE STREETS AND INTO THE SQUARE, AND BRING IN THE POOR, AND THE NEEDY. AND THE LAME, AND THE BLIND.

22. AND THE SERVANT SAID, MASTER, I HAVE DONE EVERYTHING AS THOU HAST COMMANDED, AND YET THERE IS ROOM LEFT.

23. AND THE MASTER SAID TO THE SERVANT, GO OUT INTO THE STREETS AND SQUARES, AND PERSUADE ALL TO COME, THAT MY HOUSE MAY BE FILLED.

24. FOR I TELL YOU, NONE OF THOSE WHO WERE FIRST INVITED WILL EAT MY SUPPER.

Matt. xxii. 2. THE KINGDOM OF GOD IS LIKE THIS: A CERTAIN KING MADE A MARRIAGE FOR HIS SON,

3. AND SENT OUT HIS SERVANTS TO INVITE THE GUESTS TO THE FEAST, AND THEY WOULD NOT COME.

4. AGAIN HE SENT OTHER SERVANTS, SAYING, TELL THE GUESTS THAT THE DINNER IS PREPARED; ALL THE FATTED OXEN ARE KILLED. EVERYTHING IS READY, COME TO THE FEAST.

5. BUT THE GUEST DID NOT ACCEPT THE CALL: ONE WENT TO THE FIELD, AND ANOTHER TO THE MARKET,

6. AND OTHER AGAIN SEIZED THE SERVANTS, TREATED THEM BADLY, AND BEAT THEM.

7. THE KING WAS OFFENDED, AND HE SENT HIS SOLDIERS AGAINST THEM, AND DESTROYED THEM, AND BURNED CITY.

8. THEN THE KING SAID TO HIS SERVANTS, THE DINNER IS READY, BUT THE GUESTS DID NOT AGREE.

9. GO NOW TO THE LANES, AND WHOMSOEVER YOU FIND INVITE TO THE FEAST.

10. AND THE SERVANTS WENT ALONG THE ROADS AND GATHERED AS MANY AS THEY FOUND, BOTH BAD AND GOOD, AND THE ROOMS WERE FULL OF GUESTS.

11. AND THE KING CAME OUT TO SEE THE FEAST, AND HE SAW A MAN WHO HAD NOT ON A WEDDING GARMENT.

12. AND HE SAID TO HIM, FRIEND, HOW DIDST THOU COME HERE WITHOUT A WEDDING GARMENT? THE GUEST WAS SILENT.

13. THEN THE KING SAID TO THE SERVANTS, BIND HIM HAND AND FOOT, AND TAKE HIM INTO THE DARKNESS AWAY FROM HERE.

14. FOR MANY ARE CALLED, BUT FEW ARE CHOSEN.

PARABLE OF THE RICH MAN AND THE STEWARD

Luke xvi. 1. THERE WAS A RICH MAN, WHO HAD A STEWARD; AND THE STEWARD WAS ACCUSED OF WASTING THE MASTERS GOODS.

2. AND HE CALLED HIM, AND SAID, THERE ARE RUMOURS ABOUT THEE. GIVE ME AN ACCOUNT OF THY STEWARDSHIP, FOR THOU CANST NO LONGER BE A STEWARD.

3. AND THE STEWARD SAID TO HIMSELF, WHAT SHALL I DO WHEN THE MASTER TAKES A WAY FROM ME THE STEWARDSHIP? I HAVE NO STRENGTH TO PLOUGH; TO BEG I AM ASHAMED.

4. I KNOW WHAT TO DO THAT, WHEN I AM PUT OUT OF THE STEWARDSHIP, GOOD PEOPLE MAY RECEIVE ME IN THEIR HOUSES.

5. SO HE CALLED EVERYONE OF HIS MASTERS DEBTORS, AND SAID, HOW MUCH DOST THOU OWE MY MASTER?

6. AND HE SAID, A HUNDRED PAILS OF OIL. AND HE SAID TO HIM, TAKE THY BILL, AND SIT DOWN AND WRITE QUICKLY FIFTY.

7. THEN HE SAID TO ANOTHER, HOW MUCH DOST THOU OWE? A HUNDRED MEASURES OF BREAD. AND HE SAID TO HIM, TAKE THY BILL, AND WRITE EIGHTY.

8. AND THE MASTER COMMENDED THE STEWARD OF THE IRREGULAR WEALTH, BECAUSE HE HAD DONE WISELY: FOR THE CHILDREN OF THIS WORLD ARE WISER THAN THE CHILDREN OF LIGHT AMONG THEIR OWN.

9. AND I TELL YOU, MAKE FOR YOURSELVES FRIENDS OF THE WEALTH OF UNRIGHTEOUSNESS, THAT, WHEN IT FAIL YOU, YOU MAY BE RECEIVED UNDER THE EVERLASTING ROOFS.

10. HE WHO DOES RIGHT IN LITTLE THINGS WILL DO RIGHT IN GREAT THINGS. AND HE WHO DOES WRONG IN LITTLE THINGS WILL DO WRONG IN GREAT THINGS.

11. IF THEREFORE YOU DO WRONG IN THE UNRIGHTEOUSNESS WEALTH, WHO WILL COMMIT TO YOUR TRUST THE REAL WEALTH?

12. AND IF YOU DO NOT RIGHT IN WHAT IS ANOTHER'S, WHO WILL GIVE YOU WHAT IS YOUR OWN.

13. NO SERVANT CAN SERVE TWO MASTERS: EITHER HE WILL ESTEEM THE ONE LITTLE, AND WILL PLEASE THE OTHER, OR HE WILL WORK WELL FOR THE ONE, AND WILL NEGLECT THE OTHER. YOU CANNOT WORK FOR GOD AND FOR WEALTH.

PARABLE OF THE RICH MAN AND OF LAZARUS

Luke xvi. 14. AND THE PHARISEES, WHO ARE FOUND OF MONEY, HEARD THIS, AND BEGAN TO DERIDE HIM.

15. AND HE SAID TO THEM, YOU JUSTIFY YOURSELVES BEFORE MEN; BUT GOD KNOWS YOUR HEARTS: WHAT IS HIGHLY ESTEEMED AMONG MEN IS AN ABOMINATION IN THE SIGHT OF GOD.

16. THE LAW AND THE PROPHETS WERE UNTIL JOHN; SINCE THEN THE KINGDOM OF GOD IS ANNOUNCED, AND EVERY MAN IS FORCING HIS WAY INTO IT.

19. THERE WAS A RICH MAN, WHO WAS CLOTHED IN SILK AND VELVET, AND HE MADE MERRY EVERYDAY.

20. AND THERE WAS A POOR VAGRANT NAMED LAZARUS. AND LAZARUS WAS FULL OF SORES AND LAY AT THE GATE OF THE RICH MAN.

21. LAZARUS WANTED TO LIVE ON THE REMNANTS FROM THE RICH MAN'S TABLE; BUT THE DOGS CAME AND EVEN LICKED HIS SORES.

22. AND THE POOR VAGRANT DIED, AND THE ANGELS CARRIED HIM TO ABRAHAM; THE RICH MAN ALSO DIED, AND HE WAS BURIED.

23. AND IN HELL HE LIFTED UP HIS EYES, AND SAW ABRAHAM AFAR OFF, AND LAZARUS WITH HIM.

24. AND THE RICH MAN SPOKE, AND SAID, FATHER ABRAHAM, HAVE PITY ON ME, AND SEND LAZARUS TO ME, THAT HE MAY DIP HIS FINGER IN WATER, AND COOL MY THROAT; FOR IT IS HOT IN THIS FIRE.

25. AND ABRAHAM SAID, REMEMBER, MY SON, THAT THOU RECEIVEDST IN THY LIFETIME AS MANY GOOD THINGS AS LAZARUS RECEIVED EVIL THINGS: HE HAS BEEN CALLED HERE, BUT THOU ART TORMENTED.

26. AND MORE THAN ALL THAT BETWEEN US AND YOU THERE IS A GREATER GULF. EVEN IF ONE WANTED TO PASS FROM US TO YOU, HE COULD NOT DO SO.

27. AND THE RICH MAN SAID, I PRAY THEE, FATHER, SEND LAZARUS TO MY HOUSE:

28. I HAVE FIVE BROTHERS. LET HIM EXPLAIN THINGS TO THEM, LEST THEY COME TO THIS PLACE OF TORMENT.

29. AND ABRAHAM SAID TO HIM, THEY HAVE MOSES AND THE TEACHERS: LET THEM HEAR THEM.

30. BUT HE SAID, NO, FATHER ABRAHAM: IF ONE WENT TO THEM FROM THE DEAD, THEY WOULD COME TO THEIR SENSES.

31. AND ABRAHAM SAID TO HIM, THEY HAVE NOT HEARD MOSES AND THE PROPHETS; NEITHER WILL THEY OBEY, THOUGH ONE ROSE FROM THE DEAD AND WENT TO THEM.

THE CHIEF COMMANDMENTS

Matt. xxii. 35. AND ONE OF THE LAWYERS, TEMPTING HIM, ASKED HIM,

36. TEACHER, WHICH IS THE GREAT COMMANDMENT IN THE LAW?

37. JESUS SAID TO HIM, THOU SHALT LOVE THE LORD THY HEART, WITH ALL THY SOUL, AND WITH ALL THY POWER.

38. THIS IS THE FIRST GREAT COMMANDMENT.

39. THE SECOND IS LIKE IT: THOU SHALT LOVE THY NEIGHBOR AS THYSELF.

40. IN THESE TWO COMMANDMENTS IS ALL THE LAW AND THE PROPHETS.

32. AND THE LAWYER SAID AGAIN, WELL HAST THOU SAID, TEACHER, THAT HE IS ONE, AND THERE IS NO OTHER BUT HE.

33. AND TO LOVE HIM WITH ALL THY HEART, WITH ALL THY UNDER-STANDING, WITH ALL THY LIFE, AND WITH ALL THE STRENGTH, AND TO LOVE THY NEIGHBOR AS THYSELF IS MORE IMPORTANT THAN ALL THE SERVICES.

34. AND JESUS LOOKING AT HIM, SAID TO HIM, THOU ART NOT FAR FROM THE KINGDOM OF GOD.

OF THE RICH MAN AND OF RICHES

Mark x. 17. ONE DAY A COMMANDER CAME RUNNING UP TO JESUS, AND KNEELED BEFORE HIM, GOOD TEACHER, TELL ME WHAT GOOD I MUST DO THAT I MAY INHERIT ETERNAL LIFE?

18. AND JESUS SAID TO HIM, WHAT IS THE USE OF TALKING ABOUT THE GOOD? THERE IS NONE GOOD, BUT GOD.

Matt. xix. 17. IF THOU WILT HAVE LIFE, KEEP THE COMMANDMENTS.

18. HE SAID TO HIM, WHICH? JESUS SAID, THOU SHALT NOT KILL, THOU SHALT NOT COMMIT ADULTERY, THOU SHALT NOT STEAL, THOU SHALT NOT BEAR FALSE WITNESS.

19. HONOR THY FATHER AND LOVE THY NEIGHBOR AS THYSELF.

20. AND THE COMMANDER SAID TO HIM, ALL THAT I HAVE KEPT FROM MY YOUTH. WHAT DO I LACK?

Mark x. 21. JESUS LOOK AT HIM AND SMILED, AND SAID, ONE THING THOU LACKEST:

Matt. xix. 21. IF THOU WILT FULFILL EVERYTHING, GO AND SELL EVERY-THING WHICH THOU HAST, AND GIVE TO THE POOR, AND THOU SHALT HAVE TREASURE IN GOD: THEN COME AND FOLLOW ME.

Mark x. 22. THE MAN WAS SAD AT THESE WORDS, AND WENT AWAY; FOR HE HAD GREAT POSSESSIONS.

23. AND SEEING HOW HE WAS SADDENED, JESUS LOOKED ROUND AND SAID TO HIS DISCIPLES, NOW YOU SEE HOW INCOMPATIBLE IT IS FOR THOSE WHO HAVE POSSESSIONS TO ENTER INTO THE KINGDOM OF GOD!

24. THE DISCIPLES WERE FRIGHTENED AT THESE WORDS. BUT JESUS TURNED TO THEM AND SAID, YES, CHILDREN, I TELL YOU AGAIN, IT IS INCOMPATIBLE FOR THOSE WHO HAVE POSSESSIONS TO ENTER INTO THE KINGDOM OF GOD!

25. IT IS MORE POSSIBLE FOR A CAMEL TO GO THROUGH THE EYE OF NEE-DLE, THAN FOR A RICH MAN TO ENTER INTO THE KINGDOM OF GOD.

26. THEY WERE EVEN MORE FRIGHTENED, AND SAID TO ONE ANOTHER, WHO THEN CAN PRESERVE HIS LIFE?

27. AND JESUS LOOKING AT THEM SAID, ACCORDING TO THE HUMAN UNDER-STANDING IT SEEMS IMPOSSIBLE, BUT ACCORDING TO GOD IT IS POSSIBLE.

JESUS AND ZACCHEUS

Luke xix. 1. AND ENTERING JERICHO, JESUS WALKED THROUGH THE CITY.

2. AND THERE WAS A MAN NAMED ZACCHEUS, WHO WAS THE CHIEF OF THE TAX COLLECTORS, AND HE WAS RICH.

3. AND HE WANTED TO SEE JESUS, WHAT KIND OF A MAN HE WAS; AND HE COULD NOT MAKE HIS WAY THROUGH THE CROWD, BECAUSE HE WAS SMALL OF STATURE.

4. SO HE RAN AHEAD CLIMBED UP A TREE TO SEE HIM WHEN HE PASSED THAT WAY.

5. WHEN JESUS PASSED BY, HE LOOKED AT HIM, AND SAID, ZACCHEUS, MAKE HASTE, AND CLIMB DOWN; FOR TODAY I WANT TO STAY AT THY HOUSE.

6. ZACCHEUS CLIMBED DOWN AT ONCE AND JOYFULLY RECEIVED HIM IN HIS HOUSE.

7. AND THEY SAW IT, AND BEGAN TO GRUMBLE, SAYING, WHY DID HE STOP AT THE HOUSE OF A SINNER?

8. AND ZACCHEUS WENT UP TO JESUS, AND SAID TO HIM, SIR, HALF OF MY GOODS I WILL GIVE TO THE BEGGARS, AND IF I HAVE WRONGED ANYONE, I WILL GIVE HIM FOURFOLD.

9. AND JESUS SAID IN REPLY, NOW THE CHILD OF THIS HOUSE WILL BE SAVED, FOR HE IS A SON OF ABRAHAM.

10. FOR THE WORK OF THE SON OF MAN CONSISTS IN FINDING AND SAVING WHAT HAS PERISHED AND IS PERISHING.

Mark xii. 41. AND JESUS SAT DOWN OPPOSITE THE MONEY-BOX AND WATCHED THE PEOPLE PUT THE MONEY INTO THE BOX; AND MANY RICH PEOPLE PASSED BY AND THREW IN MUCH MONEY.

42. AND THERE CAME A CERTAIN POOR WIDOW AND SHE PUT INTO THE BOX TWO MITES, WHICH MAKE A FARTHING.

43. AND HE CALLED HIS DISCIPLES, AND SAID TO THEM, VERILY, I TELL YOU, THIS POOR WIDOW HAS PUT MORE THAN THE REST INTO THE BOX.

44. FOR THEY THREW IN OF THEIR ABUNDANCE; BUT SHE OF HER WANT THREW IN EVERYTHING SHE HAD—ALL HER LIVING.

THE MEASURE OF GOOD

Mark xiv. 3. JESUS HAPPENED TO BE IN THE HOUSE OF SIMON THE LEPER. A WOMAN CAME UP TO HIM: SHE WAS RICH IN THE POSSESSION OF A PITCHER OF PRECIOUS OIL. SHE BROKE THE PITCHER, AND POURED THE OIL ON JESUS' HEAD.

John xii. 3. AND THE WHOLE ROOM WAS FILLED WITH THE PLEASANT ODOR OF THE OIL.

Matt. xxvi. 8. AND THE DISCIPLES WERE DISPLEASED, AND THEY SAID TO ONE ANOTHER, TO WHAT PURPOSE IS THIS WASTE OF THE PRECIOUS OIL?

9. THIS OIL MIGHT HAVE BEEN SOLD FOR MUCH, AND GIVEN TO THE POOR.

John xii. 4. THEN ONE OF HIS DISCIPLES, JUDAS ISCARIOT, THE ONE WHO BETRAYED HIM, SAID,

5. IT OUGHT TO HAVE BEEN SOLD: THE OIL IS WORTH THREE HUNDRED PENCE, AND IT OUGHT TO BE GIVEN TO THE POOR.

6. HE SAID THIS, NOT THAT HE CARED FOR THE POOR; BUT BECAUSE HE WAS A THIEF, AND HAD THE BOX FOR THE POOR UPON HIM.

Matt. xxvi. 10. JESUS UNDERSTOOD IT, AND SAID, WHY DO YOU TROUBLE THIS WOMAN? LEAVE HER ALONE, FOR SHE HAS DONE A GOOD ACT ON ME.

Mark xiv. 7. YOU ALWAYS HAVE THE POOR AMONG YOU, AND YOU CAN DO THEM GOOD WHENEVER YOU PLEASE; BUT I AM NOT ALWAYS WITH YOU.

8. WHAT SHE HAD SHE GAVE AWAY: SHE HAS BEFOREHAND ANOINTED MY BODY FOR BURIAL.

9. VERILY I TELL YOU, WHEREVER IN THE WORLD THE TRUE GOOD WILL BE TOLD, A WORD WILL BE SAID OF WHAT SHE HAS DONE.

Mark ix. 31. AND HE TAUGHT HIS DISCIPLES, AND SAID TO THEM, THE SON OF MAN IS DELIVERED INTO THE POWER OF MEN, AND HE WILL RISE ON THE THIRD DAY AFTER HE IS KILLED.

32. BUT THEY DID NOT UNDERSTAND HIS SAYING, AND WERE AFRAID TO ASK HIM.

Luke xii. 33. SELL YOUR ESTATES, AND GIVE ALMS. PROVIDE YOURSELVES WITH BAGS WHICH DO NOT GROW OLD, AN INEXHAUSTIBLE TREASURE WITH GOD, WHERE NO THIEF CAN APPROACH AND NO MOTH CAN FLY.

Luke xiv. 12. AND IF THOU WISHEST TO GIVE A DINNER OR A SUPPER, DO NOT CALL THY FRIENDS, BROTHERS, RELATIVES OR RICH NEIGHBORS, FOR THE PURPOSE THAT THEY MAY CALL YOU ALSO AND PAY YOU BACK.

13. BUT WHEN THOU MAKEST A FEAST, CALL THE POOR, THE MAIMED, THE LAME, THE BLIND:

14. AND THOU WILT HAPPY; FOR THEY CANNOT PAY YOU BACK, BUT THOU WILT BE RECOMPENSED AT THE REËSTABLISHMENT OF THE JUST.

Matt. xxi. 28. WHAT DO YOU THINK? A MAN HAD TWO SONS; AND HE CAME TO THE FIRST, AND SAID, GO WORK TODAY IN THE GARDEN.

29. HE WILL REPLIED, AND SAID, I WILL NOT; BUT AFTERWARD HE THOUGHT IT OVER, AND WENT.

30. AND THE FATHER CAME TO THE SECOND, AND SAID THE SAME. BUT HE SAID IN REPLY YES, FATHER; AND HE DID NOT GO.

31. WHICH OF THE TWO DID HIS FATHER'S WILL? THEY SAY TO HIM, THE FIRST.

Matt. xxi. 21. NOT EVERYONE WHO SAYS TO ME, LORD, LORD, WILL ENTER THE KINGDOM OF GOD, BUT HE WHO DOES THE WILL OF MY FATHER IN HEAVEN.

TOLSTOY'S COMMENTARY

For the life of the spirit there can be no difference between relatives and strangers. Jesus says that his mother and brothers signify nothing to him as mother and brothers: close to him are only those who do the will of the common Father.

Man's blessedness and life do not depend on his domestic relations, but on the life of the spirit. Jesus says that blessed are those who keep the understanding of the Father. For a man living by the spirit there is no home. Animals have homes, but man lives by the spirit, and so cannot have a home. Jesus says that he has no definite place for himself. To do the will of the Father one does not need any definite place—it is everywhere and at all times possible. Carnal death cannot be terrible to men who give themselves to the will of the Father, for the life of the spirit does not depend on the death of the flesh. Jesus says that he who believes in the life of the spirit cannot be afraid of anything. No cares can keep a man from living by the spirit. To the words of the man, that he will later fulfill the teaching of Jesus, but that first he wants to bury his father, Jesus replies, Only the dead can trouble themselves about burying the dead, but the living always live in the fulfillment of the will of the Father.

The cares about family and domestic matters cannot interfere with the life of the spirit. He who troubles himself to find out what his carnal life will profit from doing the will of the Father, is doing the same that the ploughman does, when he ploughs and looks backward, and not forward. The cares for the joys of the carnal life, which seem so important to people, are a dream. The only real work of life is the announcement of the will of the Father, the attention paid to it, and the fulfillment of it. To Martha's rebuke that she is attending herself to the supper, while her sister Mary is not helping her, but is listening to his teaching, Jesus says, Why dost thou rebuke her? Look after thy cares, if thou needest that which thy cares give thee, but let those who do not need carnal pleasures do that one thing which is necessary for life. Jesus says, He who wants to attain the true life, which consists in doing the will of the Father, must first of all renounce his personal wishes: he must not only keep from arranging his life as he wishes, but must also be prepared for all privations and sufferings. He who wants to arrange his carnal life as he wishes will lose the true life of the fulfillment of the will of the Father.

There is no advantage in acquiring for the carnal life, if this acquisition causes the life of the spirit to perish. Nothing causes the life of the spirit to perish so much as selfishness, the acquisition of wealth. Men forget that, no matter how much wealth and how much property they may acquire, they are liable to die at any moment, and their possessions are not needed for their life. Death hangs over every one of us: sickness, murder, unfortunate accidents, may at any second cut our life short. Carnal death is an inevitable condition of every second of life. If a man lives, he must look at every hour of his life as at an hour of grace, given to him by somebody's favour. We must remember this, and not say that we do not know it. We know and foresee what happens in heaven and on earth, but we forget the death which, we know, is lying in wait for us at any second.

If we do not forget this, we cannot abandon ourselves to the life of the flesh—we cannot count on it. In order to follow my teaching, a man must count up the advantages from serving the carnal life of his will and the advantages from doing the will of the Father. Only he who has clearly figured that out can be my disciple. He who has made the correct account will not be sorry to give up the seeming good and the seeming life in order to obtain the true good and the true life.

The true life has been given to men, and men know and hear its call, but deprive themselves of it, as they are distracted by momentary cares. The true life is like a feast, which a rich man gave, when he invited the guests. He called the guests, just as the voice of the spirit of God calls all men to him. But some of the guests were busy with commerce, others with their farms, and others again with domestic matters—and they did not come to the feast. But the poor, who have no carnal cares, came to the feast and were made happy. Even so men, being distracted by the cares of the carnal life, deprive themselves of the true life. He who will not completely renounce all cares and terrors of carnal life cannot do the will of the Father, for it is impossible to serve oneself a little and God a little. It is necessary to figure out whether it is advantageous to serve one's flesh, whether it is possible to arrange life as one wants to arrange it. We must do the same that a man does who wants to build a house or go to war. He will make his account, to see whether he can finish building, or whether he will obtain a victory. When he sees that he cannot, he does not waste his labors, nor his army. Or else he will waste it and will become a laughingstock of people. If it were possible to arrange the carnal life as one wants to arrange it, one ought to serve his flesh; but, since it is impossible to do so, it is better to abandon everything carnal, and to serve the spirit, or else it will be neither this nor that. You cannot arrange your carnal life, and the life of the spirit you will lose, and so, to do the will of the Father, it is necessary completely to renounce the carnal life.

The carnal life is that seeming wealth which is entrusted to us by others, and which we must use in such a way as to obtain the true wealth. If a steward is living with a rich man, and knows that, no matter how much he may serve his master, the master will discharge him and leave him without anything, the steward acts wisely if, as long as he is still in charge of the wealth, which is not his own, he will do good to people. If then the master will abandon him, those to whom he has done good will receive him and will feed him.

The same ought men to do with their carnal life. The carnal life is that foreign wealth of which they are in charge for but a short time.

If they make good use of this wealth, they will receive their own true wealth. If we do not give up our false possessions, we shall not receive the true possessions. It is impossible to serve the false life of the flesh and the spirit—one has to serve the one or the other. One cannot serve wealth and God. What is great before men is an abomination before God. Before God wealth is evil. The rich man is guilty for the very reason that he eats much and luxuriously, while the poor starve at his door. Everybody knows that the property which thou dost not give up to others is a non-fulfillment of the will of the Father.

An Orthodox rich chief once came to Jesus, and began to boast of keeping the commandments of the law. Jesus reminded him that there was a commandment to love all men as oneself, and that in this consisted the will of the Father. The chief said that he kept also this commandment. Then Jesus told him, That is not true. If thou wantest to do the will of the Father, thou wouldst not have any possessions. It is impossible for thee to do the will of the Father, if thou hast any property which thou hast not distributed to others. And Jesus said to the disciples, People think that it is impossible to live without possessions, but I tell you, The true life consists in giving to others what belongs to one.

A man named Zaccheus heard the teaching of Christ and believed him. He invited him to his house, and said to him, I give half of my possessions to the poor, and I will give fourfold to whomsoever I have offended. And Jesus said, Here is a man who does the will of the Father, for there is not any one position in which a man does the will of God, but our whole life is its fulfillment, and this man fulfills it.

The will of the Father is that all men should return to it.

The good cannot be measured: it cannot be said who has done more, who less. The widow who gives away her last mite gives more than the rich man who gives away thousands. Nor can the good be measured by its being useful or useless. As an example of how the good ought to be done may serve the woman who pitied Jesus and senselessly poured three hundred pence' worth of oil on his feet. Judas said that she acted foolishly, that with that money the poor could have been fed. But Judas was a thief: he lied and, speaking of the carnal profit, was not thinking of the poor. What is needed is not profit, not quantity, but the doing of the will of the Father: to love and to live for others.

One day Jesus' mother and brothers came to him, and could not see him, for there was a great multitude about him. And a man, seeing them, went up to Jesus and said:

Thy family, thy mother and thy brothers, are standing outside: they want to see thee.

My mother and brothers are those who understand the will of the Father and do it.

And a woman said, Blessed is the womb that bore thee, and the teats which thou hast sucked. To this Jesus said, Blessed are always those who have understood the understanding of the Father, and who keep it.

And a man said to Jesus, I will follow thee, wherever thou mayest go. And Jesus said to him, There is no place for thee to go to, for I have no home, no place, where I live. Only animals have lairs and dens, but man is spirit, and he is everywhere at home, if he lives by the spirit.

One day Jesus was sailing in a ship with his disciples. He said, Let us sail to the other side.

A storm rose on the sea and began to drench them, and they were almost drowned. But he was lying at the stern, and sleeping. They awakened him, and said, Teacher, does it not make any difference to thee that we are drowning? And when the storm subsided, he said, Why are you so timid, and have no faith in the life of the spirit?

Jesus said to a man, Follow me. And the man said, My old father has died. Let me first bury him, and then I will follow thee. And Jesus said to him, Let the dead bury the dead: and if thou wishest to be alive, do the will of the Father and proclaim it.

And another man said, I will be thy disciple, and will do the will of the Father, as thou commandest, but allow me first to arrange matters at home. And Jesus said to him, If a ploughman looks back, he cannot plough. No matter how much you may look back, you cannot plough. A man must forget everything but the furrow which he is making, and then only will he be able to plough. If thou discussest what it will profit the life of the flesh, thou hast not understood the real life, and thou canst not live by it.

After this it once happened that Jesus and his disciples entered a village. And a woman named Martha invited them to her house.

And Martha had a sister Mary, and she sat down at the feet of Jesus and listened to his teaching. And Martha was trying to give them a good entertainment. And Martha went up to Jesus, and said, Thou dost not even care that my sister has left me alone to serve. Tell her to work with me.

And Jesus replied to her, Martha, Martha, thou carest and troublest thyself about many things, but there is only one thing necessary, and

Mary has chosen the one thing which she needs and which no one will take from her. For life nothing but the food of the spirit is needed.

And Jesus said to all, He who wants to follow me must renounce his will and must be prepared at all times for all privations and for all sufferings of the flesh, and then only can he follow me.

For he who wants to care for his carnal life will lose the true life. But he who loses the carnal life, doing the will of the Father, will save the true life; for what profit is it to a man if he has the whole world, and loses or injures his life?

And hearing this, a man said, It is well, if there is a life of the spirit; but how if we give up everything, and there is not that life?

To this Jesus said, You know that the doing of the will of the Father gives life to all; but you are drawn away from this life by false cares, and you reject it. You do like this: a man prepared a dinner, and sent out the servants to call the guests, but the guests excused themselves.

One said, I have bought a piece of land, and I must go and see it. Another said, I have bought some oxen, and I must go and try them. The third said, I have married, and I am going to have a wedding.

And the servants came, and told their master that no one was coming. Then the master sent the servants out to call in the beggars. The beggars did not excuse themselves, but came. And when they came, there was still room left.

And the master sent the servants to invite more men, saying, Go and tell them all to come to my dinner. Let there be as many as possible at the dinner; but those who have refused on the ground of being busy will miss it.

Everybody knows that the doing of the will of God gives life, but they do not come, because they are distracted by the deception of wealth.

And Jesus said, Beware of riches, for thy life does not depend on having more than others have.

There was a rich man, and he had a good harvest of corn. And he said to himself, I will build new barns, I will make them large, and will gather all my wealth in them. And I will say to my soul, Here, soul, is everything in abundance for thee: eat, drink, and live for thy pleasure.

And God said to him, Fool! This very night will thy soul be taken, and everything which thou hast gathered will be left for others. Thus is done to all who prepare for the carnal life, and do not live in God.

And Jesus said to them, You say that Pilate killed the Galileans. Were these Galileans worse than other men, that this has happened with them?

Not at all. We are all such men, and all of us will perish in the same way, if we do not find salvation from death. And those eighteen men who were killed by the tower, when it fell in, were they some special men, worse than the rest of the inhabitants of Jerusalem? Not at all. If we do not save ourselves from death, we shall die in the same way, if not one day, then another.

If we have not yet perished like them, we ought to think in this manner: a man has an apple tree growing in his garden. The master comes into the garden to look at the tree, and sees that it has no fruit on it. So the master says to the gardener, I have been coming here these three years, and the apple tree is still barren. It has to be cut down, for it wastes the ground. And the gardener says, Let us wait awhile, master. I will dig it round, and will put manure all about it, and we shall see whether it will give fruit next summer. If it does not, we shall cut it down then.

Even so we are a barren apple tree, as long as we live in the flesh and do not bear the fruit of the life of the spirit. Only through somebody's favour are we left until the next summer. If we do not bear fruit, we shall perish like the one who built the barns, like the Galileans, like the eighteen men killed by the tower, and like all who do not bear fruit, dying an everlasting death.

In order to understand this, no wisdom is needed, for anybody can see it. Not only in domestic matters, but in everything which is going on in the world we are able to reflect and guess in advance. If the wind is from the west, we say, It is going to rain, and so it happens. How is this? The weather we can predict, and yet we cannot foresee that we shall all die and perish, and that the only salvation for us is the life of the spirit, the doing of its will.

And a great multitude went with Jesus, and he once more said to all, He who wants to be my disciple must esteem little his father, mother, wife, children, brothers, sisters, and all his property, and must at all times be prepared for everything. Only he who does what I am doing follows my teaching, and only that man will be saved from death.

For each man will figure out, before he begins anything, whether what he is doing is profitable, and if it is, he will do it; and if not, he gives it up. Every man who builds a house first sits down and figures out how much money he needs, how much he has, and whether he will have enough with which to finish building it, lest he begin and do not finish it, and men laugh at him.

Even so he who wants to live the carnal life must first figure out whether he can finish what he has begun.

Every king, who wants to wage war, first considers whether he can go with ten thousand against twenty thousand. If he figures out that he cannot, he will send messengers to make peace, and will give up the idea of fighting. So let each man, before giving himself up to the carnal life, consider whether he can wage war against death, or whether death is stronger than he. And if it is, let him make peace with it in advance.

Thus every one of you must first settle with what he considers to be his own, his family, his money, his possessions, and when he figures out what advantage he will derive from them, and understands that there is none, he will be able to be my disciple, and not before.

The kingdom of heaven does not come in an external manner. Of the kingdom of heaven, which saves from death, we cannot say that it has come, or that it will come; that it is here, or there; it is within you, in your souls.

For, if the time comes and you want to find salvation in life and you look for it in a certain time, you will not find it. And if they will tell you, Salvation is here, salvation is there, do not look for it anywhere, but within yourselves, for salvation is sudden, like lightning, and everywhere; there is no time and space for it—it is in your souls.

And as salvation was for Noah and for Lot, so it is always for the son of man. Life remains the same for all men: all eat and drink and get married, but some perish, and others are saved.

There was an evil judge, who feared neither God nor man, and a poor widow begged him; but the judge did not decide in her favour. The widow begged the judge day and night. The unjust judge said, What shall I do? I will decide as the widow wishes, for she gives me no rest.

You must understand that even the unjust judge did what the widow asked him to do. How, then, will the Father refuse to do what men ask him for day and night without cessation?

But besides the Father there is the son of man who is seeking the truth, and we cannot fail to believe in him.

He who will give up the false, temporal wealth for the true life according to the will of the Father will do the same as did the wise steward.

A man was a steward of a rich master; he saw that his master would discharge him, and that he would be left without bread and without a home.

And the steward said to himself, This is what I will do: I will quietly distribute the master's goods to the peasants and will cut down their debts; then, if the master sends me away, the peasants will remember the good I have done to them, and will not abandon me.

And so the steward did. He called up the peasants, those who were in debt to the master, and rewrote their bills. Instead of one hundred he wrote fifty, and instead of sixty he wrote twenty, and so he did to all.

And the master heard of it, and said to himself, Indeed, he has done wisely, for else he would have to go a-begging. He has caused me a loss, but he has calculated well, for in the carnal life we all understand how to calculate correctly, but in the life of the spirit we do not wish to understand.

Even so we must do with the unjust wealth: we must give it away in order to receive the life of the spirit. If we shall regret giving up such trifles as wealth for the life of the spirit, it will not be given to us. If we do not give up the false wealth, our own life will not be given to us. It is impossible to serve at once two mastery, God and wealth—the will of God and our own will. Either the one, or the other.

When the Orthodox heard that, they laughed at Jesus, for they love wealth.

And he said to them, You think that because men respect you for your riches, you are really respected. No, God does not look without, but within, into the heart. What is high before men is insignificant before God. The kingdom of God is now on earth, and great are they who enter into it; but it is not the rich, but the poor, who enter. That has always been so according to your law, and according to Moses and the prophets. Hear what the rich and the poor are according to your faith.

There was a rich man. He dressed himself in costly garments and made merry every day. And there was a vagrant named Lazarus, who was scurfy. And Lazarus came into the yard of the rich man, thinking that he might get the remnants from the rich man's table, but he did not get even those; for the rich man's dogs ate the remnants clean and even licked the wounds of Lazarus.

And both Lazarus and the rich man died. In hell the rich man saw Abraham a long way off, and Lazarus the scurfy was sitting with him.

The rich man said, Father Abraham, Lazarus the scurfy is sitting with thee: he used to wallow at the gate of my house. I dare not trouble thee. Send Lazarus the scurfy to me: let him dip his finger in water and refresh my throat, for I am burning in fire. But Abraham said, Why should I send Lazarus to thee, in hell? Thou hadst everything thou wantedst in the other world, while Lazarus saw nothing but sorrow there. It is time for him to have pleasure now. Even if he wanted to do it for thee, he cannot, for between you and us there is a great gulf, and it is impossible to cross it. We are living, but you are dead.

Then the rich man said, Father Abraham, at least send Lazarus the scurfy to my house: I have five brothers, and I am sorry for them: let him tell them how dangerous wealth is, or else they will have to suffer torment themselves. But Abraham said, They know, as it is, that wealth is dangerous, for Moses and all the prophets have told them that.

But the rich man said, Still it would be better if one risen from the dead came to them, for that would bring them to their senses. And Abraham said, If they do not listen to Moses and the prophets, they will not listen to one risen from the dead.

All know that we should divide with our brother and do good to men, and the whole law of Moses and all the prophets say nothing else. You know it, but do not wish to do it, because you love wealth.

And a rich Orthodox chief went up to Jesus, and said to him, Thou art a good teacher! Tell me what I must do that I may receive eternal life.

Jesus said, Why dost thou call me good? Good is only the Father. If thou wishest to receive life, do the commandments.

The chief said, There are many commandments; which must I keep? Jesus said, Do not kill, do not commit debauchery, do not steal, do not lie, and also honor thy Father and do his will, and love thy neighbor as thyself.

And the Orthodox chief said, All these commandments I have been keeping from childhood; but I ask what else I must do according to thy teaching.

Jesus looked at him, at his rich garments, and he smiled and said, Thou lackest one little thing: thou hast not fulfilled what thou sayest. If thou wishest to do these commandments, Do not kill, do not commit debauchery, do not steal, do not lie, and, above all, the commandment, Love thy neighbor as thyself, go and sell thy estate and give it to the poor, and then thou wilt do the will of the Father.

When the chief heard this, he frowned and went away, for he was sorry to part from his possessions.

And Jesus said to his disciples, You see that it is absolutely impossible to be rich and do the will of the Father.

The disciples were frightened at these words. But Jesus repeated, and said, Yes, children, he who has wealth cannot be in the will of God. Much easier it is for a camel to pass through the eye of a needle than for a rich man to do the will of the Father.

And they were frightened more than before, and said, If so, it is impossible to save one's life.

And he said, To a man it seems impossible to save one's life without possessions, but God will save a man without possessions.

One day Jesus happened to pass through the town of Jericho. In this city there was a rich farmer of taxes named Zaccheus. This Zaccheus had heard of Jesus' teaching and believed in it. When he heard that Jesus was in Jericho, he wanted to see him. There were so many people all about him, that it was not possible to make one's way through them.

Then he ran forward and climbed a tree, that he might see Jesus as he passed by.

And indeed, as Jesus went by, he saw Zaccheus, and, having learned that Zaccheus believed in his teaching, he said, Climb down from the tree and go home, and I will go to thy house. Zaccheus climbed down, ran home, and prepared a reception for Jesus.

The people began to judge and to say about Jesus, He has gone into the house of a tax collector, a rascal.

In the meantime Zaccheus said to Jesus, Sir, this is what I will do: I will give half of my possessions to the poor, and from the rest I will pay all whom I have injured.

And Jesus said, Now thou art saved. Thou art dead, and art alive; thou wert lost, and hast found thyself, for thou hast done like Abraham, when he wished to sacrifice his son, in order to show his faith. For the whole life of man consists in finding and saving what is perishing in one's soul.

It is impossible to measure a sacrifice by its size. One day Jesus and his disciples happened to sit opposite a money-box. Men were placing what they had into the box for God. And rich men walked up to the box, and placed a great deal in it. And then a poor widow came up and placed two mites in it.

And Jesus pointed to her, and said to his disciples, You saw the poor widow put in two mites: she has put in more than the rest, for the others put in what they did not need for life, while she put in everything she had, her whole life.

Jesus happened to be in the house of Simon the leper. And a woman entered the house. This woman had a pitcher with precious oil worth three hundred pence.

Jesus said to his disciples that his death was near. When the woman heard this, she took pity on Jesus, and wanted to show him her love and anoint his head with oil. And she forgot everything, how much her oil cost, and broke the pitcher, and anointed his head and feet, and spilled all the oil.

And the disciples began to judge her, saying that she had done badly. And Judas, the one who later betrayed Jesus, said, How much has been wasted!

The oil could have been sold for three hundred pence, and so many poor might have profited by it. And the disciples began to rebuke the woman, and she was troubled and did not know whether she had done right or wrong.

Then Jesus said to them, In vain do you trouble the woman, for she has truly done well. Why do you mention the poor? If you wish to do good to the poor, do it: they are always present, so there is no need of speaking of them. If you pity the poor, go and pity them and do good to them. She has pitied me and has done me a real good, for she has given me everything which she had. Who of you can tell what is needed, and what not? How do you know that it was not necessary to pour the oil over me? She has at least poured oil over me, so as to prepare my body for burial, and so it is necessary. She has truly done the will of the Father: she forgot herself and pitied another; she forgot the carnal calculation and gave away everything which she had.

PROOF OF THE TRUTH OF THE TEACHING. DEMANDING PROOFS OF CHRIST

Mark viii. 11. AND THE PHARISEES CAME OUT, AND BEGAN TO DISPUTE WITH HIM, TRYING TO GET THE PROOFS FROM HIM AND INVESTIGATING HIS TEACHING.

12. AND SUFFERING IN SPIRIT, HE SAID, WHAT? THESE PEOPLE WANT PROOFS? CAN THERE BE ANY PROOFS FOR THESE MEN?

Luke xii. 54. AND HE SAID TO THE PEOPLE, WHEN YOU SEE A CLOUD IN THE WEST, YOU SUPPOSE THAT THERE WILL BE RAIN, AND SO IT HAPPENS.

55. AND WHEN IT BLOWS FROM THE SOUTH, YOU SUPPOSE THAT IT WILL BE GOOD WEATHER, AND SO IT HAPPENS.

56. YOU ARE ABLE TO COMPREHEND THE APPEARANCE OF EARTH AND OF HEAVEN, BUT THIS IS LIFE YOU DO NOT COMPREHEND.

57. WHY DO YOU NOT JUDGE CORRECTLY ABOUT YOURSELVES?

Matt. xii. 38. THEN SOME OF THE DISCIPLES TURNED TO JESUS, AND SAID, TEACHER, WE SHOULD LIKE TO SEE PROOFS OF THY TEACHING.

Luke xi. 29. AND WHEN THE PEOPLE WERE GATHERED, HE BEGAN TO SPEAK, THIS TRIBE SEEKS PROOFS, BUT THEY SHALL HAVE NO OTHER PROOF THAN WHAT JONAH HAD.

30. AND SINCE JONAH WAS A PROOF FOR THE NINEVITES, THE SAME WILL THE PROOF OF THE SON OF MAN FOR THIS TRIBE.

31. IF THE QUEEN OF THE SOUTH WERE BROUGHT TO LIFE AND COMPARED WITH THE MEN OF THIS GENERATION, SHE WOULD STILL APPEAR MORE JUST THAN THEY, FOR SHE CAME FROM THE UTMOST PARTS OF THE EARTH TO HEAR THE WISDOM OF SOLOMON, BUT HERE IT IS MORE IMPORTANT FOR YOU.

32. IF THE MEN OF NINEVEH WERE BROUGHT BACK TO LIFE AND COMPARED WITH THE MEN OF THIS GENERATION, THEY WOULD APPEAR MORE JUST, FOR THEY CAME TO THEIR SENSES AFTER JONAH'S PREACHING, BUT HERE IS ONE MORE IMPORTANT THAN JONAH.

John vii. **1.** AFTER THIS, JESUS WALKED IN GALILEE: HE DID NOT WANT TO WALK THROUGH JUDEA, BECAUSE THE JEWS HAD CONDEMNED HIM TO DEATH.

2. AND A JEWISH FEAST WAS AT HAND,

3. AND HIS BROTHERS SAID TO HIM, GO AWAY FROM HERE, AND GO TO JUDEA, THAT THY DISCIPLES MAY SEE BEFORE THE OTHERS HOW THOU SERVEST GOD.

4. FOR NO MAN WILL CONCEAL HIS SERVICE OF GOD, BUT EVERY MAN SEEKS TO SHOW HIMSELF. IF THOU ṢERVEST GOD IN THIS MANNER, SHOW THY-SELF TO THE WORLD.

5. FOR HIS BROTHERS DID NOT BELIEVE IN HIS TEACHING.

6. JESUS SAID TO THEM, MY TIME HAS NOT YET COME; BUT FOR YOU THE TIME HAS, OF COURSE, COME.

7. THE WORLD WILL NOT HATE YOU; BUT ME IT HATES, BECAUSE I PROVE THAT THE WORLD'S WAY OF SERVING GOD IS EVIL.

8. GO TO THIS FEAST; BUT I CANNOT GO TO THIS FEAST, FOR MY TIME HAS NOT YET COME.

9. SO HE SPOKE, AND HE REMAINED IN GALILEE.

10. AND WHEN THEY WENT AWAY, HE WENT THERE, NOT FOR THE FEAST, BUT SIMPLY.

11. THE JEWS SOUGHT HIM AT THE FEAST, AND SAID, IS HE HERE, OR NOT?

12. AND THERE WAS MUCH CONTENTION ABOUT HIM AMONG THE PEOPLE: SOME SAID THAT HE WAS A GOOD MAN, AND OTHERS SAID, NO, HE MISLEADS THE PEOPLE.

13. BUT NO ONE SPOKE OPENLY OF HIM FOR THE FEAR OF THE JEWS.

JESUS' DISCOURSES WITH THE PHARISEES

John vii. 14. IN THE MIDDLE OF THE FEAST JESUS ENTERED THE TEMPLE, AND BEGAN TO TEACH.

15. AND THE JEWS MARVELLED, AND SAID, HOW DOES HE KNOW, HAVING NEVER LEARNED?

16. TO THIS JESUS REPLIED, MY TEACHING IS NOT MINE, BUT HIS WHO SENT ME.

17. HE WHO WILL DO HIS WILL, HE WILL KNOW OF THE TEACHING, WHETHER IT IS FROM GOD, OR WHETHER I SPEAK OF MYSELF.

18. HE WHO SPEAKS OF HIMSELF DISCUSSES WHAT SEEMS PROPER TO HIM; BUT HE WHO DISCUSSES WHAT SEEMS PROPER TO HIM WHO SENT HIM, IS TRUE, AND THERE IS NO UNTRUTH IN HIM.

19. MOSES DID NOT GIVE YOU THE LAW, AND NONE OF YOU LIVES ACCORDING TO THE LAW, SO HOW DO YOU CONDEMN ME TO DEATH?

20. AND THE PEOPLE REPLIED TO HIM, THOU ART UNSTABLE THYSELF.

21. AND JESUS ANSWERED THEM, I HAVE MADE THE SERVICE OF GOD TO BE ONE, AND AT THAT YOU MARVEL.

22. FOR MOSES GAVE YOU CIRCUMCISION, NOT BECAUSE IT IS FROM MOSES, BUT FROM THE FATHER (AS A COVENANT WITH GOD TO KEEP THE COMMANDMENTS AND THE SABBATH), AND YET YOU CIRCUMCISE ON A SABBATH.

23. IF A MAN RECEIVES THE CIRCUMCISION ON A SABBATH, THAT THE LAW OF MOSES SHOULD NOT BE BROKEN, WHY ARE YOU ANGRY AT ME, BECAUSE I HAVE MADE A MAN RIGHT ON THE SABBATH?

24. DO NOT JUDGE ACCORDING TO THE APPEARANCE, BUT IN TRUTH.

25. THEN SOME OF THE INHABITANTS OF JERUSALEM SAID, IS THIS HE WHOM THEY WANT TO KILL?

26. HE SPEAKS OPENLY, AND THEY DO NOT ANSWER HIM. HAVE NOT THE RULERS ACKNOWLEDGED HIM TO BE THE ANOINTED ONE?

27. THE ONLY THING IS WE KNOW THIS MAN. WHEN THE ANOINTED ONE COMES, NO MAN WILL KNOW WHENCE HE COMES.

28. AND TEACHING IN THE TEMPLE, JESUS SAID LOUDLY, YOU KNOW ME, AND YOU KNOW WHENCE I COME; BUT I DO NOT COME OF MYSELF: HE WHO HAS SENT ME IS TRUE, AND HIM YOU DO NOT KNOW.

29. I KNOW HIM; I KNOW THAT I AM FROM HIM AND THAT HE HAS SENT ME.

30. THEY WANTED TO OVERCOME HIM, BUT COULD NOT VANQUISH HIM, FOR IT WAS NOT YET TO BE.

31. AND MANY OF THE PEOPLE BELIEVED IN HIS TEACHING, AND SAID, WHEN CHRIST COMES, HE WILL HARDLY PROVE BETTER THAN THIS ONE.

32. THE PHARISEES HEARD THAT THE PEOPLE WERE DISTURBED ABOUT HIS TEACHING; AND THE PHARISEES AND CHIEF PRIESTS SENT SERVANTS TO TAKE HIM.

33. AND JESUS SAID, ONLY FOR A SHORT TIME DO I WALK WITH YOU AND LEAD YOU TO HIM WHO HAS SENT ME.

34. YOU WILL SEEK ARGUMENTS AGAINST ME, AND YOU WILL NOT FIND THEM; AND WHITHER I GO YOU CANNOT COME.

35. AND THE JEWS SAID, WHITHER WILL HE GO, THAT WE SHALL NOT FIND HIM? DOES HE WANT TO GO TO THE GREEKS AND TEACH THEM?

36. WHAT DOES IT MEAN, YOU WILL SEEK AND WILL NOT FIND, AND YOU WILL NOT COME WHITHER I GO?

37. ON THE LAST CHIEF DAY OF THE FEAST, JESUS STOOD AND SPOKE LOUDLY, IF ANY MAN IS THIRSTY, LET HIM COME TO ME AND DRINK.

38. HE WHO BELIEVES IN MY TEACHING, AS THE SCRIPTURE HAS SAID, OUT OF HIS BELLY WILL FLOW RIVERS OF LIVING WATER.

39. THIS HE SPOKE OF THE SPIRIT OF GOD, WHICH THEY WHO BELIEVED IN HIM WOULD RECEIVE; FOR THE SPIRIT WAS NOT YET, BECAUSE JESUS WAS NOT YET UNDERSTOOD.

40. MANY OF THE PEOPLE, HAVING UNDERSTOOD HIS TEACHING, SAID, HE IS TRULY A PROPHET.

41. OTHERS SAID, THIS IS THE CHOSEN ONE OF GOD. SOME SAID, SHALL THE CHOSEN ONE COME OUT OF GALILEE?

42. THE SCRIPTURE SAYS THAT HE IS OF THE SEED OF DAVID, AND OUT OF THE VILLAGE OF BETHLEHEM.

43. AND THERE WAS A DIVISION AMONG THE PEOPLE BECAUSE OF HIM.

44. SOME OF THEM WANTED TO OVERCOME HIM, BUT NO ONE VANQUISHED HIM.

45. THEN THE SERVANTS CAME TO THE PRIESTS, AND THE PRIESTS SAID, WHY HAVE YOU NOT TAUGHT HIM?

46. THE SERVANTS REPLIED, NO MAN EVER SPOKE LIKE THIS ONE.

47. AND THE PHARISEES SAID, HAVE YOU, TOO, ERRED?

48. FOR NONE OF THE RULERS AND NONE OF THE PHARISEES BELIEVE IN HIM.

49. BUT THIS RABBLE, ACCURSED PEOPLE, DOES NOT KNOW THE LAW.

50. NICODEMUS SAID TO THEM (IT WAS HE WHO HAD COME TO JESUS IN THE NIGHT, AND HE WAS WITH THEM):

51. DOES OUR LAW ALLOW US TO CONDEMN A MAN WITHOUT LEARNING FIRST HOW HE TEACHES?

52. THEY ANSWERED HIM, ART THOU ALSO OF GALILEE? SEARCH IN THE LAW, AND SEE WHETHER THERE CAN BE A PROPHET OUT OF GALILEE.

53. AND ALL WENT HOME.

John viii. 12. ANOTHER TIME JESUS SAID, I AM THE LIGHT OF THE WORLD. HE WHO WILL FOLLOW ME WILL NOT WALK IN THE DARKNESS, BUT WILL HAVE THE LIGHT OF LIFE.

13. AND THE PHARISEES SAID TO HIM, THOU BEAREST WITNESS OF THY-SELF, AND SO THY TESTIMONY IS NOT TRUE.

14. AND JESUS REPLIED TO THEM, THOUGH I BEAR WITNESS OF MYSELF, MY TESTIMONY IS TRUE, FOR I KNOW WHENCE I CAME, AND WHITHER I LEAD: IT IS YOU ONLY WHO DO NOT KNOW WHENCE I COME AND WHITHER I LEAD.

15. YOU JUDGE AFTER THE FLESH; BUT I JUDGE NO MAN.

16. AND IF I JUDGE MY JUDGMENT IS TRUE: FOR I AM NOT ALONE—THERE IS ALSO THE FATHER WHO SENT ME.

17. IT IS ALSO WRITTEN IN YOUR LAW, THAT THE TESTIMONY OF TWO MEN IS SUFFICIENT.

18. I BEAR WITNESS OF MYSELF, AND THE FATHER WHO SENT ME BEARS WITNESS OF ME.

19. THE JEWS SAID TO HIM, WHO IS THIS FATHER OF THINE? AND JESUS SAID TO THEM, YOU DO NOT KNOW ME, AND YOU DO NOT KNOW MY FATHER. IF YOU KNEW ME, YOU WOULD KNOW MY FATHER.

20. THESE WORDS JESUS SPOKE NEAR THE TREASURY IN THE TEMPLE, AND NO MAN OVERCAME HIM; FOR EVIDENTLY HIS TIME HAD NOT YET COME.

21. AND AGAIN JESUS SAID TO THEM, I LEAD, AND YOU WILL DISCUSS WHO I AM, AND THROUGH YOUR ERROR YOU WILL DIE. YOU WILL NOT GO WHITHER I LEAD.

22. AND THE JEWS SAID, DOES HE MEAN TO KILL HIMSELF? FOR HE SAID, YOU WILL NOT GO WHITHER I LEAD.

23. AND HE SAID TO THEM, YOU ARE FROM BENEATH, BUT I AM FROM ABOVE. YOU ARE OF THIS WORLD, BUT I AM NOT OF THIS WORLD.

24. I SAID THAT YOU WILL DIE IN YOUR ERRORS IF YOU DO NOT TRUST IN ME.

25. THEN THEY SAID TO HIM, WHO ART THOU? AND JESUS SAID TO THEM, FIRST OF ALL I AM WHAT I TELL YOU.

28. AND JESUS SAID TO THEM, WHEN YOU HAVE LIFTED UP THE SON OF MAN, THEN YOU WILL KNOW WHAT I AM. I DO NOTHING OF MYSELF; BUT AS MY FATHER HAS TAUGHT ME, SO I SPEAK.

29. AND HE WHO SENT ME IS WITH ME. THE FATHER HAS NOT LEFT ME ALONE; FOR I DO ALWAYS AND EVERYWHERE WHAT PLEASE HIM.

30. AND WHEN HE SAID THIS, MANY BELIEVED IN HIS TEACHING.

31. THEN JESUS SAID TO THOSE WHO BELIEVED IN HIM, IF YOU ARE FIRM IN YOUR BELIEF OF MY WORDS, YOU WILL BE TAUGHT BY ME,

32. AND YOU WILL KNOW THE TRUTH, AND THE TRUTH WILL MAKE YOU FREE.

33. THEY ANSWERED HIM, WE ARE OF ABRAHAM'S NATION, AND WERE NEVER ANYBODY'S SLAVES. HOW, THEN, DOST THOU SAY THAT THOU WILT MAKE US FREE?

34. AND JESUS ANSWERED THEM, YOU KNOW YOURSELVES THAT EVERY MAN WHO MAKES MISTAKES BECOMES THE SLAVE OF MISTAKES.

35. BUT THE SLAVE DOES NOT ALWAYS REMAIN IN THE FAMILY, BUT THE SON ALWAYS.

36. IF, THEREFORE, THE SON WILL FREE YOU, YOU WILL BE FREE INDEED.

37. I KNOW THAT YOU ARE OF ABRAHAM'S TRIBE; BUT YOU WANT TO KILL ME, BECAUSE MY WORDS HAVE NO PLACE IN YOU.

38. I SPEAK WHAT I HAVE COMPREHENDED OF YOUR NON-TEMPORAL FATHER.

39. AND THEY SAID TO HIM, ABRAHAM IS OUR FATHER. JESUS SAID TO THEM, IF YOU WERE ABRAHAM'S CHILDREN, YOU WOULD SERVE GOD LIKE HIM.

40. BUT NOW YOU DELIBERATE HOW YOU MAY KILL ME, A MAN WHO HAS TOLD YOU THE TRUTH, WHICH I HAVE HEARD OF GOD. ABRAHAM DID NOT DO THIS.

41. YOU SERVE YOUR FATHER. THEY SAID TO HIM, WE ARE NOT BORN OF FORNICATION: WE HAVE ONE FATHER—GOD.

42. JESUS SAID TO THEM, IF GOD WERE YOUR FATHER, YOU WOULD LOVE ME: FOR I PROCEEDED FROM GOD AND GO TO HIM. I DID NOT COME TO MYSELF, BUT HE SENT ME.

43. YOU DO NOT UNDERSTAND MY WORDS OF THE MEANING OF LIFE, BECAUSE YOU CANNOT UNDERSTAND MY DISCUSSION.

44. YOU ARE OF THE DEVIL, AND YOU WILL DO THE LUST OF YOUR FATHER: HE WAS A MURDERER IN THE BEGINNING, AND DID NOT LIVE IN THE TRUTH, BECAUSE THERE IS NO TRUTH IN HIM. WHEN HE SPEAKS, HE SPEAKS HIS

OWN LIE, AND THERE IS NO TRUTH IN HIM, FOR HE IS A LIAR, AND THE FATHER OF LIES.

45. BUT WHEN I SPEAK THE TRUTH, YOU DO NOT BELIEVE ME.

46. WHO OF YOU WILL ACCUSE ME THAT I AM IN ERROR? IF I SAY THE TRUTH, WHY DO YOU NOT BELIEVE ME?

47. HE WHO IS OF GOD UNDERSTANDS THE WORKS OF GOD. YOU DO NOT HEAR, BECAUSE YOU ARE NOT OF GOD.

48. AND THE JEWS REPLIED TO HIM, DID WE NOT SAY RIGHT THAT THOU ART A MAD SAMARITAN?

49. JESUS ANSWERED, I AM NOT MAD; BUT I HONOR MY FATHER, AND YOU DISHONOR ME.

50. I DO NOT DISCUSS WHAT SEEMS GOOD TO ME: THERE IS ONE WHO DISCUSSES AND PUNISHES.

51. VERILY I TELL YOU, IF A MAN UNDERSTANDS MY COMPREHENSION TEACHING AND FULFILLS ITS MEANING, HE WILL NEVER SEE DEATH.

52. THE JEWS SAID TO HIM, NOW WE SEE THAT THOU ART MAD. ABRAHAM DIED, AND THE PROPHETS; AND THOU SAYEST, IF A MAN FULFILLS MY TEACHING, HE WILL NEVER SEE DEATH.

53. IF THOU ART GREATER THAN OUR FATHER ABRAHAM—AND HE DIED, AND SO DID THE PROPHETS—WHOM MAKEST THOU THYSELF?

54. JESUS ANSWERED, IF I ACKNOWLEDGED IT MYSELF, WHAT SEEMS GOOD TO ME WOULD HAVE NO MEANING; BUT THERE IS ONE WHO ACKNOWLEDGES ME, HE WHOM YOU CALL YOUR GOD.

55. YOU HAVE NOT KNOWN HIM, BUT I KNOW HIM; AND IF I SHOULD SAY THAT I DO NOT KNOW HIM, I WOULD BE A LIAR LIKE YOURSELVES. BUT I KNOW HIM, AND KEEP HIS COMPREHENSION.

56. YOUR FATHER ABRAHAM LOVED MY LIGHT; AND HE SAW IT AND WAS GLAD.

57. THE JEWS SAID TO HIM, THOU ART NOT YET FIFTY YEARS OLD, AND HAST THOU SEEN ABRAHAM?

58. AND JESUS SAID TO THEM, VERILY I TELL YOU, BEFORE ABRAHAM WAS, I AM.

59. THEN THEY TOOK UP STONES TO THROW THEM AT HIM; BUT JESUS HID HIMSELF, AND WENT OUT OF THE TEMPLE.

John ix. 1. AND AS JESUS PASSED BY, HE SAW A MAN WHO WAS BLIND BY HIS NATURE.

2. AND HIS DISCIPLES ASKED HIM, TEACHER, IN WHAT WAY DID THIS MAN OR HIS PARENTS SIN, THAT HE WAS BORN BLIND?

3. JESUS ANSWERED, NEITHER HAS THIS MAN SINNED, NOR HIS PARENTS, BUT THAT THE SERVING OF GOD SHOULD BE MADE MANIFEST IN HIM.

4. WE MUST SERVE HIM WHO HAS SENT US, WHILE IT IS DAY; WHEN THE NIGHT COMES, NOBODY CAN DO ANYTHING.

5. WHEN I AM IN THE WORLD, I AM THE LIGHT OF THE WORLD.

7. AND SAID TO HIM, GO, WASH IN THE POOL OF HIM WHO IS SENT. HE CLEANSED HIMSELF, AND BEGAN TO SEE.

8. THE NEIGHBORS AND THOSE WHO HAD SEEN HIM BEFORE, THAT HE WAS A BEGGAR, SAID, IS NOT THIS HE WHO SAT AND BEGGED?

9. SOME SAID, THIS IS THE SAME. OTHERS SAID, HE IS LIKE HIM. BUT HE SAID, I AM HE.

10. AND THEY SAID TO HIM, HOW WERE THY EYES OPENED?

11. AND HE REPLIED TO THEM, A MAN CALLED JESUS TAUGHT ME HOW TO CLEANSE MYSELF WITH THE CLEANSING OF HIM WHO IS SENT, AND I CLEANSED MYSELF, AND NOW I SEE.

12. THEN THEY SAID TO HIM, WHERE IS HE? HE SAID, I DO NOT KNOW.

13. THEN THEY BROUGHT TO THE PHARISEES HIM WHO HAD BEEN BLIND.

14. IT WAS THE SABBATH WHEN JESUS OPENED THE EYES OF THE BLIND MAN.

15. AND AGAIN THE PHARISEES ASKED HIM HOW HE RECEIVED THE SIGHT. HE SAID TO THEM, I CLEANSED MYSELF, AND NOW I SEE.

16. AND SOME OF THE PHARISEES SAID, THIS MAN IS NOT IN A COVENANTS WITH GOD, FOR HE DOES NOT KEEP THE SABBATH. OTHERS SAID, HOW CAN A SINNER SHOW SUCH EXAMPLES? AND THERE WAS A DISSENSION AMONG THEM.

17. AND AGAIN THEY SAID TO HIM WHO HAD BEEN BLIND, WHAT DOST THOU SAY ABOUT THIS, THAT HE HAS OPENED THY EYES? AND HE SAID, I SUPPOSE THAT HE IS A PROPHET.

18. AND THE JEWS DID NOT BELIEVE THAT HE HAD BEEN BLIND AND RECEIVED HIS SIGHT, UNTIL THEY CALLED HIS PARENTS.

19. AND THEY ASKED THEM, IS THIS YOUR SON, WHO YOU SAY WAS BORN BLIND? HOW, THEN, DOES HE SEE NOW?

20. AND THE PARENTS REPLIED TO THEM, WE KNOW THAT THIS IS OUR SON, AND THAT HE WAS BORN BLIND.

21. BUT HOW HE SEES NOW, AND WHO HAS OPENED HIS EYES, WE DO NOT KNOW. HE IS OF AGE; ASK HIM: HE WILL SPEAK FOR HIMSELF.

22. HIS PARENTS SPOKE SO, BECAUSE THEY WERE AFRAID OF THE JEWS; FOR THE JEWS HAD AGREED ALREADY THAT IF ANY MAN TOOK HIM TO BE CHRIST, HE WOULD BE PUT OUT OF THE ASSEMBLY.

23. THEREFORE HIS PARENTS SAID, HE IS OF AGE; ASK HIM.

24. THEN THEY AGAIN CALLED UP THE ONE WHO HAD BEEN BLIND, AND SAID TO HIM, CONFESS GOD: WE KNOW THAT THIS MAN IS A SINNER.

25. AND HE ANSWERED THEM, WHETHER HE IS A SINNER OR NOT, I DO NOT KNOW. ONE THING I KNOW, THAT I WAS BLIND, AND NOW I SEE.

26. AGAIN THEY SAID TO HIM, WHAT DID HE DO TO THEE? HOW DID HE OPEN THY EYES?

27. AND HE REPLIED TO THEM, I HAVE TOLD YOU ALREADY, BUT YOU DO NOT BELIEVE. WHY DO YOU WANT TO HEAR IT AGAIN? DO YOU WANT TO BECOME HIS DISCIPLES?

28. AND THEY REVILED HIM, AND SAID, THOU ART HIS DISCIPLE, BUT WE ARE MOSES' DISCIPLES.

29. WE KNOW THAT GOD SPOKE TO MOSES: BUT WE DO NOT KNOW THIS MAN, NOR WHENCE HE COMES.

30. AND HE ANSWERED THEM, AND SAID, THIS IS THE MARVEL THAT YOU DO NOT KNOW WHENCE HE IS, AND YET HE HAS OPENED MY EYES.

31. WE KNOW THAT GOD DOES NOT HEAR SINNERS; BUT HE HEARS THOSE WHO ARE GODLY AND DO THE WILL OF GOD.

32. SINCE THE WORLD BEGAN IT WAS NOT HEARD THAT ANY MAN OPENED THE EYES OF ONE BORN BLIND.

33. IF THIS MAN WERE NOT OF GOD, HE COULD DO NOTHING.

34. AND THEY ANSWERED HIM, THOU WAST ALL BORN IN SINS, AND YET THOU TEACHEST US. AND THEY DROVE HIM AWAY.

35. JESUS HEARD THAT THEY HAD DRIVEN HIM AWAY; AND WHEN HE MET HIM, HE SAID, DOES THOU TRUST IN THE SON OF GOD?

36. AND HE REPLIED, WHO IS HE, THAT I SHOULD TRUST IN HIM?

37. AND JESUS SAID TO HIM, THOU HAST SEEN HIM AND SEES HIM, AND HE TALKS WITH THEE.

38. AND HE SAID, I TRUST IN HIM, SIR; AND HE BOWED TO HIM.

39. AND JESUS SAID, I CAME INTO THIS WORLD FOR THE DIVISION: THAT THEY WHO DO NOT SEE MIGHT SEE; AND THOSE WHO SEE MIGHT BE MADE BLIND.

40. AND THE PHARISEES AND OTHERS WITH THEM HEARD THIS, AND SAID, DOST THOU CONSIDER US BLIND ALSO?

41. JESUS SAID TO THEM, IF YOU WERE BLIND, THERE WOULD BE NO ERROR IN YOU; BUT NOW YOU CONSIDER YOURSELVES SEEING, AND SO THERE IS ERROR IN YOU.

John x. 19. AND THERE WAS DISCORD AMONG THE JEWS ON ACCOUNT OF THESE WORDS.

20. MANY OF THEM SAID, HE IS STUBBORN AND MAD; WHY DO YOU LISTEN TO HIM?

21. OTHERS SAID, YOU WILL NOT HEAR SUCH WORDS FROM A MADMAN. A MADMAN CANNOT OPEN THE EYES.

CHRIST THE DOOR OF LIFE

John x. 1. VERILY, I TELL YOU, HE WHO DOES NOT ENTER INTO THE SHEEP-FOLD BY THE DOOR, BUT CLIMBS IN SOMEWHERE, IS A THIEF AND A ROBBER.

2. HE WHO ENTERS BY THE DOOR IS THE SHEPHERD OF THE SHEEP.

3. TO HIM THE WATCHMAN OPENS, AND THE SHEEP HEAR HIS VOICE. AND HE CALLS EACH SHEEP BY NAME, AND LETS THEM OUT INTO THE FIELD.

4. AND WHEN HE LETS OUT HIS OWN SHEEP, HE GOES BEFORE THEM; AND THE SHEEP FOLLOW HIM, FOR THEY KNOW HIS VOICE.

5. AND A STRANGER THEY WILL NOT FOLLOW, BUT WILL RUN AWAY FROM HIM, FOR THEY DO NOT KNOW THE VOICE OF STRANGERS.

6. THIS PARABLE JESUS SPOKE TO THEM; BUT THEY DID NOT UNDERSTAND WHAT HE SAID.

7. AND AGAIN JESUS SAID TO THEM, VERILY, I TELL YOU, MY TEACHING IS THE DOOR FOR THE SHEEP.

8. ALL THOSE WHO EVER CAME BEFORE ME ARE THIEVES AND ROBBERS: BUT THE SHEEP DID NOT OBEY THEM.

9. I AM THE DOOR. IF ANY MAN ENTERS THROUGH ME, HE WILL BE SAFE: HE WILL GO IN AND OUT, AND WILL FIND PASTURE.

10. THE THIEF GOES ONLY TO STEAL, AND TO KILL, AND TO DESTROY. I CAME AS THE DOOR, THAT THEY MIGHT HAVE LIFE MORE ABUNDANTLY.

11. I AM THE GOOD SHEPHERD: THE GOOD SHEPHERD GIVES HIS LIFE FOR THE SHEEP.

12. A HIRELING IS NOT A SHEPHERD: THE SHEEP ARE NOT HIS OWN; HE SEES THE WOLF COMING, AND LEAVES THE SHEEP, AND RUNS AWAY; AND THE WOLF CATCHES AND SCATTERS THE SHEEP.

13. THE HIRELING FLEES, BECAUSE HE IS A HIRELING, AND DOES NOT CARE FOR THE SHEEP.

14. I AM THE GOOD SHEPHERD: I KNOW MY SHEEP, AND THEY KNOW ME.

15. AS THE FATHER KNOWS ME, EVEN SO I KNOW THE FATHER; AND I LAY DOWN MY LIFE FOR THE SHEEP.

16. AND I HAVE OTHER SHEEP, WHICH ARE NOT OF THIS FOLD: I MUST LEAD THEM OUT, AND THEY WILL HEAR MY VOICE; AND THERE WILL BE ONE FOLD, AND ONE SHEPHERD.

17. THEREFORE MY FATHER LOVES ME, BECAUSE I LAY DOWN MY LIFE THAT I MAY RECEIVE IT AGAIN.

18. NO MAN TAKES IT FROM ME, BUT I LAY IT DOWN OF MY OWN WILL, AND I CAN RECEIVE IT. THIS COMMANDMENT I RECEIVED FROM MY FATHER.

24. THEN THE JEWS SURROUNDED HIM, AND SAID TO HIM, HOW LONG WILT THOU TORMENT US? IF THOU ART CHRIST, TELL US SO.

25. JESUS ANSWERED THEM, I HAVE TOLD YOU ALREADY, BUT YOU DO NOT BELIEVE. THE WAY I LIVE ACCORDING TO MY FATHER'S TEACHING SHOWS YOU WHO I AM.

26. BUT YOU DO NOT BELIEVE, BECAUSE YOU ARE NOT OF MY SHEEP, AS I TOLD YOU.

27. MY SHEEP KNOW MY VOICE, AND I RECOGNIZE THEM, AND THEY FOLLOW ME.

28. AND I GIVE THEM NON-TEMPORAL LIFE; AND THEY WILL NEVER PERISH, AND NO ONE WILL TAKE THEM FROM ME.

29. MY FATHER, WHO ENTRUSTED THEM TO ME, IS GREATER THAN ALL, AND NO ONE CAN TAKE THEM FROM MY FATHER.

30. I AND MY FATHER ARE ONE.

31. THEN THE JEWS TOOK UP STONES AGAIN TO STONE HIM.

32. JESUS SAID TO THEM, I HAVE SHOWED YOU MANY GOOD WORKS OF MY FATHER; FOR WHICH OF THOSE WORKS DO YOU WANT TO STONE ME?

33. AND THE JEWS REPLIED TO HIM, WE WILL NOT STONE THEE FOR A GOOD WORK, BUT FOR BLASPHEMY, BECAUSE, BEING A MAN, THOU MAKEST THYSELF A GOD.

34. AND JESUS ANSWERED THEM, IS IT NOT WRITTEN IN YOUR LAW, I GOD, SAID, YOU ARE GODS?

35. IF HE CALLED THOSE GODS, TO WHOM HE SPOKE, AND THE SCRIPTURE CANNOT BE BROKEN;

36. HOW, THEN, DO YOU SAY TO ME, WHOM GOD HAS LOVED AND SENT INTO THE WORLD, THAT I BLASPHEME, BECAUSE I SAID THAT I WAS THE SON OF GOD.

37. IF I DO NOT DO AS MY FATHER, DO NOT BELIEVE ME.

38. BUT IF I DO AS MY FATHER, DO NOT BELIEVE ME; BELIEVE THE WORK, THEN YOU WILL UNDERSTAND THAT THE FATHER IS IN ME, AND I AM IN HIM.

John xi. 25. AND JESUS SAID TO HER, MY TEACHING IS THE TEACHING OF THE AWAKENING AND OF LIFE. HE WHO BELIEVES IN MY TEACHING, THOUGH HE DIED, WILL BE ALIVE.

26. AND HE WHO BELIEVES IN MY TEACHING WILL NOT DIE.

John x. 39. AND THE JEWS DELIBERATED AGAIN HOW TO OVERTHROW HIM. BUT HE COULD NOT BE VANQUISHED.

40. AND HE WENT AGAIN BEYOND THE JORDAN, TO THE PLACE WHERE JOHN THE BAPTIST USED TO BAPTIZE. AND HE STOPPED THERE.

41. AND MANY TOOK UP HIS TEACHING, AND SAID THAT JOHN HAD GIVEN NO PROOFS, BUT THAT EVERYTHING HE HAD SAID OF THIS MAN WAS TRUE.

42. AND MANY BELIEVED IN HIS TEACHING THERE.

Matt. xvi. 13. AND JESUS WENT INTO THE VILLAGES OF CESAREA, INTO PHILIPPI, AND ASKED HIS DISCIPLES, SAYING, HOW DO PEOPLE UNDERSTAND THIS, THAT I AM THE SON OF GOD?

14. THEY SAID, SOME TAKE YOU TO BE JOHN THE BAPTIST; SOME, ELIJAH; OTHERS, JEREMIAH, OR ONE OF THE PROPHETS.

15. AND HE SAID TO THEM, AND HOW DO YOU JUDGE OF ME?

16. AND SIMON, NAMED THE ROCK (PETER), REPLIED TO HIM, THOU ART CHRIST, THE SON OF THE LIVING GOD.

John vi. 68. THOU HAST THE WORDS OF THE ETERNAL LIFE.

Matt. xvi. 17. AND JESUS REPLIED TO THEM, HAPPY ART THOU, SIMON, SON OF JONAH, FOR NO MORTAL HAS REVEALED THIS TO YOU, BUT GOD MY FATHER.

18. AND I TELL THEE THAT THOU ART A ROCK, AND ON THIS ROCK WILL I BUILD MY ASSEMBLY OF MEN, AND DEATH WILL NOT OVERCOME THIS ASSEMBLY OF MEN.

20. THEN HE EXPLAINED TO THE DISCIPLES THAT THEY SHOULD TELL NO MAN THAT HE WAS CHRIST.

TOLSTOY'S COMMENTARY

To receive the true life one must give up the carnal life. The carnal life is the food for the true life. The teaching of Jesus consists in giving up the carnal life for the true life.

The Pharisees and learned men began to ask Jesus, Thou sayest that it is necessary to give up the carnal life and all its pleasures in order to receive the true life, but how dost thou prove this?

And Jesus groaned from pity for these men. Their asking for proofs showed him that they did not understand him. And he said, Men want proofs, and proofs cannot be given to them.

And he said to them, What carnal proofs do you want for a non-carnal life? Have you no proofs for everything which you know? Looking at the beautiful evening glow you assume that next day there will be fair weather, and when it looks gloomy in the morning, you assume that it will rain. You have no proofs, but you judge of this from the appearance of the sky, and you are able to draw your conclusions. Why, then, do you not draw the same correct conclusions in regard to yourselves? If you judged just as correctly about yourselves as you do about the signs of the weather, you would know that just as certainly as the west wind brings rain, death follows after the temporal life.

And so there is no other proof, and there can be none, for the proof of my teaching, except the teaching itself.

There can be no proofs of the understanding.

The southern queen went to see Solomon, not to ask for proofs, but to listen to his wisdom. The Ninevites did not ask Jonah for proofs, but listened to his teaching, and were converted; even so you must do, and must not ask for any proofs.

After this the Jews tried to sentence Jesus to death, and Jesus went into Galilee, and there lived with his relatives.

There came the Jewish feast of the tabernacles.

The brothers of Jesus got ready to go to the feast, and asked Jesus to go with them. They did not believe in his teaching, and said to him, Thou sayest that the Jewish way of serving God is not right, and that thou knowest the right way of serving him with deeds. If thou truly believest that none but thee know the true service of God, go with us to the feast, for a large multitude will be there. There thou canst announce in the presence of the whole people that the teaching of Moses is false. If all of them will believe thee, all thy disciples will see that thou art right. What is the sense in concealing thyself? Thou sayest that our service is wrong, that thou knowest the true way of serving God, so show it to all.

And Jesus said to them, For you there is a special time and place for serving God; but I have no such special time and place. I always and everywhere work for God. It is this that I show people: I show them that their service of God is false, and for this they hate me. Go yourselves to the feast, and I will go whenever I wish.

And the brothers went away, but he remained at home; later he went to the feast when it was half over.

The Jews were troubled, because he did not honor their holiday and did not come. And they disputed a great deal about his teaching: some said that he was telling the truth; and others said that he only agitated the people.

In the middle of the holiday Jesus entered the temple and began to teach the people, saying that their worship was false, and that God must be worshipped not in the temple and with sacrifices, but in the spirit and with works. All listened to him and marvelled at his wisdom.

And Jesus, hearing that they marvelled at his wisdom, said to them, My wisdom consists in this, that I teach what I know from my Father. My teaching consists in doing the will of the spirit, which gives me life. He who does this will know that it is the truth, for he will not do what seems good to him, but what seems good to the spirit which lives within him. Your law of Moses is not the eternal law, and so those who follow it do not execute the eternal law, and do wrong and what is untrue. I teach you to do the one will, and in my teaching there can be no contradiction, but your written law of Moses is all filled with contradictions. I give you a teaching, with which man stands higher than all decrees and finds the law within himself.

And many said, They have said that he is a false prophet, and he has been condemning the law, and yet no one says anything to him. Maybe he is indeed real, and maybe the rulers have acknowledged him. There is one thing, however, which does not fit: it is said that when he who is sent by God shall come, no one will know whence he comes, but we know whence he comes, and we know his whole family.

The people did not understand his teaching, and kept looking for external proofs.

Then Jesus said to them, You know whence I come in a carnal way, but you do not know whence I come in the spirit. You do not know him from whom I come in the spirit, and it is only him that you ought to know. If I said that I am Christ, you would believe me as a man, but you would not believe God who is in me and in you. You must believe in the one God. I am here among you for a brief space of time: I show you the way of salvation, the return to that source of life from which I came. And you ask me for proofs and want to condemn me. If you do not know the way, you will certainly not find me when I am gone. You must not condemn me, but follow me. He who will do what I say will find out whether what I say is true or not. He for whom the life of the flesh has not become the food of the spirit, who does not seek the truth, as the thirsty person seeks water, cannot understand me. But he who thirsts for water may follow me and drink. And he who will believe in my teaching will receive the true life. He will receive the life of the spirit.

And many believed in his teaching, and said, What he says is true and from God. Others did not understand him, and kept looking in the prophecies for proofs of his being sent by God. And many disputed with him, but could not prevail against him. The Pharisees and learned men seat their assistants to contend with him. But their assistants returned to them, saying, We can do nothing with him.

And the high priests said, Why did you not accuse him?

And they replied, Never has a man spoken like him.

Then the Pharisees said, It does not mean anything, that you cannot prevail against him, and that the people believe in his teaching. We do not believe, and none of the rulers believe, but the accursed people are always stupid and ignorant.

And Jesus said to the Pharisees, There can be no proofs of the truth of my teaching, just as there can be no illumination of the light. My teaching is the true light, that light when men see what is good and what bad, and so it is impossible to prove my teaching: it proves everything else. He who will follow me will not be in the dark, but with him life and light is the same.

But the Pharisees still demanded proofs of the truth of his teaching, and said, Thou art the only one who says this.

And he replied to them, If I am the only one who says this, I am still in the right, for I know whence I come and whither I go. Besides, not I alone teach this, but the Father, my spirit, teaches it also. But you do not know him, and so this proves the falseness of your teaching. You do not know whence you come and whither you go. I am leading you, but, instead of following me, you discuss who I am; and so you cannot come to salvation and to life, to which I lead you. And you will perish, if you abide in this error and do not follow me.

And the Jews asked, Who art thou?

He said, I am not any special man; as a man I am nothing; but, above all, I am what I tell you: I am the way and the truth—I am the understanding. And when you make the spirit of the son of man your God, you will know what I am, because what I do and say is not from me, as a man, but what my Father has taught me.

Only he who keeps the understanding, who does the will of the Father, can be taught by me. To understand the truth, it is necessary to do good. He who does evil loves the darkness and goes toward it; he who does good goes toward the light. And so, in order to understand my teaching, it is necessary to do good. He who will do good will know the truth, and he who will know the truth will be free from evil and from death; for every man who errs becomes the slave of his error.

And as the slave does not always live in the house of his master, while the master's son is always there, even so a man, who errs in life and becomes the slave of his error, does not live forever, but dies. Only he who is in the truth lives forever. But the truth consists in being a son, and not a slave. And so, if you err, you will be slaves, and you will die; but if you abide in the truth, you will be free sons, and will live.

You say of yourselves that you are the children of Abraham, and that you know the truth; and yet you want to kill me, because I tell you the truth. Abraham did not do so. If you wish to do this—to kill a man, you are not the sons of God the Father, and you do not serve him, but serve your father. You are not with me the sons of the same Father: you are the slaves of error, and its sons. If you had the same Father with me, you would love me, for I, too, come from God. I was not born of myself, but am also from God. For this reason you do not understand my words, and the understanding has no place in you. If I am from the Father, and you are from the same Father, you cannot wish to kill me. But since you wish to kill me, we are not of one Father. I am from God, but you are from the devil. You want to do the will of your father: he has always been a murderer and liar, and there is no truth in him. If he, the devil, says anything, he says his own personal matters, and not what is common to all, and he is the father of lying and error; and so you are the slaves of error, and his children.

You see how easy it is to accuse you of error. If I err, accuse me; but if there is no error, why do you not believe me?

And the Jews began to scold him, and said that he was mad.

He said, I am not mad, but honor my Father, and you want to kill me, the son of the Father; consequently you are not my brothers, but children of another father. Not I affirm that I am right, but the truth speaks for me. And so I repeat to you, He who will grasp and execute my teaching will not see death.

And the Jews said, Do we not tell the truth, when we say that he is a mad Samaritan? Thou accusest thyself. The prophets are dead; Abraham is dead, and thou sayest that he who will execute thy teaching will not see death. Abraham is dead, and thou wilt not die! Or art thou greater than Abraham?

The Jews kept discussing whether he, Jesus of Galilee, was an important prophet or not, and forgot everything which he had said, and that he said nothing of himself as a man, but spoke of the spirit of God which was within him.

And Jesus said, I make nothing of myself. If I spoke of what seems good to me, everything I say would be without meaning; but there is a beginning of all things, which you call God, and of him I speak. You have not known the true God, but I know him. I cannot help saying that I know him. I should be a liar, such as you are, if I said that I did not know him. I know him, and I know his will, and do it. Your father Abraham is holy for this reason only, that he saw my understanding and rejoiced in it.

The Jews said, Thou art thirty years old; how could you have lived in the days of Abraham?

He said, Before Abraham was, I was, that I, of whom I have told you—the understanding.

The Jews picked up stones, to stone him, but he went away from them.

I am the light of the world. He who will follow me will not walk in darkness, but will have the light of life. If a man does not see the light, neither his parents, nor he, are to blame; but if he has light, it is his duty to shine for others. While we are in the world, we are the light of the world. If we see men who are deprived of light, we reveal the light to them from the principle which has produced us. And if a man sees the light, he will all be changed so that no one can tell him. A man remains the same man; but there is this difference that, having learned that he is a son of God, he receives the light and sees what he never saw before.

A man who did not see the light and has come to see it can say nothing as to whether it is true that he has regained his sight; all he can say is, I am regenerated; I am different from what I was; before this I was blind and did not see the true good, but now I see it. I do not know how I came to see, but I think that he who revealed the light to me is a man from God.

And no matter how much they may say to a man who has seen the light, that it is not the true light; that he must pray to another God, the one he does not see; that he who gave him the light is mistaken, the man will not believe it. He will say, I know nothing about your God, nor whether the man who opened my eyes was mistaken, or not; but I know that formerly I did not see, and now I see.

And no matter how much you may ask such a man how his eyes were opened, he will tell you the same. They were opened in this way, that I found out that the beginning of my life is the spirit, and, having learned this, I was regenerated. No matter how much you may say that the law of Moses is the true law of God; that God himself revealed it to Moses; that God communes with the saints, and that he who opened his eyes is a sinner, the man will repeat the one answer, I know nothing about all that, but I know that I was blind, and now I see. And I know that he who opened my eyes is from God. For, if he were not from God, he could not do it.

Such a man trusts only in the spirit of the son of God, which is in him, and that is all he needs.

And Jesus said, The teaching separates men: the blind receive their sight, and those who think that they see become blind. If men do not see the light from their birth, they are not to blame, and they may receive their sight. Only those who affirm that they see, when they see nothing, are to blame indeed.

And the Jews began to dispute. Some said, He is simply mad; and others said, A madman cannot open men's eyes.

Men abandon themselves to my teaching, not because I prove it to them: it is impossible to prove the truth, but the truth proves everything else. But people abandon themselves to my teaching, because it is one, and familiar to people, and promises them life. My teaching is for people what the familiar voice of the shepherd is for the sheep, when he enters to them by the door and gathers them, to drive them into the pasture. But nobody believes your teaching, because it is foreign to men, and men see in it your lusts. It is for men what for the sheep is the sight of a man who does not enter by the door, but climbs over the enclosure: the sheep do not know him, and they feel that he is a robber.

My teaching is the only true one, as one door is for the sheep. All your teachings of the law of Moses are a lie—as the thieves and robbers are lies for the sheep. He who abandons himself to my teaching will find the true life, just as the sheep will go out and find food, if they follow the shepherd. For a thief comes only to steal, rob, and destroy, while a shepherd comes to feed and give life. And it is only my teaching which promises the true life.

The shepherds are masters, whose lives are formed by the sheep and who give their lives for the sheep; they are true shepherds. But there are hirelings, who do not trouble themselves about the sheep, because they are hirelings, and the sheep are not their own, such as, when a wolf comes, forsake their sheep, and these are not true shepherds. Even so there are untrue teachers, such as have no thought for the life of men, and true teachers, such as give their souls for the life of men. I am such a teacher.

My teaching consists in giving the life for other men. No one takes it from me, but I of my own will give it for men, in order that I may receive the true life. This commandment I received from my Father. And as the Father knows me, so I know the Father, and so I lay my life down for the sake of men. And so the Father loves me, for I fulfill his commandments.

And all men, not only here and now, but all men, will understand my voice and will all come together, and will be one, and the teaching will be one.

And the Jews surrounded him, and said, Everything which thou sayest is hard to understand and does not agree with our Scripture. Do not torment us, but tell us outright, Art thou that Messiah who according to our books is to come into the world?

And Jesus replied to them, I have already told you who I am. I am what I have told you; but you do not believe my words. Believe my works—the life in God, which I lead—you will understand by them who I am, and wherefore I have come. But you do not believe, for you do not follow me. He who walks in my path and does what I say understands me. And he who understands my teaching and fulfills it will receive the true life. My father united them with me, and nobody can sever them. I and the Father are one.

And the Jews were offended by this, and laid hold of stones to stone him.

But he said to them, I have shown you much good through my Father, so for what deed do you want to stone me?

They said, Not for a good deed do we wish to stone thee, but because thou, a man, makest thyself a God.

And Jesus answered them, But the same is said in your Scripture: it says that God himself said to the bad rulers, You are gods. If vicious people were called gods, why should you consider it a blasphemy to call God that which God, loving it, sent into the world? Every man according to the spirit is a son of God. If I do not live in godly fashion, do not believe that I am a son of God; but if I do, believe according to my life that I am in God. And then you will understand that God is in me, and I am in God, that I and the Father are one.

And Jesus said, My teaching is the awakening of life. He who believes in my teaching retains his life, though he dies carnally. He who lives does not die.

And the Jews did not know what to do with him, and were not able to sentence him.

And he went once more beyond the Jordan, and remained there. And many believed in his teaching, and said that it was as true as John's teaching. And so many believed in his teaching.

And Jesus once asked his disciples, and said, Tell me how people understand my teaching about the son of God and the son of man.

They said, Some understand it like John's teaching; others, like the prophecy of Elijah; others again say that it resembles the teaching of Jeremiah, and take you to be a prophet.

He said, And how do you understand my teaching? And Simon Peter said to him, In my opinion thy teaching consists in this, that thou art the chosen son of God, of life. Thou teachest that God is the life in man.

And Jesus said to him, Happy thou art, Simon, to have understood this. No man could have revealed this to thee, for God within thee has revealed it to thee. Not carnal reflection and not I with my words, but God, my Father, has directly revealed it to thee.

And on this understanding is based the assembly of men, for whom there is no death.

CHAPTER EIGHT

THERE IS NO OTHER LIFE. OF THE REWARDS IN THE KINGDOM OF GOD

Matt. x. 37. HE WHO LOVES FATHER OR MOTHER MORE THAN ME, DOES NOT AGREE WITH ME: AND HE WHO LOVES SON OR DAUGHTER MORE THAN ME, DOES NOT AGREE WITH ME.

38. AND HE WHO IS NOT PREPARED FOR CARNAL PRIVATIONS AND DOES NOT FOLLOW ME, DOES NOT AGREE WITH ME.

39. HE WHO ACQUIRES CARNAL LIFE WILL LOSE IT; AND HE WHO LOSES HIS CARNAL LIFE ACCORDING TO MY TEACHING, WILL RECEIVE LIFE.

Matt. xix. 27. THEN SIMON PETER SAID TO HIM, BEHOLD, WE HAVE FORSAKEN ALL, AND FOLLOWED THEE; WHAT SHALL WE HAVE FOR IT?

29. AND JESUS ANSWERED THEM, YOU KNOW YOURSELVES THAT EVERY ONE WHO FORSAKES HIS FAMILY, HIS BROTHERS AND SISTERS, OR FATHER, OR MOTHER, OR WIFE AND CHILDREN, AND FIELDS FOR THE SAKE OF MY TEACHING—THE TRUE GOOD,

30. WILL RECEIVE A HUNDRED TIMES MORE HERE, IN THIS LIFE, AMID PERSECUTIONS, FAMILIES, BROTHERS, SISTERS, CHILDREN, AND FIELDS, AND ETERNAL LIFE IN THE PASSING WORLD.

31. AND MANY WHO ARE FIRST WILL BE LAST, AND WHO WERE LAST WILL BE FIRST.

PARABLE OF THE LABORERS IN THE VINEYARD

Matt. xx. 1. FOR THE KINGDOM OF GOD IS LIKE THIS: A MASTER WENT OUT IN THE MORNING TO HIRE LABORERS.

2. WHEN HE HAD AGREED WITH THE LABORERS FOR A PENNY A DAY, HE SENT THEM INTO HIS GARDEN.

3. THEN HE WENT OUT AT BREAKFAST TIME TO LOOK AROUND, AND FOUND OTHER LABORERS, WHO WERE NOT OCCUPIED,

4. AND HE SAID TO THEM, GO YOU ALSO TO WORK IN MY GARDEN, AND I WILL PAY YOU WHAT IS RIGHT. AND THEY WENT.

5. AND AGAIN THE MASTER WENT OUT TO THE MARKETPLACE AT THE SIXTH AND AT THE NINTH HOUR, AND HE FOUND OTHER LABORERS WHO WERE NOT OCCUPIED, AND HE DID THE SAME WITH THEM.

6. AT NOON THE MASTER WENT AGAIN TO THE MARKETPLACE, AND SAW LABORERS STANDING IDLE; AND HE SAID TO THEM, WHY DO YOU STAND HERE THE WHOLE DAY IDLE?

7. THEY SAID, BECAUSE NO MAN HAS HIRED US. AND HE SAID TO THEM, GO YOU ALSO INTO THE GARDEN, AND YOU WILL RECEIVE WHAT IS RIGHT.

8. WHEN EVENING CAME, THE MASTER SAID TO HIS STEWARD, CALL THE LABORERS, AND GIVE THEM THEIR WAGES; FIRST TO THE LAST, AND THEN TO THE FIRST.

9. AND THOSE THAT CAME AT NOON RECEIVED A PENNY.

10. AND THOSE WHO CAME FIRST SUPPOSED THAT THEY WOULD RECEIVE MORE; BUT THEY RECEIVED ONLY A PENNY EACH.

11. THEY TOOK IT, BUT THEY BEGAN TO MURMUR AGAINST THE MASTER.

12. HOW IS THIS? THEY SAID. THEY HAVE DONE BUT ONE HOUR'S WORK, AND THOU HAST MADE THEM EQUAL WITH US. WE HAVE WORKED HARD AND SWEATED ALL DAY.

13. BUT THE MASTER ANSWERED ONE OF THEM, FRIEND, I DO THEE NO WRONG; DID WE NOT AGREE FOR A PENNY?

14. TAKE WHAT IS THINE, FRIEND, AND GO THY WAY. I WANT TO GIVE THE LAST AS MUCH AS TO THEE.

15. HAVE I NO RIGHT OVER WHAT IS MINE? OR DOST THOU SEE THAT I AM GOOD, AND SO THY EYE HAS BECOME ENVIOUS?

16. SO THE LAST SHALL BE LIKE THE FIRST, AND THE FIRST LIKE THE LAST.

GREATEST IS HE WHO IS A SERVANT TO ALL

Mark x. 35. AND JAMES AND JOHN, THE SONS OF ZEBEDEE, CAME TO JESUS, SAYING, TEACHER, WE WISH THOU WOULDST DO FOR US WHAT WE SHALL ASK THEE.

36. AND HE SAID TO THEM, WHAT DO YOU WANT ME TO DO FOR YOU?

37. AND THEY SAID TO HIM, MAKE US BOTH EQUAL TO THEE IN THY TEACHING.

38. AND JESUS REPLIED TO THEM, YOU DO NOT KNOW WHAT YOU ASK. ON EARTH YOU CAN DO THE SAME AS I AM DOING, AND YOU MAY BE REGENE-RATED IN THE SPIRIT, JUST I AM REGENERATED.

Matt. xx. 22. THEY SAID TO HIM, WE CAN.

23. AND HE SAID TO THEM, YOU CAN LIVE AND BE REGENERATED THE SAME AS I; BUT TO MAKE YOU SUCH AS I AM IS NOT IN MY POWER, BUT IN THE POWER OF MY FATHER.

24. WHEN THE OTHER TEN HEARD THIS, THEY WERE ANGRY AT THE TWO BROTHERS.

25. AND JESUS CALLED THEM UP, AND SAID, YOU KNOW THAT THOSE WHO CONSIDER THEMSELVES RULERS OF THE PEOPLE HAVE POWER OVER THEM. AND THE OFFICERS EXERCISE AUTHORITY OVER THEM.

26. BUT IT OUGHT NOT TO BE SO AMONG YOU: WHOEVER WILL BE GREAT AMONG YOU LET HIM BE A SERVANT;

27. AND WHOEVER WILL BE FIRST, LET HIM BE A SLAVE.

Luke xxii. 26. HE WHO IS AS THE YOUNGER IS GREATEST, AND HE WHO IS AS THE SERVANT IS FIRST.

Matt. xx. 28. FOR THE SON OF MAN DID NOT DECLARE HIMSELF TO BE MINISTERED TO, BUT TO MINISTER AND LAY DOWN HIS LIFE, AS A RANSOM FOR WHAT IS GREAT.

Matt. xviii. 11. IT IS THE BUSINESS OF THE SON OF MAN TO SAVE WHAT IS PERISHING.

12. HOW DO YOU THINK? IF A MAN HAS A HUNDRED SHEEP, AND ONE OF THEM GOES ASTRAY, DOES HE NOT LEAVE THE NINETY-NINE, AND GO EVERYWHERE TO FIND THE ONE WHICH HAS GONE ASTRAY?

13. AND IF IT HAPPENS THAT HE FINDS IT, YOU KNOW YOURSELVES THAT HE REJOICES MORE AT THIS ONE SHEEP, THAN AT THE NINETY-NINE THAT HAVE NOT GONE ASTRAY.

Luke xv. 6. AND WHEN HE COMES HOME, HE CALLS HIS NEIGHBORS, AND SAYS, I REJOICE, I HAVE FOUND THE SHEEP THAT WENT ASTRAY.

Matt. xviii. 14. EVEN SO IT IS THE WILL OF YOUR FATHER IN HEAVEN THAT NOT ONE OF THESE LITTLE MEN SHOULD PERISH.

Luke xv. 8. IF A WOMAN LOSES ONE OUT OF TEN DIMES, SHE WILL LIGHT A CANDLE, AND SWEEP THE HOUSE AND SEEK DILIGENTLY, TILL SHE FINDS IT.

9. AND WHEN SHE FINDS IT, SHE SAYS TO HER NEIGHBORS, I REJOICE, FOR I HAVE FOUND THE DIME I HAD LOST.

10. EVEN SO YOUR FATHER IN HEAVEN WISHES THAT NOT ONE OF THESE LITTLE PEOPLE BE LOST.

Luke xiv. 7. AND HE SAID TO THEM,

8. WHEN THOU ART CALLED TO A WEDDING, DO NOT SIT DOWN IN THE FRONT CORNER, FOR IT MIGHT HAPPEN THAT A MORE HONORED GUEST THAN THOU IS INVITED;

9. AND THE HOST WILL COME AND SAY TO THEE, YIELD THY PLACE TO HIM; FOR THEN THOU WILT IN SHAME SIT DOWN IN THE LOWEST PLACE.

10. BUT WHEN THOU ART INVITED, GO AND SIT DOWN IN THE LOWEST PLACE, THAT WHEN THE HOST SEES THEE, HE MAY SAY, FRIEND, SIT UP HIGHER; THEN THOU WILT BE HONORED IN THE PRESENCE OF THE GUESTS.

11. FOR WHOEVER EXALTS HIMSELF WILL BE ABASED; AND HE WHO HUMBLES HIMSELF WILL BE EXALTED.

Luke ix. 47. AND JESUS KNEW THEIR THOUGHTS,

Mark ix. 35. AND SAID TO THEM, HE WHO WANTS TO BE FIRST WILL BE THE LAST OF ALL, AND A SERVANT OF ALL.

THE PARABLE OF THE PRODIGAL SON

Luke xv. 11. AND JESUS SAID, A CERTAIN MAN HAD TWO SONS:

12. AND THE YOUNGER OF THEM SAID TO HIS FATHER, FATHER, GIVE ME MY PORTION. AND THE FATHER GAVE IT TO HIM.

13. AND SOON AFTER THE YOUNGER SON TOOK HIS WHOLE PORTION, AND WENT AWAY; AND HE SQUANDERED ALL HIS SUBSTANCE.

14. WHEN HE HAD SPENT ALL, THERE AROSE A GREAT FAMINE IN THAT LAND; AND HE BEGAN TO SUFFER WANT.

15. AND HE JOINED A CITIZEN; AND HE SENT HIM INTO THE FIELD TO HERD SWINE.

16. NOBODY GAVE HIM ANYTHING, AND HE WAS GLAD TO EAT THE ACORNS THAT THE SWINE ATE.

17. AND HE REFLECTED, AND SAID, HOW MANY HIRED SERVANTS OF MY FATHER'S HAVE BREAD ENOUGH TO EAT, AND I PERISH WITH HUNGER!

18. I WILL GO TO MY FATHER, AND WILL SAY TO HIM, FATHER, I AM GUILTY TOWARD GOD AND TOWARD THEE,

19. AND AM NOT WORTHY TO BE CALLED THY SON: TAKE ME FOR A HIRED SERVANT.

20. AND HE GOT UP AND WENT TO HIS FATHER. AND HIS FATHER RECOGNIZED HIM AT A DISTANCE, AND GROANED, AND RAN TOWARD HIM, AND EMBRACED HIS NECK, AND KISSED HIM.

21. AND THE SON SAID, FATHER, I AM GUILTY TOWARD GOD AND TOWARD THEE, AND AM NOT WORTHY TO BE THY SON.

22. BUT THE FATHER SAID TO HIS SERVANTS, BRING THE BEST COAT, AND DRESS HIM; AND I WILL PUT A COSTLY RING ON HIS HAND, AND GIVE HIM GOOD SHOES;

23. AND BRING THE FATTED CALF, AND KILL IT; AND WE SHALL REJOICE.

24. FOR THIS SON OF MINE WAS LIKE ONE DEAD, AND IS ALIVE AGAIN. HE WAS LOST, AND IS FOUND. AND HE BEGAN TO BE MERRY.

25. BUT HIS ELDER SON WAS AT THAT TIME IN THE FIELD: AND AS HE CAME UP, HE HEARD MUSIC AND DANCING.

26. AND HE CALLED UP A BOY, AND ASKED, WHAT IS GOING ON AT OUR HOUSE?

27. AND THE BOY SAID, THY BROTHER HAS COME AND THY FATHER HAS HAD THE FATTED CALF KILLED, BECAUSE HE HAS RETURNED SAFE.

28. AND THE ELDER BROTHER WAS ANGRY, AND WOULD NO GO IN. HIS FATHER WENT OUT, AND CALLED HIM.

29. AND THE ELDER SON SAID, THESE MANY YEARS HAVE I SERVED THEE, AND HAVE NOT DISOBEYED THY COMMAND, AND THOU HAST NOT AS MUCH AS GIVEN ME A KID, THAT I MIGHT MAKE MERRY WITH MY FRIENDS.

30. BUT THIS SON OF THINE HAS SQUANDERED THY POSSESSIONS WITH HARLOTS, AND AS SOON AS HE CAME HOME, THOU HAST KILLED FOR HIM THE FATTED CALF.

31. AND THE FATHER SAID TO HIM, THOU ART ALWAYS WITH ME, AND ALL THAT I HAVE IS THINE.

32. BUT HOW CAN I HELP BEING HAPPY, SINCE THY BROTHER WAS DEAD, AND IS ALIVE AGAIN; HE WAS LOST, AND IS FOUND.

Matt. xviii. 14. EVEN SO YOUR FATHER IN HEAVEN DOES NOT WANT ONE MAN, EVEN THE LEAST TO PERISH.

THE PARABLE OF THE VINEYARD

Mark xii. 1. AND HE BEGAN TO SPEAK TO THEM IN PARABLES. A MAN PLANTED A GARDEN, AND HEDGED IT IN, AND DUG A POND, AND BUILT A HOUSE, AND LET IT OUT TO PEASANTS, AND HIMSELF DEPARTED.

2. AND AT THE PROPER TIME HE SENT TO THE PEASANTS A SERVANT, TO RECEIVE FROM THEM BY AGREEMENT THE FRUITS OF THE GARDEN.

3. THE PEASANTS CAUGHT THE SERVANT, AND BEAT HIM, AND SENT HIM AWAY EMPTY.

4. THE MASTER SENT ANOTHER SERVANT; AND THEY STONED HIM, AND WOUNDED HIM IN THE HEAD, AND HANDLED HIM DISGRACEFULLY, AND SENT HIM AWAY.

5. THE MASTER SENT AGAIN ANOTHER. AND THEY KILLED HIM. AND THEY BEAT AND KILLED MANY OTHER SERVANTS WHO WERE SENT TO THEM.

6. THE MASTER HAD A BELOVED SON, AND FINALLY HE SENT HIM TO THEM, SAYING, MAYBE THEY WILL RESPECT MY SON.

7. BUT THE PEASANTS SAID TO THEMSELVES, THIS IS THE MASTER HIM-SELF. LET US KILL HIM, AND EVERYTHING WILL BE OURS.

8. AND THEY TOOK HIM, AND KILLED HIM, AND THREW HIM OUT OF THE GARDEN.

9. WHAT WAS THE MASTER OF THE GARDEN TO DO?

Matt. xxi. 41. THEY REPLIED TO HIM, LET HIM KILL THESE MURDERERS, AND LET OUT THE GARDEN TO OTHERS, WHO WILL GIVE HIM THE FRUITS OF THE GARDEN.

42. AND JESUS SAID TO THEM, DID YOU NEVER READ IN THE SCRIPTURE, THE STONE WHICH THE BUILDERS REJECTED BECAME THE KEYSTONE. THIS KEYSTONE IS FROM GOD, AND IT IS MARVELOUS IN OUR EYES.

43. THEREFORE I TELL YOU, YOU WILL BE DEPRIVED OF THE KINGDOM OF GOD, AND IT WILL BE GIVEN TO THOSE WHO BRING FORTH ITS FRUITS.

Luke xvii. 5. AND THE DISCIPLES SAID TO JESUS, CAUSE US TO BELIEVE.

6. AND JESUS SAID, IF YOU HAD FAITH LIKE A BIRCH SEED, YOU WOULD SAY, TREE, GO AND TRANSPLANT THYSELF INTO THE SEA, AND IT WOULD OBEY YOU.

7. IF THOU HAST A LABORER PLOUGHING OR HERDING AND HE RETURNS FROM THE FIELD, WILT THOU SAY TO HIM AT ONCE, SEAT THYSELF AT THE TABLE?

8. NO, THOU WILT SAY, FRIEND, GET MY SUPPER READY, AND SERVE ME WHILE I EAT AND DRINK; AND THEN SIT DOWN THYSELF, AND EAT AND DRINK.

9. DOST THOU THANK THE LABORER VERY MUCH, BECAUSE HE HAS DONE WHAT THOU HAST COMMANDED HIM TO DO? HARDLY.

10. EVEN SO YOU, WHEN YOU SHALL HAVE DONE WHAT YOU ARE COMMANDED TO DO, MUST THINK OF YOURSELVES THAT YOU HAVE NOT DONE MORE THAN UNPROFITABLE LABORERS, AND ONLY WHAT WAS WANTED OF YOU.

OF THE COMING OF THE KINGDOM OF GOD

Luke xvii. 20. HE SAID TO THEM, THE KINGDOM OF GOD DOES NOT COME THROUGH ANYTHING HAPPENING.

21. YOU WILL NOT BE TOLD, HERE IT IS; OR, THERE IT IS; FOR IT IS WITHIN YOU.

22. AND HE SAID TO THE DISCIPLES, THE TIME WILL COME, WHEN YOU WILL WISH TO SEE ONE OF THE DAYS OF SALVATION OF THE SON OF MAN, AND YOU WILL NOT SEE IT.

23. AND IF THEY SAID TO YOU, HERE IT IS, THERE IT IS, DO NOT GO AFTER IT, DO NOT SEEK IT.

24. FOR IT SHINES LIKE LIGHTNING FROM ONE END OF THE HEAVENS TO THE OTHER. LET THE SON OF MAN BE SUCH IN THE DAY OF HIS SALVATION.

25. BUT FIRST HE MUST SUFFER AND BEAR FROM HIS BIRTH.

26. AND AS IT WAS IN THE LIFE OF NOAH, SO IT WILL BE IN THE DAY OF SALVATION OF THE SON OF MAN.

27. THEY ATE, THEY DRANK, THEY MARRIED, UNTIL THE DAY THAT NOAH ENTERED INTO THE ARK, AND THE FLOOD CAME, AND DESTROYED THEM ALL.

28. EVEN SO IT WAS IN THE DAYS OF LOT: THEY ATE, THEY DRANK, THEY BOUGHT, THEY SOLD, THEY PLANTED, THEY BUILT:

29. BUT ON THE DAY THAT LOT WENT OUT OF SODOM, IT RAINED FIRE AND BRIMSTONE, AND ALL WERE DESTROYED.

30. EVEN THUS IT WILL BE IN THE DAY WHEN THE SON OF MAN IS REVEALED.

31. IN THE DAY OF SALVATION HE WHO IS ON THE ROOF, AND HIS CLOTHES IN THE HOUSE, LET HIM NOT COME DOWN TO FETCH THEM; AND HE WHO IS IN THE FIELD, LET HIM NOT LOOK BACK.

32. REMEMBER LOT'S WIFE (SHE LOOKED BACK, HATED TO LOSE WHAT WAS OF EARTH, AND SO PERISHED).

33. WHOEVER WANTS TO SAVE HIS EARTHLY LIFE WILL LOSE IT; AND WHOEVER LOSES IT, WILL GIVE IT AN INCREASE—ETERNITY.

Matt. xxiv. 3. AND AS HE SAT ON THE MOUNT OF OLIVES, HIS DISCIPLES CAME PRIVATELY TO HIM, AND SAID, TELL US, WHEN WILL IT BE, AND WHAT IS THE SIGN OF THE COMING OF THY TEACHING AND OF THE GETTING OF THE ETERNAL LIFE?

Mark xiii. 32. AND NO ONE KNOWS OF THE DAY OF SALVATION AND OF THE TIME, NEITHER THE POWERS OF GOD, NOR THE SON.

Luke xvii. 37. AND AGAIN THEY SAID TO HIM, WHERE? AND HE SAID TO THEM, WHERE THE CARCASS IS, THERE THE CROWS GATHER.

Mark xiii. 28. WHEN THE BRANCHES OF THE FIG-TREE BECOME SOFT, AND THE LEAVES BEGIN TO COME OUT, YOU KNOW THAT SUMMER IS NEAR.

29. SO YOU, WHEN YOU WILL SEE THAT THESE THINGS HAVE COME TO PASS, SHALL KNOW THAT THE KINGDOM OF GOD IS AT THE DOOR.

Luke xxi. 28. BUT WHEN THESE THINGS COME TO PASS, STRAIGHTEN YOURSELVES UP AND LIFT UP YOUR EYES, FOR YOUR SALVATION IS NEAR.

OF PRAYER

Luke xviii. 1. AND JESUS GAVE THEM AN INSTRUCTION TO THIS END, THAT MEN SHOULD ALWAYS PRAY, AND NEVER STOP.

Luke xi. 2. AND JESUS SAID TO THEM, WHEN YOU PRAY, SAY, FATHER, BE HOLY IN US. THY KINGDOM COME, THAT IS, THY WILL BE DONE. THY SPIRIT COME DOWN UPON US AND CLEANSE US.

3. GIVE US THE FOOD OF THE SPIRIT, WHICH GIVES US LIFE.

4. AND DO NOT REQUEST EVERYTHING OF US WHICH WE OWE, FOR WE DO NOT REQUEST OF THOSE WHO OWE US. HAVE NO ACCOUNTING WITH US.

11. IF ANY SON WILL ASK BREAD OF ANY OF YOU WHO IS A FATHER, WILL HE GIVE HIM A STONE? OR IF HE ASKS A FISH, WILL HE GIVE HIM A SNAKE?

12. OR IF HE ASKS AN EGG, WILL HE GIVE HIM A SPIDER?

13. IF YOU LIVE BADLY, AND KNOW HOW TO GIVE GIFTS TO YOUR CHIL-
DREN; SO MUCH THE MORE WILL GOD GIVE THE HOLY SPIRIT TO THOSE
WHO ASK HIM.

5. AND HE SAID TO THEM, IF THOU HAST COME TO HIM AT MIDNIGHT, AND
SAYEST TO HIM, FRIEND, GIVE ME THREE LOAVES,

6. FOR A FRIEND OF MINE IS STOPPING WITH ME IN HIS JOURNEY, AND I
HAVE NOTHING TO SET BEFORE HIM;

7. THAT NEIGHBOR WILL NOT SAY FROM WITHIN, DO NOT TROUBLE ME:
THE DOOR IS ALREADY SHUT, AND THE CHILDREN ARE WITH ME IN BED; I
CANNOT GET UP AND GIVE YOU THE LOAVES.

8. I SUPPOSE, IF HE WILL NOT GET UP BECAUSE OF HIS FRIENDSHIP AND
GIVE IT, HE WILL JUMP UP BECAUSE OF HIS SHAME (BEFORE HIM) AND GIVE
HIM WHAT HE WANTS.

9. AND I TELL YOU, ASK, AND IT WILL BE GIVEN TO YOU; HE WHO SEEKS
FINDS, AND TO HIM WHO KNOCKS IT IS OPENED.

Luke xviii. 2. HE SAID, THERE WAS IN A CITY A JUDGE, WHO NEITHER
FEARED GOD, NOR WAS ASHAMED BEFORE MEN.

3. AND THERE WAS A WIDOW IN THAT CITY, AND SHE KEPT GOING TO
THE JUDGE AND SAYING TO HIM, JUDGE BETWEEN ME AND HIM WHO HAS
OFFENDED ME.

4. AND FOR A LONG TIME THE JUDGE WOULD NOT JUDGE; BUT AFTER-
WARD HE SAID TO HIMSELF, THOUGH I DO NOT FEAR GOD, AND DO NOT
REGARD MEN,

5. YET THAT I MAY NOT BE ANNOYED BY THIS WIDOW, I WILL DECIDE THE
CASE, LEST SHE LOSE HER PATIENCE AND SCRATCH OUT MY EYES.

6. AND JESUS SAID, HEAR WHAT THE JUDGE OF UNRIGHTEOUSNESS SAID.

7. HOW, THEN, WILL GOD NOT ACT RIGHTEOUSLY WITH HIS OWN ELECT,
WHO CRY DAY AND NIGHT TO HIM, AND ENDURE.

8. I TELL YOU THAT HE WILL TREAT THEM RIGHTEOUSLY AT ONCE. BESIDES, THE SON OF MAN WILL COME AND FIND FAITH ON EARTH.

Luke xii. 22. AND HE SAID TO HIS DISCIPLES, THEREFORE TAKE NO THOUGHT FOR YOUR LIFE.

25. WHO OF YOU WITH TAKING THOUGHT CAN ADD ONE HOUR TO HIS LIFE?

31. SEEK ONLY TO BE IN THE WILL OF GOD, AND EVERYTHING ELSE WILL COME OF ITSELF.

35. BE GIRDED AND READY, AND LET THE NIGHT CANDLES BURN ALL THE TIME.

36. BE ALWAYS LIKE SERVANTS, WHEN THEY WAIT FOR THEIR MASTER TO RETURN FROM A VISIT, THAT, WHEN HE KNOCKS, THEY MAY OPEN TO HIM AT ONCE.

37. HAPPY ARE THE SERVANTS, WHOM THE MASTER FINDS PREPARED. YOU KNOW YOURSELVES THAT HE WILL MAKE THEM SIT DOWN AT THE TABLE, AND WILL SERVE THEM.

38. AND IF HE COMES AT THE FIRST, THE SECOND, OR THE THIRD HOUR, THE SERVANTS WILL ALWAYS BE SATISFIED.

39. YOU KNOW, THAT IF THE HOUSEHOLDER KNEW WHEN THE THIEF WOULD COME, HE WOULD NOT SLEEP, AND WOULD NOT ALLOW THE HOUSE TO BE BROKEN INTO.

40. EVEN THUS BE YOU READY, FOR YOU DO NOT KNOW THE TIME WHEN THE SON OF MAN WILL GO AWAY.

Matt. xxiv. 45. WILL HE BE A FAITHFUL AND WISE SLAVE WHOM THE MASTER HAS PUT IN CHARGE OF HIS SERVANTS, TO FEED THEM IN TIME?

46. HAPPY IS THE SLAVE, IF THE MASTER COMES AND FINDS HIM DOING SO.

47. TRULY I TELL YOU, THE MASTER WILL PUT HIM IN CHARGE OF ALL HIS POSSESSIONS.

48. BUT IF THE EVIL SLAVE SHALL SAY TO HIMSELF, MY MASTER WILL BE LATE IN COMING BACK,

49. AND SHALL BEGIN TO BEAT THE SERVANTS, AND TO EAT AND DRINK WITH THE DRUNKARDS;

50. AND THE SLAVE'S MASTER SHALL COME AT A TIME WHEN HE DOES NOT EXPECT HIM, THE SLAVE WILL FARE ILL.

Mark xiii. 33. AND SO DO NOT FALL ASLEEP, FOR YOU DO NOT KNOW WHEN THE TIME WILL COME.

34. WHEN A MAN GOES AWAY FROM HIS HOUSE (GIVING FREEDOM TO HIS SERVANTS AND EACH HIS WORK), AND ORDERS HIS WATCHMAN NOT TO SLEEP,

35. DO NOT SLEEP, FOR YOU DO NOT KNOW WHEN THE MASTER OF THE HOUSE WILL RETURN, IN THE EVENING, OR AT MIDNIGHT, OR AT COCK-CROW, OR IN THE MORNING:

36. LEST, COMING BACK, HE FIND YOU SLEEPING.

37. IT IS THIS THAT I SAY TO YOU, BE ALWAYS READY.

Luke xxi. 34. RESTRAIN YOURSELVES, LEST YOUR HEARTS BE SURFEITED WITH EATING AND DRINKING, AND WORDLY CARES, AND THAT DAY FIND YOU UNAWARES.

35. FOR IT IS THROWN LIKE A SNARE OVER ALL WHO LIVE ON EARTH.

36. BE WAKEFUL THEREFORE, FEARING AT ALL TIMES, SO THAT YOU MAY AT ALL TIMES BE WORTHY OF ESCAPING EVERYTHING WHICH WILL BE, AND BE WORTHY OF THE SON OF MAN.

PARABLE OF THE VIRGINS AND THE LAMPS

Matt. xxiv. 42. DO NOT SLEEP, FOR YOU DO NOT KNOW WHAT HOUR THE MASTER WILL COME.

44. THEREFORE BE PREPARED; FOR AT AN HOUR THAT YOU DO NOT KNOW THE SON OF MAN WILL COME.

Matt. xxv. 1. THEN WILL THE KINGDOM OF GOD BE LIKE THE TEN GIRLS, WHO TOOK THEIR LAMPS, AND WENT OUT TO MEET THE BRIDEGROOM.

2. FIVE OF THEM WERE WISE, AND FIVE FOOLISH.

3. THE FOOLISH GIRLS TOOK THE LAMPS, BUT TOOK NO OIL WITH THEM.

4. AND THE WISE GIRLS TOOK THEIR LAMPS AND OIL IN THE VESSELS.

5. THE BRIDEGROOM TARRIED, AND THEY WERE SLEEPY AND FELL ASLEEP.

6. IN THE NIGHT THEY SUDDENLY CRIED, THE BRIDEGROOM IS COMING. GO OUT TO MEET HIM.

7. THEN ALL THE GIRLS AWOKE, AND TRIMMED THEIR LAMPS.

8. THE FOOLISH GIRLS SAID TO THE WISE, GIVE US OF YOUR OIL, FOR OUR LAMPS HAVE GONE OUT.

9. BUT THE WISE GIRLS ANSWERED THEM, THAT IS IMPOSSIBLE: THERE WILL NOT BE ENOUGH FOR US AND YOU; GO INTO THE SHOP, AND BUY SOME.

10. AND WHILE THEY WENT TO BUY, THE BRIDEGROOM CAME. THOSE WHO WERE READY WENT WITH THE BRIDEGROOM TO THE WEDDING, AND THE DOOR WAS SHUT.

11. THEN CAME THE OTHER GIRLS, AND SAID, MASTER, OPEN THE DOOR.

12. AND HE SAID TO THEM, TRULY, I DO NOT KNOW WHO YOU ARE.

13. SO DO NOT SLEEP, FOR YOU DO NOT KNOW THE DAY AND THE HOUR WHEN THE SON OF MAN WILL COME.

Matt. xxiv. 43. BUT YOU KNOW ALSO THAT IF THE MASTER OF THE HOUSE KNEW WHEN THE THIEF WAS COMING, HE WOULD NOT SLEEP AND WOULD NOT ALLOW HIS HOUSE TO BE BROKEN INTO.

Luke xiii. 23. AND A MAN SAID TO HIM, SIR, ARE THERE FEW WHO ARE SAVED?

24. FIGHT TO ENTER THROUGH THE NARROW GATE, FOR MANY, I TELL YOU, WILL STRIVE TO ENTER, AND BUT FEW WILL PREVAIL.

25. IF, FROM THE TIME THAT THE MASTER COMES, AND SHUTS THE DOOR, YOU BEGIN TO STAND OUTSIDE, AND TO PUSH AT THE DOOR, SAYING, MASTER, MASTER, OPEN TO US, HE WILL SAY TO YOU, I DO NOT KNOW YOU, AND I DO NOT KNOW WHENCE YOU COME.

26. THEN YOU WILL BEGIN TO SAY, WE HAVE EATEN AND DRUNK IN THY PRESENCE, AND THOU HAST TAUGHT AMONG US.

27. AND HE WILL SAY, I TELL YOU, I DO NOT KNOW YOU, WHENCE YOU ARE. GO AWAY FROM ME, ALL YOU WORKERS OF INIQUITY.

OF THE COMING OF THE SON OF MAN

Matt. xvi. 27. FOR THE SON OF MAN WILL ENTER WITH HIS POWERS, AND WILL REWARD EVERY MAN ACCORDING TO HIS WORKS.

Matt. xxv. 31. WHEN THE SON OF MAN WILL ENTER INTO HIS MEANING, AND ALL HIS POWERS WITH HIM, HE WILL SETTLE HIMSELF IN THE SEAT OF HIS MEANING.

32. THEN ALL MEN WILL APPEAR BEFORE HIM, AND HE WILL SEPARATE THEM ONE FROM ANOTHER, AS A SHEPHERD SEPARATES THE SHEEP FROM THE GOATS;

33. AND HE WILL DRIVE THE SHEEP TO THE RIGHT, AND THE GOATS TO THE LEFT.

Matt. xxv. 34. THEN THE LORD WILL SAY TO THOSE WHOM HE HAS SEPARATED AND PLACED ON THE RIGHT, COME HITHER, YOU BELOVED OF MY FATHER, AND INHERIT THE KINGDOM PREPARED FOR YOU FROM THE BEGINNING OF THE WORLD.

35. FOR I WAS HUNGRY, AND YOU FED ME; I WAS THIRSTY, AND YOU GAVE ME TO DRINK; I WAS A STRANGER, AND YOU TOOK ME IN;

36. I WAS NAKED, AND YOU CLOTHED ME; I WAS SICK, AND YOU TENDED ON ME; I WAS IN PRISON, AND YOU CAME TO SEE ME.

37. THEN THE RIGHTEOUS WILL ANSWER HIM, AND SAY, WHEN DID WE SEE THEE HUNGRY, AND FED THEE? OR THIRSTY, AND GAVE THEE TO DRINK?

38. WHEN DID WE SEE THEE SICK, OR IN PRISON, AND CAME TO SEE THEE?

40. AND THE LORD WILL SAY TO THEM IN REPLY, YOU KNOW YOURSELVES THAT WHATEVER YOU HAVE DONE TO THE LEAST OF THESE MY BRETHREN, YOU HAVE DONE TO ME.

41. THEN HE WILL SAY TO THOSE WHO ARE ON THE LEFT, GO AWAY FROM ME, UNBELOVED, INTO THE OUTER FIRE, PREPARED FOR EVIL AND ITS POWERS.

42. FOR I WAS HUNGRY, AND YOU DID NOT GIVE ME TO EAT; I WAS THIRSTY, AND YOU DID NOT GIVE ME TO DRINK;

43. I WAS A STRANGER, AND YOU DID NOT RECEIVE ME; I WAS NAKED, AND YOU DID NOT CLOTHE ME; I WAS SICK AND IN PRISON, AND YOU DID NOT LOOK AFTER ME.

44. THEN THESE WILL ANSWER HIM, SAYING, LORD, WHEN DID WE SEE THEE HUNGRY, OR THIRSTY, OR A STRANGER, OR NAKED, OR SICK, OR IN PRISON, AND DID NOT SERVE THEE?

45. THEN HE WILL ANSWER THEM, YOU KNOW YOURSELVES THAT WHAT-SOEVER YOU DID NOT DO TO THE LEAST OF YOUR BRETHREN, YOU DID NOT DO TO ME.

46. AND THEY WILL GO INTO THE EVERLASTING SEGREGATION, BUT THE RIGHTEOUS INTO LIFE ETERNAL.

TOLSTOY'S COMMENTARY

You will be mendicants and vagrants, you will be humbled. But he who loves father or mother, son or daughter, more than me, has not understood my teaching. He who is not prepared for all carnal sufferings has not understood me. He who acquires everything which is best for the carnal life will lose the true life. And he who loses the carnal life will receive the true life.

In response to these words Peter said to him, That is true, and we have listened to you, and have given up all cares and all property, and have become vagrants, and have followed thee. What will be our reward?

Jesus said to them, Thou knowest thyself what thou hast given up; and every man who gives up his family, sisters, brothers, father, mother, wife, children, and property, and follows my teaching of the true good, will he not receive a hundred times more even in this life, now, sisters, and brothers, and fields, and everything which he needs? And besides, in this life, he receives the life outside of time. But thou art mistaken in supposing that thou wilt get a reward for what thou hast done. There are no rewards in the kingdom of God. The kingdom of God is the aim and the reward. In the kingdom of God all are equal, and there are no first, and no last.

The kingdom of God is like this: A master went out in the morning to hire laborers for the garden. He hired them at a penny a day, and brought them to the garden, where he set them to work.

And he went out again at noontime, and hired more laborers, and sent them to the garden to work. And he agreed with all of them to give them a penny.

When the time for paying came, the master commanded that all the laborers be paid an equal amount, first those who came last, and then those who came first.

When the first saw that the last were getting a penny each, they thought that they would get more. But the first received but a penny each. And they murmured, and said, How is this? They have done but one plot, and we have done all four, and yet we are paid the same: this is not fair.

And the master came up, and said, Why do you grumble? Have I not treated you right? I have paid to you as much as we agreed upon. Take what belongs to you, and go. If I want to pay the last as much as I have paid you, have I not the right to do so? Or are you envious, because you see that I am good?

In the kingdom of God there are no first and no last—all are the same. He who does the will of God and gives up the carnal life has the life of the spirit. And those who fulfill it are in the will of God. Nobody else can bring man nearer to the will of God. The kingdom of God is taken by assault.

One day, two of the disciples, James and John, came up to Jesus, saying, Teacher, promise us that thou wilt do for us what we shall ask thee.

He said, What do you wish?

They said, We want to be as thou art.

And Jesus said to them, You ask what is not in my power. You can live like me, and be regenerated in spirit like me, but it is not in my power to make you like myself. All men are variously born, and to each a different degree of the understanding is given, but all may alike do the will of God and receive life.

When the other disciples heard this, they grew angry at the two brothers, because they wanted to be like the teacher, and the eldest of the disciples.

But Jesus called them up, and said, If you, brothers James and John, asked me to make you like myself, in order to be the leading disciples, you were in error; if you, the other disciples, are angry at them, because these two want to be of greater authority than you, you, too, are in error. Only in the world do they count by kings and rulers, who are of greater authority, to rule the nations; but among you there can be no greater and no smaller. In order that one of you may be greater than another, he must be a servant to all, for the teaching of the son of man consists even in this, that he does not live to be ministered to, but to minister to all, and that we should give up our life as a ransom for the life of the spirit. God the spirit seeks the salvation of him who perishes. God wishes the salvation of men, and rejoices at it, as rejoices the shepherd, when he has found his lost sheep. And when one has been lost, he leaves the ninety-nine, and goes to save the one which is lost. And if a woman loses a penny, she will sweep her whole house, until she finds it. God loves what perishes and calls it to himself.

And he told them another parable, saying that those who lived in the will of God should not exalt themselves. He said, If thou art called to a dinner, do not seat thyself in the front corner, lest someone more honored should come, and the host say to thee, Go away from there, and let him sit down who is better than thou; and then thou wilt be put to shame. Rather seat thyself in the lowest place, for then the host will find thee and call thee to the place of honor, and thou wilt be honored.

Even thus there is no place of pride in the kingdom of God. He who exalts himself, by that very act abases himself, and he who humbles himself (considers himself unworthy), by that very act raises himself in the kingdom of God.

A man had two sons. The younger one said, Father, give me my portion. And the father gave it to him.

The younger son took his portion and went to a foreign country, where he squandered his possessions, and fell into misery. And he became a swineherd in that foreign land. And he suffered so much hunger that he ate the acorns with the swine. And one day he reflected on his life, and said to himself, Why did I leave my father's house? My father has plenty of everything. At my father's the laborers get their fill to eat, while I eat the same food as the swine. I will go to my father, fall down before his feet, and say, Father, I have sinned before thee; I am not worthy of being thy son, so take me as a laborer.

So he thought, and went to his father. And as he was coming near to the house, and his father saw him in the distance, he ran to meet his son, and embraced him, and began to kiss him.

And the son said, Father, I have sinned before thee, I am not worthy of being thy son.

But the father would not listen to him, and said to the servants, Go and bring at once the best raiment, and the best shoes, and dress him. And run and catch the fatted calf and kill it: we shall rejoice, because this son of mine was dead, and has been made alive. He was lost, and now he has been found.

The elder brother was returning from the field, and as he came near the house he heard them singing at home. He called up a boy, and asked him, What merriment is this in our house?

And the boy said, Hast thou not heard? Thy brother has returned, and thy father is rejoicing, and has commanded that the fatted calf be killed, to make merry at the return of his son.

The elder brother was angry, and did not go into the house. But the father came out to him, and called him.

Father, I have worked for the these many years, and have not disobeyed thee, but thou hast never killed a calf for me. My younger brother left the house and spent all his portion with drunkards, and thou hast ordered the fatted calf to be killed for him.

And the father said, Thou art always with me, and everything I have is thine. How can I help rejoicing, since thy brother was dead, and has come to life; he was lost, and has been found.

Even thus your Father in heaven does not want a single man, not even the least worthy, to be lost, but wants him to live.

The life of men, who do not understand that they are not living in this world that they may eat and drink and make merry, but that they may all their life work for God, is like this: a master planted a garden, got it into good shape, and did everything that it might bring forth fruits. And he sent laborers into the garden, to work, to gather the fruits, and to pay him for the garden according to the agreement.

This master is God, the garden is the world. The laborers are men. God created the world and sent men into it that they might give to God what is God's, the understanding of life, which he has placed in them. The time came, and the master sent his servant to collect the rent. God is in the souls of men, continually speaking to them of what they ought to do for him, and continually calling them.

The laborers drove away the messenger of the master without anything, and continued to live, imagining that it was their own garden, and that they were settled in it for their own sakes. Men have driven away the admonition of the will of God, and continue to live, imagining that they are living for themselves, for the pleasures of the carnal life.

Then the master sent more of his favourites, and his son, to remind the laborers of their duty. But the laborers entirely lost their reason and imagined that if they killed the master's son, who reminded them of the fact that the garden was not theirs, they would be left in peace, and so they killed him. Men do not like to be reminded of the spirit which dwells within them and shows them that it is eternal, while they are not, and they have killed, as much as they could, the consciousness of the spirit, wrapped it in a handkerchief, and hid in the ground the talent which was given to them.

What was the master to do? Only this, to drive the laborers away, and to send others in their place. What is God to do? To sow while there is any fruit. And this he does. Men have not understood that the consciousness of the spirit, which is in them, and which they are hiding, because it interferes with them, is the very understanding which is the foundation of life. They reject the very stone by which everything is supported. And those who will not take the spirit as the foundation of life, do not enter into the kingdom of God and do not receive life. In order to receive life and the kingdom of God, a man must remember his situation, not wait for rewards, but feel himself under obligations.

Then the disciples said to Jesus, Increase our faith. Tell us something which will make us believe more firmly in the life of the spirit so that we may not regret the life of the flesh. See how much we must give away, and it is necessary to give up everything for the life of the spirit. And thou sayest thyself that there is no reward.

And to this Jesus replied, If your faith were as strong as is your faith that out of a birch seed there will grow up a large tree, you would believe that within you there is the only germ of the life of the spirit, out of which grows the true life. Faith does not consist in believing in something miraculous, but in understanding our condition and that in which our salvation is. If thou understandest thy condition, thou wilt not be waiting for rewards, but wilt work to retain what has been given thee. If thou comest from the field with thy laborer, thou wilt not seat him at the table, but wilt command him to put away the cattle and get thy supper ready, and only then wilt thou say to him, Eat and drink. Thou dost not thank the laborer for doing his duty. And the laborer is not offended, but works and waits for his due.

Even thus do what is right, and think that you are worthless laborers, and have done only what was right, and wait for no reward. The care ought to be, not about receiving the reward, but about not being a guilty and bad laborer. We must not have a thought for this, that we believe that there will be a reward and that there will be life—this cannot be otherwise; but we must have a thought for this, that we may not lose this life, and that we may not forget that it is given to us, that we may bring forth its fruits and do the will of God. We must not think of what we have accomplished, and that a reward is coming to us.

Only then will you understand that there is a kingdom of God, of which I tell you, and that this kingdom of God is the only salvation from death, and will not appear in such a way as to be visible. Of the kingdom of God which saves from death we cannot say, Here it has come, or, It will come; Here it is, or, There it is. It is within you, in your soul: and so, if the time ever comes that you wish to find salvation in life, you will be searching for it in some time, and you will not find it. And if they tell you, Salvation is here, salvation is there, do not seek this salvation anywhere but within you; for salvation is like lightning, sudden, and for it there is no time, and there is no death—it is within you.

And as was salvation for Noah, and as it was for Lot, such it always is for the son of man. Life remains the same for all men: all eat, drink, marry, but when the flood comes, and the rain from heaven, when carnal death comes, some perish, and others are saved. When the kingdom of God within you shall come, each one of you will no longer think of the carnal; and do not look around, like Lot's wife. It is impossible for you to plough, if you look back. Remember only the present.

Then the disciples asked how they could tell that the day of salvation had come and that we had attained eternal life.

And Jesus replied to them, Nobody can know when and where this is going to happen to man. It is impossible to show and prove it. The one thing which we can know is that, when this takes place in you, you will feel the true life. What will happen to you, is what happens to a tree in the spring: it was dead, and now you see the branches growing soft, and the buds filling up, and the leaves growing. It is this that you will feel in yourselves. You will feel in yourselves life which proceeds from you. When you feel this, you may know that the kingdom of God and the day of salvation are near. Consequently, have no thought for the carnal life. Seek only to be in the will of God—everything else will come of itself.

And he said that it was necessary to wish for this one thing only, and not to lose courage.

And the disciples said, Teach us to pray.

And he said, Your prayer shall be this only: Father, thy spirit be holy in us, thy will be in us. Let us feed on the carnal life for the life of the spirit. Do not importune us, asking for what we owe thee, as we will not importune those who are indebted to us. Have no accounting with us.

If a son asks his father for bread, his father will certainly not give him a stone; nor will he give him a snake instead of a fish. If we, evil men, give to our children what is good, and not what is bad for them; how then will our Father, from whom we come, the Father of the spirit, refuse us that spirit, for which alone we ask him? Not only no father, but no stranger can refuse another, when he is persistently asked to give him a thing. If thou goest at midnight to thy neighbor to ask him for bread, in order to entertain thy guest, thou knowest that, if not out of friendship, certainly out of shame, he will give thee what thou wantest, if thou askest him persistently. If thou wilt ask, thou wilt receive; if thou wilt knock, it will be opened to thee. Certainly you cannot expect God to give you of the spirit, which saves from death, if you do not seek, and ask him.

And Jesus said, There was an evil judge, who feared neither God nor men. And a poor widow begged him, but he would not pass judgment. And the widow clung to the judge day and night, begging him all the time. And the judge said, What can I do? I will settle the case as the widow wants me to, or else she will give me no rest.

Consider this, that, though the judge was unrighteous, he did it. How then will God refuse to do what they pray to him for day and night? If there is God, he will do it. If there is no God, and instead of God there is an unrighteous judge, there is still the son of man, who is seeking truth, and we cannot help but believe in him. Seek the kingdom of God and his truth at all times, in every place, and all else will come of itself. Do not trouble yourselves about the future, and try only to avoid the present evil.

Be always ready, like servants waiting for the master, to open the door, the moment he comes. The servants do not know when he will return, whether early or late, and must always be ready. And if they meet the master and have done his will, they fare well. The same is in life: always, at every minute of the present, we must live the life of the spirit, without thinking of the past and the future, and without saying to ourselves, I will do this or that at such and such a time. If the master knew when the thief would come, he would not sleep; even thus you must not sleep, because for the son of man there is no time: he lives only in the present, and does not know when the beginning and the end of his life are. Our life is like the life of a slave whom the master left as a watchman in his house. Happy is the slave who always does the will of his master, But if he says, My master will not come back immediately, and forgets his master's business, the master will return unawares, and will drive him away. And so do not lose your courage, but always live in the spirit in the present. For life there is no time.

Look after yourselves, lest you burden and bedim yourselves with too much eating and drinking and with cares, and lose the time of salvation. The time of salvation is thrown over you like a snare—it is always here. And so always live the life of the son of man.

The kingdom of heaven is like this: Ten maidens went out with their lamps to meet the bridegroom. Five of them were wise, and five foolish. The foolish girls took the lamps, but forgot the oil, while the wise maidens took both the lamps and a supply of oil. As they were waiting for the bridegroom, they fell asleep.

When the bridegroom came near, the foolish maidens saw that they did not have enough oil; they begged the wise girls for some and went to buy it; while they were gone, the bridegroom came, and the wise maidens, who had oil, went in with him, and the doors were closed. The only reason the maidens had to go out was to meet the bridegroom with their lamps, and they had forgotten that what was important was that the lamps should burn at the proper time. But that they should burn then, it was necessary for them to have burned all the time. Life is given only for the purpose of exalting the son of man, and the son of man is always; he is not in time, and so we must serve him outside of time, in the present only. And so make an effort, do works, that you may enter into the life of the spirit; if you make no effort, you will not enter into it.

You will say, We have said this and that, but you will not do good deeds, and so there will not be the whole life: for the son of man in his power will give to each what he has done.

Men are all divided according to their manner of serving the son of man. By their works they are divided into two classes, as a flock of sheep is separated from the goats. Some will live, and others will die. Those who have served the son of man will receive what belonged to them from the beginning of the world—the life which they have preserved. But they have preserved their life by serving the son of man: they have fed the hungry, clothed the naked, received the stranger, visited the prisoner. Some have lived the life of the son of man, feeling that he is one in all men, and so loved him. He is one in all. But those who have not lived the life of the son of man did not serve him and did not understand that he is one in all, and so they have not united with him, and have lost the life in him, and perished.

CHAPTER NINE

THE OFFENCES

Mark x. 13. AND THEY BROUGHT CHILDREN TO JESUS, THAT THEY MIGHT WALK UP TO HIM; BUT HIS DISCIPLES DID NOT ADMIT THOSE WHO BROUGHT THEM.

14. WHEN JESUS SAW IT, HE WAS GRIEVED, AND HE SAID TO THEM, LET THE CHILDREN COME TO ME, AND DO NOT HINDER THEM; FOR THEY ARE SUCH AS ARE IN THE KINGDOM OF GOD.

15. YOU KNOW YOURSELVES THAT IF THE KINGDOM OF GOD IS NOT UNDER-STOOD AS A CHILD UNDERSTANDS IT, YOU WILL NOT ENTER INTO IT.

Matt. xviii. 2. AND JESUS CALLED A LITTLE BOY, AND PLACED HIM AMONG HIS DISCIPLES.

3. AND SAID, TRULY I TELL YOU, IF YOU DO NOT TURN BACK, AND BECOME AS LITTLE CHILDREN, YOU WILL NOT ENTER INTO THE KINGDOM OF HEAVEN.

5. AND WHOEVER UNDERSTANDS ONE SUCH CHILD, AS HE UNDERSTANDS ME, UNDERSTANDS MY TEACHING.

Mark ix. 37. AND HE WHO UNDERSTANDS ME UNDERSTANDS HIM WHO HAS SENT ME.

Matt. xviii. 10. TAKE HEED THAT YOU DO NOT DESPISE ONE CHILD, FOR I TELL YOU, THEIR SOULS ALWAYS SEE GOD THEIR FATHER.

14. THUS NOT ONE CHILD PERISHES BY THE WILL OF GOD YOUR FATHER.

6. AND HE WHO WILL ALLURE AWAY EVEN ONE OF THESE CHILDREN WHO BELIEVE IN ME, DOES THIS FOR HIM, THAT A MILLSTONE MAY BE HANGED AROUND HIS NECK, AND HE BE DROWNED IN THE SEA.

7. THE WORLD OF MEN IS UNHAPPY BECAUSE OF THE OFFENCES, FOR IT IS IMPOSSIBLE FOR THE OFFENCES NOT TO EXIST; BUT UNHAPPY IS THE MAN WHO BECOMES A DECEIVER.

8. IF THY HAND OR THY FOOT LEADS THEE INTO DECEPTION, CUT THEM OFF, AND CAST THEM FROM THEE; FOR IT IS GOOD TO LIVE EVEN ARMLESS OR LAME, BUT NOT TO PERISH WITH TWO HANDS AND TWO FEET.

9. AND IF THY EYE LEADS THEE INTO DECEPTION, TEAR IT OUT, AND CAST IT FROM THEE. IT IS GOOD TO LIVE WITH ONE EYE, AND NOT TO PERISH WITH TWO EYES.

Luke xvii. 3. BEWARE; IF THY BROTHER OFFENDS THEE, REBUKE HIM; AND IF HE CHANGES HIS CONDUCT, FORGIVE HIM.

Matt. xviii. 21. THEN PETER CAME UP TO HIM, AND SAID, NO MATTER HOW MUCH A BROTHER OFFENDS ME, I WILL FORGIVE HIM SEVEN TIMES.

22. AND JESUS SAID TO HIM, I DO NOT SPEAK OF FORGIVING SEVEN TIMES, BUT SEVENTY TIMES SEVEN.

23. THEREFORE THE KINGDOM OF GOD IS LIKE THIS: A RICH MAN WANTED TO SETTLE HIS AFFAIRS WITH HIS CLERKS.

24. AND WHEN HE HAD BEGUN TO MAKE THE ACCOUNT, THEY BROUGHT TO HIM A CLERK WHO OWED HIM TEN THOUSAND DOLLARS.

25. BUT HE COULD NOT PAY IT, AND SO THE MASTER ORDERED HIS WIFE, HIS CHILDREN, AND EVERYTHING HE HAD TO BE SOLD, FOR THE SAKE OF THE PAYMENT.

26. AND THE CLERK FELL DOWN BEFORE THE MASTER, AND BEGAN TO BOW TO HIM, SAYING, MASTER, HAVE PATIENCE WITH ME, AND I WILL PAY THEE ALL.

27. THEN THE MASTER TOOK PITY UPON THE SERVANT, AND FREED HIM AND FORGAVE HIM HIS DEBT.

28. AND THE CLERK WENT OUT, AND FOUND ONE OF HIS SERVANTS, WHO OWED HIM ONE HUNDRED CENTS. AND CALLING HIM UP, HE BEGAN TO CHOKE HIM, SAYING, PAY ME WHAT THOU OWEST ME.

29. AND THAT SERVANT FELL DOWN AT HIS FEET, AND BESOUGHT HIM, SAYING, HAVE PITY ON ME, AND I WILL PAY THEE ALL.

30. BUT THE CLERK WOULD NOT LISTEN: HE WENT AND TOOK HIM TO THE PRISON, TILL HE SHOULD PAY HIS DEBT.

31. AND THE OTHER SERVANTS SAW WHAT WAS DONE, AND THEY WERE MUCH GRIEVED, AND WENT AND TOLD THEIR MASTER EVERYTHING WHICH HAD HAPPENED.

32. THEN THE MASTER CALLED UP THE CLERK, AND SAID TO HIM, THOU WICKED SLAVE, I FORGAVE THEE THE WHOLE DEBT, BECAUSE THOU DIDST ASK ME,

33. AND THOU OUGHTEST TO HAVE FORGIVEN THY SERVANT, AS I HAD PITY ON THEE.

34. AND THE MASTER WAS ANGRY, AND TURNED HIM OVER TO THE TORMENTORS, TILL HE SHOULD PAY EVERYTHING WHICH HE OWED HIM.

35. EVEN THUS MY HEAVENLY FATHER WILL DO TO YOU, IF EVERYONE OF YOU WILL NOT IN HIS HEART FORGIVE HIS BROTHER HIS TRESPASSES.

Matt. xviii. 15. IF THY BROTHER OFFENDS THEE, GO AND TELL HIM HIS FAULT FACE TO FACE. IF HE SHALL HEAR THEE, THOU ART THE GAINER, FOR THOU HAST FOUND A BROTHER.

16. BUT IF HE SHALL NOT HEAR THEE, THEN TAKE WITH THEE ONE OR TWO MORE, THAT THE TWO OR THREE MAY PERSUADE HIM.

17. AND IF HE SHALL NOT HEAR THEM EITHER, TELL IT TO THE ASSEMBLY; AND IF HE DOES NOT HEAR THE ASSEMBLY, LET HIM BE TO THEE AS A STRANGER OR AS A TAX COLLECTOR.

18. VERILY I TELL YOU, WHATEVER YOU WILL BIND ON EARTH, WILL BE BOUND WITH GOD, AND WHATEVER YOU WILL LOOSE ON EARTH, WILL BE LOOSED WITH GOD.

19. AGAIN YOU KNOW, THAT IF TWO OR THREE OF YOU HAVE AGREED ON EARTH IN EVERYTHING, THEN WHOMEVER THEY ASK, THEY WILL GET WHAT THEY ASK BEFORE MY FATHER IN HEAVEN.

20. FOR WHERE TWO OR THREE ARE UNITED THROUGH MY TEACHING, I AM WITH THEM ALSO.

ON MARRIAGE AND DIVORCE

Matt. xix. 3. AND THE PHARISEES CAME UP TO HIM, AND, TEMPTING HIM, SAID TO HIM, IS IT LAWFUL FOR A MAN TO DIVORCE HIS WIFE FOR EVERY CAUSE?

4. AND JESUS REPLIED TO THEM, DO YOU NOT KNOW THAT HE WHO MADE MALE AND FEMALE IN THE BEGINNING, MADE ALSO THEM?

5. AND SAID, FOR THIS REASON WILL A MAN LEAVE FATHER AND MOTHER, AND WILL CLEAVE TO HIS WIFE; AND THE TWO WILL BE ONE BODY.

6. SO THAT THERE WILL NOT BE TWO, BUT ONE BODY. THEREFORE, WHAT GOD HAS UNITED, NO MAN SHALL DIVIDE.

7. AND THEY SAID TO HIM, WHY, THEN, DID MOSES COMMAND US TO GIVE A WRITING OF DIVORCEMENT, AND TO DIVORCE A WIFE?

8. AND HE SAID TO THEM, BECAUSE OF YOUR RUDENESS DID MOSES COMMAND YOU TO DIVORCE YOUR WIVES: FROM THE BEGINNING IT WAS NOT SO.

9. I TELL YOU, WHOEVER PUTS AWAY HIS WIFE, EXCEPT FOR FORNICATION, CAUSES HER TO COMMIT ADULTERY.

Mark x. 11. AND EVERY MAN WHO MARRIES A DIVORCED WOMAN COMMITS ADULTERY.

Matt. xix. 10. AND HIS DISCIPLES SAID TO HIM, IF SUCH IS THE DUTY OF A MAN TO HIS WIFE, IT IS MORE PROFITABLE NOT TO MARRY.

11. AND HE SAID TO THEM, NOT ALL KEEP THIS COMPREHENSION IN THEIR HEART, SAVE THOSE TO WHOM IT IS GIVEN.

12. FOR THERE ARE CHASTE PEOPLE, WITHOUT ADULTEROUS PASSION, WHO WERE SO BORN FROM THEIR MOTHER'S WOMB; AND THERE ARE OTHERS WHO ARE DEPRIVED OF THEIR LUST BY MEN; AND OTHERS AGAIN, WHO HAVE MADE THEMSELVES CHASTE FOR THE KINGDOM OF GOD. HE WHO IS ABLE TO TAKE TO HEART THIS COMPREHENSION, LET HIM RECEIVE IT.

ON TRIBUTE

Matt. xvii. 24. WHEN THEY CAME TO CAPERNAUM, THOSE WHO COLLECTED DIDRACHMS CAME TO PETER, AND SAID TO HIM, YOUR TEACHER DOES NOT PAY THE DIDRACHMS.

25. HE SAID, YES. AND WHEN PETER ENTERED INTO THE HOUSE, JESUS ANTICIPATED HIM, SAYING, WHAT THINKEST THOU, SIMON? OF WHOM DO THE KINGS OF THE EARTH TAKE CUSTOM AND TRIBUTE? OF THEIR CHILDREN, OR OF STRANGERS?

26. AND PETER SAID, OF STRANGERS. JESUS SAID TO HIM, THEN ARE THE CHILDREN FREE.

27. BUT, LEST WE SHOULD LEAD THEM INTO SIN, GO AND CAST OUT A TACKLE, AND TAKE UP THE FIRST FISH WHICH THOU CATCHEST, AND GET A STATER FOR IT, AND GIVE THIS FOR ME AND THEE.

Matt. xxii. 15. THEN THE PHARISEES WENT, AND TOOK COUNSEL HOW THEY MIGHT CATCH HIM IN HIS SPEECH.

16. AND THEY SENT OUT UNTO HIM THEIR DISCIPLES WITH THE HERODIANS, SAYING, TEACHER, WE KNOW THAT THOU TEACHEST THE WAY OF GOD IN TRUTH, AND THAT THOU DOST NOT CARE FOR ANY MAN, FOR THOU PAYEST NO ATTENTION TO PERSONS.

17. TELL US THEREFORE, IS IT LAWFUL ACCORDING TO YOUR OPINION TO PAY TRIBUTE TO CÆSAR, OR NOT?

18. AND GUESSING AT THEIR CUNNING, JESUS SAID, WHY DO YOU TEMPT ME, CUNNING PEOPLE?

19. SHOW ME THE TRIBUTE MONEY. AND THEY BROUGHT HIM A PENNY.

20. AND HE SAID TO THEM, WHOSE IS THIS IMAGE AND SUPERSCRIPTION?

21. THEY SAID, CÆSAR'S. THEN HE SAID TO THEM, THEN GIVE BACK TO CÆSAR WHAT IS CÆSAR'S: AND TO GOD GIVE WHAT IS GOD'S.

22. WHEN THEY HEARD THIS, THEY MARVELED, AND LEFT HIM, AND WENT AWAY.

OF THE ADULTERESS

Luke ix. 52. ON THEIR WAY THE DISCIPLES OF JESUS ENTERED INTO A VILLAGE OF SAMARIA, TO PREPARE A NIGHT'S LODGING FOR HIM.

53. BUT THEY DID NOT RECEIVE HIM THERE.

54. AND WHEN HIS DISCIPLES JAMES AND JOHN SAW THIS, THEY SAID, DOST THOU AGREE TO THIS, THAT IT IS PROPER TO SAY, MAY THEY BE KILLED BY LIGHTNING FROM HEAVEN FOR THIS?

55. AND JESUS REPLIED TO THEM, YOU DO NOT UNDERSTAND OF WHAT SPIRIT YOU ARE.

56. FOR THE SON OF MAN HAS NOT COME TO DESTROY THE LIVES OF MEN, BUT TO SAVE THEM. AND HE WENT TO ANOTHER VILLAGE.

John viii. 3. AND THE SCRIBES AND PHARISEES BROUGHT TO HIM A WOMAN TAKEN IN ADULTERY; AND THEY PLACED HER BEFORE HIM,

4. AND SAID TO HIM, TEACHER, THIS WOMAN WAS CAUGHT IN ADULTERY.

5. ACCORDING TO THE LAW OF MOSES WE ARE COMMANDED TO STONE SUCH A ONE TO DEATH. WHAT DOST THOU SAY?

6. THEY SAID THIS, TEMPTING HIM, THAT THEY MIGHT HAVE CAUSE FOR ACCUSING HIM. BUT JESUS, BENDING DOWN, WROTE WITH HIS FINGER ON THE GROUND.

7. AND THEY CONTINUED ASKING HIM. HE LIFTED HIMSELF UP, AND SAID TO THEM, HE WHO IS WITHOUT SIN AMONG YOU, LET HIM CAST THE FIRST STONE AT HER.

8. AND AGAIN HE BENT DOWN AND BEGAN TO WRITE ON THE GROUND.

9. THEY UNDERSTOOD HIM, AND THEIR CONSCIENCE REPROVED THEM, AND ONE BY ONE, FROM THE ELDEST TO THE YOUNGEST, THEY ALL WENT AWAY. AND JESUS ALONE WAS LEFT, AND THE WOMAN STANDING BEFORE HIM.

10. JESUS LIFTED HIMSELF AND SAW NONE BUT THE WOMAN. AND HE SAID HER, WOMAN, WHERE ARE THY ACCUSERS? HAS NO ONE CONDEMNED THEE?

11. SHE SAID, NO ONE, SIR. AND JESUS SAID TO HER, NEITHER DO I CONDEMN THEE: GO, AND SIN NO MORE.

OF THE TRUE LIFE

Luke xii. 13. AND ONE OF THE PEOPLE SAID TO JESUS, TEACHER, COMMAND MY BROTHER TO DIVIDE THE INHERITANCE WITH ME.

14. AND JESUS SAID TO HIM, MAN, HAS ANYONE MADE ME A JUDGE OR DIVIDER AMONG YOU?

Luke x. 25. AND, BEHOLD, A LAWYER STOOD UP AND, TEMPTING JESUS, SAID, TEACHER, WHAT SHALL I DO TO RECEIVE ETERNAL LIFE?

26. JESUS SAID TO HIM, WHAT IS WRITTEN IN THE LAW? HOW DOST THOU READ?

27. AND THE LAWYER REPLIED, LOVE THY LORD WITH ALL THY HEART, AND WITH ALL THY SOUL, AND WITH ALL THY STRENGTH, AND WITH ALL THY MIND; AND THY NEIGHBOR AS THYSELF.

28. JESUS SAID TO HIM, THOU HAST ANSWERED RIGHT: DO THIS, AND THOU WILT LIVE.

29. BUT THE LAWYER WANTED TO JUSTIFY HIMSELF, AND SAID TO JESUS, AND WHO IS MY NEIGHBOR?

30. AND JESUS SAID TO HIM, THERE WAS A MAN WHO WENT FROM JERICHO, AND FELL AMONG ROBBERS. THE ROBBERS TOOK EVERYTHING FROM HIM, BEAT HIM, AND WENT AWAY, LEAVING HIM HALF DEAD.

31. A PRIEST HAPPENED TO COME THAT WAY. WHEN HE SAW THE MAN, HE TURNED AROUND AND WENT AWAY.

33. A SAMARITAN, AS HE TRAVELED, CAME WHERE HE WAS; HE SAW HIM AND TOOK PITY ON HIM.

34. AND HE WENT AND BOUND UP HIS WOUNDS, POURING IN OIL AND WINE, AND SET HIM ON HIS HORSE, AND BROUGHT HIM TO AN INN, AND TOOK CARE OF HIM.

35. ON THE FOLLOWING MORNING THE SAMARITAN PROCEEDED ON HIS JOURNEY, GIVING THE HOST TWO PENCE, AND SAYING, TAKE CARE OF THIS MAN. IF THOU SPENDEST MORE ON HIM, I WILL REPAY THEE ON MY WAY BACK.

36. WELL, WHAT DO YOU THINK? WHICH OF THE THREE, THE PRIEST, THE LEVITE OR THE SAMARITAN, WAS A NEIGHBOR TO HIM WHO FELL AMONG THE ROBBERS?

37. AND THE LAWYER SAID, OF COURSE, HE WHO HAD PITY ON HIM. THEN JESUS SAID, GO, AND DO LIKEWISE.

Matt. xvi. 21. AND JESUS BEGAN TO TELL HIS DISCIPLES THAT HE HAD TO GO TO JERUSALEM,

22. FOR THE SON OF MAN MUST SUFFER MUCH, AND BE REJECTED BY ELDERS, PRIESTS, AND LEARNED MEN, AND BE SLAIN, AND BE RAISED AFTER THREE DAYS.

Mark viii. 32. AND HE SPOKE THESE WORDS WITH CONFIDENCE. AND TAKING HIM BY THE HAND, SIMON PETER BEGAN TO HOLD HIM BACK.

33. BUT WHEN HE HAD TURNED AROUND AND LOOKED AT HIS DISCIPLES, HE REBUKED SIMON PETER, SAYING, GET AWAY FROM ME, OFFENDER. THOU ENTICEST ME AWAY FROM THE TRUTH, FOR THOU DOST NOT THINK OF WHAT IS DIVINE, BUT WHAT IS HUMAN.

John xi. 9. THERE ARE TWELVE HOURS IN THE DAY. AND IF THOU WALKEST IN THE DAY, THOU DOST NOT STUMBLE, FOR IT IS LIGHT.

10. BUT IF THOU WALKEST IN THE NIGHT, THOU STUMBLEST, FOR THOU DOST NOT SEE THE LIGHT.

Mark viii. 34. AND HE CALLED THE PEOPLE WITH HIS DISCIPLES, AND SAID TO THEM, HE WHO WANTS TO WALK ACCORDING TO ME, LET HIM DENY HIMSELF (LET HIM TAKE THE CROSS AND FOLLOW ME).

35. FOR HE WHO WANTS TO SAVE HIS EARTHLY LIFE, WILL LOSE THE TRUE LIFE; AND HE WHO WILL LOSE THE EARTHLY LIFE FOR ME AND THE TRUE GOOD, WILL SAVE IT.

Mark xii. 18. THEN THE SADDUCEES CAME TO HIM. THEY TOLD HIM, ON THE CONTRARY, THAT THERE WOULD BE NO AWAKENING OF LIFE, AND BEGAN TO ASK HIM,

19. TEACHER, MOSES SAID THAT IF ONE DIES AND LEAVES NO CHILDREN, THEN THE BROTHER IS TO TAKE THE WIFE OF HIM WHO DIED, TO RAISE UP A DESCENT TO HIS BROTHER.

20. THERE WERE SEVEN BROTHERS, AND THE FIRST MARRIED AND DIED, AND HAD NO CHILDREN, AND LEFT HIS WIFE TO HIS BROTHER.

21. AND SIMILARLY THE SECOND AND THE THIRD,

22. UP TO THE SEVENTH. AFTER ALL OF THESE THE WOMAN DIED.

23. WHOSE WIFE WILL SHE BE IN THE RESURRECTION, WHEN THEY WILL RISE TO LIFE? ALL SEVEN HAD HER.

24. AND JESUS REPLIED TO THEM, YOU ARE CONFUSED; YOU DO NOT UNDERSTAND THE SCRIPTURE AND THE POWER OF GOD.

Luke xx. 34. MEN OF THIS LIFE MARRY, AND WOMEN ARE GIVEN IN MARRIAGE:

35. BUT THOSE WHO BECOME WORTHY OF THE OTHER LIFE AND OF THE REËSTABLISHMENT FROM THE DEAD NEITHER MARRY, NOR ARE GIVEN IN MARRIAGE.

36. FOR THEY CANNOT DIE AGAIN; FOR THEY BECOME THE WILL OF GOD: THEY BECOME THE CHILDREN OF GOD AND THE CHILDREN OF THE REËSTABLISHMENT.

Matt. xxii. 33. AND THE PEOPLE MARVELED AT HIS TEACHING.

Luke xx. 39. AND MANY OF THE LEARNED SAID, TEACHER, THOU ART RIGHT.

40. AND THEY DID NOT DARE TO ASK HIM AGAIN.

Matt. xxii. 31. BUT AS TO THE WAKENING OF THE DEAD, HAVE YOU NOT READ THE WORD OF GOD SPOKEN TO YOU? HE SAID.

32. I AM THE GOD OF ABRAHAM, AND THE GOD OF ISAAC, AND THE GOD OF JACOB. GOD IS NOT THE GOD OF THE DEAD, BUT OF THE LIVING.

Luke xx. 38. FOR ALL ARE LIVING TO HIM.

Matt. xxii. 34. BUT WHEN THE PHARISEES HEARD THAT HE HAD PUT THE SADDUCEES TO SILENCE, THEY UNITED.

35. AND OF THEM, A LAWYER, TEMPTING HIM, SAID,

36. TEACHER, WHICH IS THE GREATEST COMMANDMENT IN THE LAW?

37. AND JESUS SAID TO HIM,

Mark xii. 29. THE FIRST THING IS, THE LORD OUR GOD IS THE ONLY LORD.

30. AND THOU WILT LOVE THE LORD THY GOD WITH ALL THY HEART, AND WITH ALL THY MIND, AND WITH ALL THY STRENGTH. THIS IS THE CHIEF COMMANDMENT.

Matt. xxii. 31. AND THE SECOND IS LIKE IT: THOU WILT LOVE THY NEIGH-BOR AS HIM.

40. ON THESE TWO COMMANDMENTS DEPEND THE WHOLE LAW AND THE PROPHETS.

41. THEN JESUS ASKED THEM,

42. IN YOUR OPINION, WHAT IS CHRIST?

Matt. xxii. 42. WHETHER HE IS A SON OF MAN? AND THEY REPLIED TO HIM, THE SON OF DAVID.

43. AND JESUS SAID TO THEM, HOW, THEN, DOES DAVID CALL HIM HIS LORD IN THE SPIRIT.

44. THE LORD HAS SAID TO MY LORD, BE ON MY RIGHT HAND, TILL I CONQUER THY ENEMIES.

45. BUT IF DAVID CALLS HIM LORD, HOW CAN HE BE HIS SON?

46. AND THEY DID NOT DARE ASK HIM MORE.

OF THE LEAVEN OF THE PHARISEES, THE SADDUCEES, AND THE HERODIANS

Matt. xvi. 6. AND JESUS SAID, TAKE HEED AND BEWARE OF THE LEAVEN OF THE PHARISEES AND OF THE SADDUCEES AND OF THE HERODIANS.

7. THE DISCIPLES THOUGHT THAT HE WAS SPEAKING OF BREAD.

11. THEN HE SAID TO THEM, WHY DO YOU NOT UNDERSTAND THAT I AM NOT SPEAKING CONCERNING BREAD; BEWARE OF THE LEAVEN OF THE PHARISEES, OF THE SADDUCEES, AND OF THE HERODIANS.

12. THEN THEY UNDERSTOOD THAT HE WAS NOT SPEAKING TO THEM THAT THEY SHOULD BEWARE OF BREAD, BUT THAT HE WAS SPEAKING OF THE TEACHING.

Luke xii. 1. BUT MOST OF ALL BEWARE OF THE LEAVEN OF THE PHARISEES, FOR IT IS HYPOCRISY.

2. FOR THERE IS NOTHING COVERED, THAT WILL NOT BE REVEALED; NOR HID, THAT WILL NOT BE KNOWN.

Luke xx. 45. AND WHEN ALL THE PEOPLE UNDERSTOOD HIM, HE SAID TO HIS DISCIPLES,

46. BEWARE OF THE PHARISEES.

Matt. xxiii. 2. THE LEARNED MEN AND THE PHARISEES HAVE TAKEN UP THE PLACE OF MOSES, THE PROPHET OF GOD.

3. SO THAT WHATEVER THEY TELL YOU, OBSERVE AND DO, YOU, FOLLOW-ING THEIR EXAMPLE, DO NOT DO, BECAUSE THEY SPEAK, AND DO NOT DO.

4. FOR THEY BIND HEAVY BURDENS AND HARD TO BEAR, AND LAY THEM ON MEN'S SHOULDERS; BUT THEY THEMSELVES WILL NOT MOVE THEM WITH ONE OF THEIR FINGERS.

5. ONLY THAT THEY MAY BE SEEN OF MEN DO THEY MAKE THEIR DEVO-TIONS IN PUBLIC, AND LET OUT THE BORDERS OF THEIR MANTLES.

6. AND THEY LOVE TO TAKE THE FIRST PLACE AT DINNERS, AND THE CHIEF SEATS IN THE CHURCHES.

7. AND LIKE TO HAVE THEIR HANDS KISSED IN THE PRESENCE OF PEOPLE, AND TO BE CALLED, MASTER, AND, TEACHER.

8. BUT DO NOT CALL YOURSELVES TEACHERS, FOR YOU HAVE THE ONE TEACHER, CHRIST; AND ALL YOU ARE BROTHERS.

9. AND DO NOT CALL ANY MAN FATHER UPON EARTH, FOR ONE IS YOUR FATHER, WHO IS IN HEAVEN.

10. AND BE NOT CALLED MASTERS, FOR ONE IS YOUR PASTOR, CHRIST.

13. WOE TO YOU, LEARNED MEN AND PHARISEES, HYPOCRITES! FOR YOU SHUT UP THE KINGDOM OF GOD AGAINST MEN: FOR NEITHER DO YOU YOUR-SELVES GO IN, NOR DO YOU LET OTHERS ENTER.

Luke xi. 52. WOE TO YOU, LAWYERS! FOR YOU HAVE TAKEN AWAY THE KEY OF THE COMPREHENSION: YOU HAVE NOT ENTERED YOURSELVES, AND YOU DO NOT LET OTHERS ENTER.

Matt. xxiii. 15. WRETCHED YOU ARE, LEARNED MEN AND PHARISEES, HYPOCRITES! FOR YOU TRAVEL OVER THE EARTH AND THE SEAS, TO MAKE MEN SWEAR TO KEEP YOUR LAW AND OBEY YOUR AUTHORITIES; AND WHEN THEY SWEAR, THEY BECOME CHILDREN OF THE ABYSS, AND TWICE AS BAD AS YOU ARE.

16. WRETCHED YOU ARE, BLIND GUIDES! YOU SAY, WHO SWEARS BY THE TEMPLE, IT IS NOTHING; BUT WHOEVER SWEARS BY THE GOLD IN THE TEMPLE MUST FULFILL.

17. FOOLISH AND BLIND MEN! WHAT IS GREATER, THE GOLD, OR THE TEMPLE WHICH SANCTIFIES THE GOLD?

18. AND WHOEVER WILL SWEAR BY THE ALTAR, IT IS NOTHING: BUT WHOEVER SWEARS BY THE GIFT ON THE ALTAR MUST FULFILL.

19. FOOLISH AND BLIND MEN! WHAT IS GREATER, THE ALTAR OR THE GIFT?

20. HE WHO SWEARS BY THE ALTAR, SWEARS ALSO BY WHAT IS UPON IT.

21. AND WHOEVER SWEARS BY THE TEMPLE, SWEARS BY IT AND BY WHAT LIVES IN IT.

22. AND HE WHO SWEARS BY HEAVEN, SWEARS BY THE THRONE OF GOD, AND BY WHAT IS OVER IT.

23. WOE TO YOU, LEARNED MEN AND PHARISEES, HYPOCRITES! YOU PAY TITHE OF MINT, ANISE, AND CUMMIN, AND DO NOT FULFILL WHAT IS DIFFICULT IN THE LAW, JUSTICE, MERCY, FAITH IN GOD; IT IS THIS THAT YOU OUGHT TO HAVE DONE.

24. BLIND GUIDES, YOU STRAIN A GNAT AND SWALLOW A CAMEL.

25. WOE TO YOU, LEARNED MEN AND PHARISEES, HYPOCRITES! FOR YOU MAKE CLEAN THE GLASSES AND VESSELS FROM THE OUTSIDE, AND WITHIN YOU SWARM WITH PILLAGE AND INJUSTICE.

26. BLIND PHARISEE! CLEANSE FIRST THE INSIDE OF THE VESSEL, AND THE OUTSIDE WILL BE CLEAN.

27. WOE TO YOU, LEARNED MEN AND PHARISEES, HYPOCRITES! FOR YOU ARE LIKE WHITED SEPULCHERS. THE SEPULCHERS LOOK BEAUTIFUL OUTWARDLY, AND WITHIN ARE FULL OF BONES AND OF ALL UNCLEANNESS.

28. EVEN THUS YOU OUTWARDLY APPEAR RIGHTEOUS, BUT WITHIN ARE FULL OF HYPOCRISY AND INIQUITY.

29. WOE TO YOU, LEARNED MEN AND PHARISEES, HYPOCRITES! FOR YOU BUILD THE CHURCHES FOR THE PROPHETS AND PAINT THE COFFINS OF THE MARTYRS,

30. AND SAY, IF WE HAD BEEN IN THE DAYS OF OUR FATHERS, WE WOULD NOT HAVE BEEN PARTAKERS IN THE BLOOD OF THE PROPHETS.

31. THEREFORE YOU WITNESS OF YOURSELVES THAT YOU ARE THE SONS OF THOSE WHO KILLED THE PROPHETS.

32. AND YOU OBSERVE THE FAITH OF YOUR FATHERS.

33. O YOU SERPENTS, GENERATION OF VIPERS, WHERE WILL YOU ESCAPE FROM THE DESTRUCTION OF GEHENNA.

34. BECAUSE, BEHOLD, I SENT TO YOU PROPHETS, WISE AND LEARNED MEN, YOU WILL KILL AND CRUCIFY THEM, AND FLOG THEM IN YOUR ASSEMBLIES, AND DRIVE THEM FROM CITY TO CITY.

35. SO THAT UPON YOU COMES ALL THE RIGHTEOUS BLOOD SHED UPON EARTH FROM RIGHTEOUS ABEL TO ZECHARIAH, WHO WAS KILLED IN THE TEMPLE.

39. FOR I TELL YOU, YOU WILL NOT UNDERSTAND MY TEACHING, TILL YOU SAY, BLESSED IS HE WHO COMES IN THE NAME OF GOD.

Mark iii. 28. FOR YOU KNOW YOURSELVES THAT ALL MISTAKES MAY BE FORGIVEN TO PEOPLE, AND ALL BLASPHEMIES, WHATEVER THEY ARE.

29. BUT IF ONE BLASPHEMES AGAINST THE SPIRIT OF GOD, HE WILL NOT BE FORGIVEN IN THIS LIFE: HE IS SUBJECT TO THE DESTRUCTION OF LIFE.

Matt. xxiii. 37. O JERUSALEM, JERUSALEM, THOU KILLEST THE PROPHETS AND STONEST THOSE WHO ARE SENT TO THEE. HOW OFTEN DID I WISH TO BRING ALL THY CHILDREN TOGETHER, JUST AS A HEN GATHERS HER CHICKENS UNDER HER WING, BUT YOU WOULD NOT!

38. AND SO YOUR HOUSE IS BEING RUINED.

39. FOR I TELL YOU, YOU WILL NOT SEE THE TRUTH, TILL YOU WILL SAY, BLESSED IS HE WHO TEACHES THE COMPREHENSION OF THE LORD.

Matt. xxiv. 1. AND LEAVING THE TEMPLE, JESUS WENT AWAY. THEN HIS DISCIPLES APPROACHED HIM, TO SHOW HIM THE BUILDINGS OF THE TEMPLE.

Mark xiii. 1. PRECIOUS STONES, AND WHAT OFFERINGS!

Matt. xxiv. 2. AND JESUS REPLIED TO THEM, PAY NO ATTENTION TO THESE THINGS. TRULY I TELL YOU, THERE WILL NOT BE LEFT HERE ONE STONE UPON ANOTHER, THAT WILL NOT BE THROWN DOWN.

3. AND WHEN HE SAT DOWN ON THE MOUNT OF OLIVES, THE DISCIPLES CAME TO HIM AND ASKED HIM PRIVATELY, WHEN WILL IT BE? AND WHAT WILL BE THE SIGN THAT THY TEACHING HAS STOPPED, AND THAT THE PRESENT LIFE IS ENDED?

4. AND JESUS ANSWERED THEM, TAKE HEED AND BEWARE THAT YOU MAKE NO MISTAKE.

5. FOR MANY WILL TEACH YOU IN THE NAME OF THE COMPREHENSION AND WILL DECEIVE MANY.

6. YOU WILL HEAR OF WARS AND DISTURBANCES: SEE THAT YOU ARE NOT AFRAID, FOR ALL THESE THINGS WILL BE, BUT THAT IS NOT THE END OF THE OFFENCES.

7. NATION WILL RISE AGAINST NATION, AND KINGDOM AGAINST KINGDOM; AND THERE WILL BE HUNGER AND EARTHQUAKE IN VARIOUS PLACES.

8. ALL THESE ARE ONLY THE TORMENTS OF LABOR.

11. AND MANY FALSE TEACHERS WILL APPEAR, AND THEY WILL DECEIVE MANY.

12. AND FROM THE INCREASE OF THE INIQUITY THE LOVE OF MANY WILL BE DIMINISHED.

14. AND WHEN THE ANNOUNCEMENT OF THE TRUE GOOD SHALL BE BORNE THROUGH THE WHOLE WORLD AS A CONFIRMATION FOR ALL THE NATIONS, THEN THERE WILL BE AN END OF THE OFFENCES.

TOLSTOY'S COMMENTARY

If a man lives for the flesh, he perishes, like all flesh. If he lives in the spirit, he acquires the true life, but the flesh offends him.

Beware of offences. For it is better that one of thy members should perish than that the whole body be lost. It is better to be deprived of a momentary joy than of the true life. The true life is given to us, and we all know it, but the deception of the flesh ensnares us.

One day they brought children to Jesus, that they might be with him. But the disciples drove the children away, saying, What is our teacher to do with the silly children?

Jesus saw that they had no respect for the children and drove them away, and he was grieved at the disciples, and said, You have no reason to drive these children away—they are the best of people, for they all live in the will of God. They are certainly already in the kingdom of God. You must not drive them, but learn from them, for, in order that you may live in the will of God, you must live like children. Children always execute the five rules, which I have given you: children do not scold, do not harbor evil against men, do not commit adultery, do not swear, do not resist abuse, do not litigate, do not know the difference between their own nation and another, and do not wage war. Children execute the five rules, and so they are better than grown people and are in the kingdom of God.

If you will not abandon all the deceptions of the flesh and will not become like children, you will not be in the kingdom of God.

Only he who understands that the children are better than we, because they do not break the law of God, understands my teaching. Only he who understands my teaching understands God.

We cannot despise the children, for they are better than we, and their souls are pure before God, and are always with God. They are all good. And not one child perishes through the will of God; they all perish through men, who entice them away from the truth.

And so we must guard them, and not entice them away from the Father and from the life of truth. And badly acts the man who entices them away from purity. To entice a child away from what is good, to offend him with anger, adultery, oaths, courts, war, is as bad as hanging a millstone around his neck and throwing him into the water: he will hardly swim out, but will rather be drowned. Even so it is hard for a child to get away from an offence into which a man has led him.

The world is unfortunate only through offences. Offences have always been in the world and always will be, and a man perishes through offences.

And so give everything away, sacrifice everything, if only you can keep out of offences. When a fox falls into a trap, he wrenches off his leg and runs away, and lives. Even so must you do: give everything away, so long as you can get away from an offence. Offences are put up against all five rules, and you must guard yourselves against all of them.

Beware then! Here is the offence against the first rule, Be not angry.

Do not ask how many times thou shalt forgive thy brother; do not imagine that thou must forgive him seven times, and mayest wreak vengeance after that. Forgive, not seven times, but seventy times seven, and then forgive again.

For the kingdom of God may be likened to this: A king was settling his accounts with the proprietors. And they brought to him one who owed him a million dollars. And he could not pay what he owed. And the king would have sold his estate, his wife, his children, and himself; but the proprietor began to beg the king's mercy, and the king had mercy on him, and forgave him his whole debt.

This proprietor went home and saw a peasant who owed him fifty cents. The proprietor took hold of him, began to choke him, and said, Give me what thou owest me. And the peasant fell down at his feet, and said, Have patience with me, and I will give thee all. But the proprietor did not have mercy on him, but put him in prison, to let him stay there until he paid all he owed.

When the peasants saw this, they went to the king, and told him what the proprietor had done. Then the king called the proprietor, and said to him, Thou dog, I forgave thee the whole rental, because thou didst beg me, so thou oughtest to have forgiven thy debtor, because I forgave thee. And the king grew angry and turned the proprietor over to be tormented, till he should pay what he owed.

Even so God the Father will do with you, if you will not forgive with all your heart those who are guilty toward you.

When a man offends thee, remember that he is the son of the same God the Father, and a brother of thine. If he has offended thee, go and admonish him face to face. If he listens to thee, thou art the gainer, for thou wilt have a new brother.

If he does not listen to thee, admonish him, and call two or three with thee to admonish him. If he does not listen to them, tell it to the assembly; and if he does not listen to the assembly, then he will be as a stranger to thee: forgive him, and have nothing to do with him.

Thou knowest that if a quarrel is taken up with a man it is better to make peace with him without letting it come before the courts. Thou knowest this, and dost so, because thou knowest that if it comes to litigating, thou wilt lose more. The same is true of any quarrel: if thou knowest that it is bad and that it will remove thee from God, then get rid of the evil at once and make thy peace, as long as he has not yet left, with whom the evil was started.

You know yourselves that as it is started on earth, so will it be before God; and if you loose it on earth, you will be loosed in heaven.

Again you must understand that if two or three have agreed in everything on earth, they will receive from their Father everything for which they shall ask. For where two or three are united by my teaching, they execute my teaching.

Beware! Here is the offence against the second rule, Do not commit adultery.

One day self-styled pastors went up to Jesus and, tempting him, said, May a man leave his wife?

But he said, Man was created male and female from the beginning—this is a natural law. And so a man leaves his father and mother and cleaves to his wife, and man and wife unite into one. Consequently a man must not break the natural, divine law, and separate what is united. But if according to your law of Moses it is permitted to send away a wife, this is untrue, for according to the natural law it is not so. And I tell you that he who sends away his wife drives into debauch both her and him who takes her up.

And the disciples said to Jesus, If it is necessary to keep the same wife which a man has once taken to himself, and never to abandon her, that is so difficult to do that it is better not to marry at all.

He said to them, You may not marry, but you must understand what it means. If a man wants to live without a wife, he must be pure and not touch a woman. There are such people who have no use for women; but if a man loves women, let him bind himself to one woman, and keep her all the time, and have nothing to do with other women.

Beware! Here is the offence against the third rule, Make no promises to anyone about anything.

Your self-styled pastors travel about everywhere and cause the people to swear that they will be true to the law and the authorities, but they only subvert them in this manner. It is impossible to promise your body for your soul, for in your soul is God, and men cannot make promises to men for God.

And one day the tax collectors went up to Peter, and asked him, Well, does your teacher not pay his taxes?

Peter said, No, he does not pay, and he went and told Jesus that he had been stopped and told that all must pay their taxes.

Then Jesus said to him, A king does not receive tribute from his sons, and they have to pay no one but the king. Even so it is with us. If we are the children of God, we are under no obligations to anyone but God, and are free before everybody. We are not bound by anything, but if they ask thee to pay taxes, give them to them, not because thou art obliged to, but because thou shouldst not resist evil. And if they want to take thy cloak away, give them also thy coat.

At another time the pastors came together with the officers of the king, and went to Jesus, trying to catch him with words.

They said to him, Thou teachest in truth, so tell us whether we are obliged to pay tribute to Cæsar or not.

Jesus saw that they wanted to condemn him for opposing himself to the oath to Cæsar. He said to them, Show me that with which you pay tribute to Cæsar.

They showed him a coin. He looked at the coin, and said, What is this? Whose image and superscription?

They said, Cæsar's.

And then he said, If so, give to Cæsar what is Cæsar's, but what is God's, your soul, do not give to anyone but God. Money, property, your labor, everything give to him who will ask you for it, but do not give your soul to anyone but God. And make no promises to anyone, for you are all in the power of God, and your soul give to God alone.

Beware! Here is the offence against the fourth rule, Do not judge, and be not judged.

One day the disciples of Jesus entered a village and begged permission to stay overnight. They were not allowed to remain. Then the disciples came to Jesus to complain about it, and they said, May they be killed by lightning.

Jesus said, Still you do not understand of what spirit you are. I do not teach how to destroy, but how to save people.

One day they brought a woman to Jesus, and said, This woman was caught in adultery. According to the law she ought to be stoned to death. What dost thou say?

Jesus made no reply, and waited for them to change their minds. But they stuck to him, and asked how he would judge this woman.

Then he said, He who among you is without error, let him cast the first stone at her. Then the Pharisees looked at each other, and their conscience smote them, and those who were in front stepped behind the others, and all went away.

And Jesus was left alone with the woman. He looked up, and saw that no one was there. Well, he said, Has no one accused thee?

She said, No one.

And he said, Neither can I accuse thee. Go, and err no more.

No matter how clear, how bad the case is, there is no one who can accuse a man of it. Only he who has not erred can accuse, but accusing is already an error.

Once there came a man to Jesus, who said, Order my brother to give me my inheritance.

Jesus said to him, No one has made me a judge over you, and I do not sit in judgment over anyone. Neither can you judge anyone.

Beware! Here is the offence against the fifth rule, There are no different nations; all men are brothers, children of one God the Father.

A lawyer wanted to offend Jesus, and said, What must I do, in order that I may obtain the true life?

Jesus said, Thou knowest what: love God thy Father and thy brother, no matter what his nationality may be.

And the lawyer said, This would be well, if there were no different nations, for how can I love the enemy of my nation?

And Jesus said, There was a Jew who fell into misfortune: he was beaten, robbed, and thrown out into the road. A Jewish priest passed by, and he looked at the beaten man, and went his way. Then a Levite passed by, and he looked at him, and went his way. Then a man of a hostile nation, a Samaritan, passed by. This Samaritan saw the Jew, and he did not consider this, that the Jews had no regard for the Samaritans, but had pity on the Jew who was beaten. He washed his wounds and dressed them, and took him on his ass to an inn, and paid the innkeeper for him, and promised to come later and pay more. Even so treat foreigners, those who have no regard for you and destroy you, and then you will get the true life.

Jesus said, The world loves its own, but despises the things that are of God, and so the people of the world, priests and scribes, will torment those who keep the law of God. And I, too, am going to Jerusalem, and shall be tormented and killed, but my spirit cannot be killed—it will live.

When Peter heard that Jesus would be tormented and killed in Jerusalem, he was grieved. He took the hand of Jesus, and said to him, If this is so, thou hadst better not go to Jerusalem.

Then Jesus said to Peter, Do not say this. What thou sayest is an offence. If thou art afraid for me, lest I should be tortured and killed, that means that thou art thinking of human, and not of divine things.

He who lives by the light of the understanding can have no evil befall him, for he is always in the light; evil can befall only him who comes out of the light of truth into the darkness of the offence of the flesh.

And calling up the people with his disciples, Jesus said, He who wants to live according to my teaching must renounce his carnal life; let him be ready for all carnal sufferings, for he who is afraid for his carnal life will lose his true life, and he who neglects the carnal life will save the true life.

And again he told them that when they kill a man who lives by the understanding, the understanding does not die, but will live.

And they did not understand it. And the Sadducees came up, and he explained to all what was meant by the true life in God, and by the rising from the dead. The Sadducees said that after the carnal death there was no life. They said, How can all rise from the dead? If they did rise, they could not all live together. For example, we had seven brothers. The first married and died. His wife married the second brother, and he died; and she married the third, and so on, until the seventh. How are the seven brothers going to live with one wife, if they shall all rise from the dead?

Jesus said to them, You purposely mix up matters, and do not understand what the life after death is. In this life people marry and are given in marriage; but those who will earn the life after the carnal death will not marry and be given in marriage, for they do not have to continue life in others: they themselves do not die, for they unite with God, having become his children.

In your Scripture it says that God said, I am the God of Abraham and Jacob. And this God said when Abraham and Jacob were already dead for men. Consequently, those who are dead for men are alive for God. If there is a God, and God does not die, those who are with God are always alive. The reëstablisbment from death is the life in God. The life in God is the fulfillment of the will of God in the carnal life. He who fulfills the will of God unites with God. For God there is no time, and so, in uniting with God, man passes out of time, consequently out of death.

When the pastors heard this, they did not know what to invent in order that they might silence him, and so united with the laymen and began together with them to tempt him.

And one of them, a pastor, said, Teacher, which, in thy opinion, is the chief commandment in the whole law?

The pastors thought that Jesus would get caught in the answer according to the law.

But Jesus said, the chief commandment is to love the Lord our God, in whose power we are, with all our soul, and another follows from it: to love our neighbor, for in him is the same Lord. In these two commandments is contained everything which is written in all your books.

And Jesus said again, Who, in your opinion, is Christ? Is he anybody's son?

They said that according to them Christ was the son of David.

Then he said to them, How, then, does David call Christ his master? Christ is not the son of David, nor the son of anybody else, except the same Lord our master, whom we know within us, as our life. Christ is that understanding which is in us.

After that they asked him no more questions.

And Jesus said, Beware of the leaven of the self-styled pastors. Beware also of the leaven of the worldly, and of the leaven of the royalty. But, above everything, beware of the leaven of the self-styled pastors, for that is deception.

When the people understood whereof he spoke, he said, Above all, beware of the teaching of the learned self-styled pastors. Beware of them, for they have usurped the place of the prophet who announces the will of God to the people. They have usurped the power to preach the will of God to the people. They preach words, and do nothing. And it turns out that they say, Do this and that, but there is nothing to do, for they do not do anything good, and only talk. And they talk of what cannot be done, but themselves do nothing. All they care to do is to retain the right of their teachership, and so they try to distinguish themselves: they dress up and want to receive honors. And so know that no one ought to call himself teacher and pastor. None but our Lord is a teacher and pastor. But the pastors call themselves teachers, and thus prevent our entering the kingdom of God, and themselves do not enter into it.

These pastors think that it is possible to lead to God by external ceremonies, by oaths, and, like blind people, they do not see that the external things do not mean anything, that everything is in the soul of man. They do those external things which are easiest, but what is necessary and difficult—love, compassion, truth—they leave out. All they care for is to be externally in the law, and to lead others externally to the law. And so they are like whited sepulchres, apparently clean without, but an abomination within. Externally they honor the holy martyrs, but in fact they are those who torture and kill the saints.

They have always been the enemies of what is good. From them proceeds all the evil in the world, for they conceal the good, and instead of the good bring forward the bad. Most of all fear these self-styled pastors. For you know yourselves that any mistake may be corrected; but if men err in what is good, such a mistake can no longer be corrected. And it is this that the self-styled pastors do.

And Jesus said, I wanted here, in Jerusalem, to unite all men into one understanding of the true good, but the teachers of this city know only how to kill the teachers of good. And so they remain the same godless people that they were, and do not know God, unless, loving, they accept the understanding of God.

And Jesus went away from the temple. Then his disciples said to him, What about this temple of God with all its adornments, which men have brought as an offering for God?

And Jesus said, Truly I tell you that this whole temple with all its adornments will be destroyed, and nothing will be left. There is one temple of God—the hearts of men, when they love one another.

And they asked him, When will this temple be?

And Jesus said to them, It will not be soon. Many people will deceive through my teaching, and there will be wars and disturbances on account of it. And there will be great lawlessness, and little love. But when the true teaching shall be disseminated among all men, there will be an end to evil and to offences.

CHAPTER TEN

THE STRUGGLE AGAINST THE OFFENCES

Luke xi. 53. AS HE SAID THIS, THE LEARNED PASTORS BEGAN TO URGE JESUS VEHEMENTLY, AND TO ASK HIM ABOUT MANY THINGS.

54. THEY DEVISED TO CATCH HIM IN HIS OWN WORDS, SO AS TO ACCUSE HIM.

John xi. 47. AND THE CHIEF PRIESTS, THE PASTORS, MET IN COUNCIL, AND SAID, WHAT SHALL WE DO? THE MAN GIVES SUCH PROOFS OF HIS TRUTH.

48. IF WE LEAVE HIM ALONE, ALL WILL BELIEVE IN HIM. AND THE ROMANS WILL COME AND WILL TAKE OUR CITY AND OUR NATION.

Luke xix. 48. AND THEY COULD NOT FIND WHAT THEY MIGHT DO, FOR THE PEOPLE CLUNG TO HIM AND LISTENED TO HIM.

47. AND THE CHIEF PRIESTS AND THE LEARNED SOUGHT TO DESTROY HIM.

John xi. 49. ONE OF THEM, NAMED CAIAPHAS, WHO WAS THE HIGH PRIEST THAT YEAR, SAID TO THEM, YOU DO NOT UNDERSTAND ANYTHING.

50. YOU DO NOT CONSIDER THAT IT IS NECESSARY THAT ONE MAN SHOULD DIE FOR THE PEOPLE, AND THAT THE WHOLE PEOPLE MAY NOT PERISH.

51. THIS HE DID NOT SPEAK OF HIMSELF, BUT, BEING THE HIGH PRIEST THAT YEAR, HE PROPHESIED THAT JESUS WOULD DIE FOR THE NATION,

52. AND NOT ONLY FOR THE NATION, BUT IN ORDER THAT THE CHILDREN OF GOD BE UNITED INTO ONE.

53. FROM THAT DAY ON THEY DECIDED TO KILL HIM.

54. BUT JESUS DID NOT APPEAR BEFORE THE JEWS; HE WENT AWAY NEARER TO THE DESERT, INTO THE CITY OF EPHRAIM, AND THERE REMAINED WITH HIS DISCIPLES.

55. THE JEWISH PASSOVER WAS NEAR, AND MANY PEOPLE CAME FROM THE VILLAGES TO JERUSALEM FOR THE PASSOVER, TO PREPARE THEMSELVES FOR THE FEAST.

56. AND THEY SOUGHT JESUS AND SPOKE AMONG THEMSELVES IN THE TEMPLE, WHAT DO YOU THINK? WILL HE COME TO THE FEAST?

57. AND THE CHIEF PRIESTS GAVE A COMMAND, THAT IF ANY MAN KNEW WHERE HE WAS, HE SHOULD ANNOUNCE IT, THAT THEY MIGHT VANQUISH HIM.

John xii. 1. SIX DAYS BEFORE THE PASSOVER, JESUS WENT TO BETHANY.

John xi. 8. AND HIS DISCIPLES SAID TO HIM, TEACHER, THE CHIEF PRIESTS WANT TO STONE THEE; AND THOU GOEST THERE AGAIN.

9. AND JESUS ANSWERED THEM, IN THE DAY THERE ARE TWELVE HOURS. IF A MAN WALKS IN THE DAY, HE DOES NOT STUMBLE, BECAUSE HE SEES THE LIGHT OF THE WORLD.

10. ONLY HE WHO WALKS AT NIGHT STUMBLES, BECAUSE THERE IS NO LIGHT IN HIM.

John xii. 2. AND THEY MADE HIM A SUPPER, AND MARTHA SERVED HIM.

3. THEN MARY, HER SISTER, TOOK A POUND OF PURE, COSTLY, PERFUMED OIL, AND ANOINTED THE FEET OF JESUS, AND WIPED THEM WITH HER HAIR. AND THE HOUSE WAS FILLED WITH THE ODOR OF THE OIL.

4. THEN SAID JUDAS ISCARIOT, ONE OF HIS DISCIPLES, WHO BETRAYED HIM,

5. THIS OIL COULD BE SOLD FOR THREE HUNDRED PENCE, AND GIVEN TO THE POOR.

6. HE DID NOT SAY THIS BECAUSE HE CARED FOR THE POOR, BUT BECAUSE HE WAS A THIEF AND CARRIED THE BAG.

7. AND JESUS SAID, LET HER ALONE: SHE DID THIS FOR THE DAY OF MY BURIAL.

8. YOU WILL ALWAYS HAVE THE POOR, BUT I WILL NOT ALWAYS BE WITH YOU.

12. ON THE NEXT DAY, THE WHOLE PEOPLE THAT CAME TO THE FEAST HEARD THAT JESUS WAS COMING TO JERUSALEM.

13. AND THEY TOOK BRANCHES, AND CAME OUT TO MEET HIM, AND CRIED, BLESSED IS HE WHO COMES IN THE NAME OF GOD, THE KING OF ISRAEL.

14. AND JESUS FOUND A YOUNG ASS, AND SAT UPON IT.

Mark xi. 11. AND JESUS ENTERED JERUSALEM.

Matt. xxi. 10. AND WHEN HE ENTERED, ALL THE CITY AROSE, AND ASKED, WHO IS THIS?

11. THE PEOPLE SAID, THIS IS JESUS, THE PROPHET OF NAZARETH OF GALILEE.

12. AND JESUS ENTERED THE TEMPLE, AND DROVE OUT ALL THOSE WHO SOLD AND BOUGHT.

John xii. 19. THE PASTORS SAID AMONG THEMSELVES, SEE THERE, WHAT ELSE WILL IT BE? THE WHOLE WORLD IS FOLLOWING HIM.

Mark xi. 18. AND THEY CONSIDERED HOW THEY MIGHT DESTROY HIM, FOR THEY WERE AFRAID OF HIM, LEST THE PEOPLE SHOULD BE CARRIED AWAY BY HIS TEACHING.

John xii. 20. AND THERE WERE SOME GREEKS AMONG THOSE WHO CAME TO THE FEAST.

21. THESE WENT UP TO PHILIP, AND SAID, SIR, WE WANT TO SEE JESUS.

22. PHILIP WENT, AND TOLD ANDREW; AND ANDREW AND PHILIP TOLD JESUS.

23. AND JESUS REPLIED TO THEM, THE HOUR HAS COME, WHEN THE SON OF MAN WILL BE RECOGNIZED.

24. YOU KNOW YOURSELVES THAT, IF A KERNEL OF WHEAT FALLS INTO THE GROUND AND DOES NOT DIE, IT REMAINS ALONE; BUT IF IT DIES, IT BRINGS FORTH MUCH FRUIT.

25. HE WHO IS AFRAID FOR HIS LIFE WILL LOSE IT; AND HE WHO DOES NOT SPARE HIS LIFE IN THIS WORLD, WILL KEEP IT IN THE TRUE LIFE.

26. IF ANY MAN SERVES ME, LET HIM FOLLOW ME. WHERE I AM, THERE IS MY SERVANT. HE WHO SERVES ME WILL BE HONORED BY MY FATHER.

27. NOW MY LIFE IS BEING DECIDED, AND WHAT SHALL I SAY? FATHER, SAVE ME FROM THIS HOUR.

28. FATHER, SHOW THYSELF.

31. NOW IS THE SENTENCE PRONOUNCED ON THE WORLD; NOW WILL HE WHO RULES THE WORLD BE CAST OUT.

32. AND IF I SHALL BE LIFTED UP ABOVE THE EARTH, I WILL DRAW ALL TOWARD ME.

34. AND THE PEOPLE ANSWERED HIM, WE KNOW FROM THE LAW THAT THE LORD DOES NEVER CHANGE; HOW, THEN, DOST THOU SAY THAT THE SON OF MAN MUST BE LIFTED UP? WHO IS THIS SON OF MAN?

35. AND JESUS SAID TO THEM, YET A LITTLE WHILE IS THE LIGHT IN YOU. LIVE SINCE THERE IS LIGHT, LEST DARKNESS COME UPON YOU. HE WHO WALKS IN DARKNESS DOES NOT KNOW WHITHER HE GOES.

36. WHILE YOU HAVE THE LIGHT, BELIEVE IN THE LIGHT, THAT YOU MAY BE THE CHILDREN OF THE LIGHT.

44. JESUS SPOKE IN A LOUD VOICE, HE WHO BELIEVES IN MY TEACHING BELIEVES NOT ME, BUT HIM WHO SENT ME.

45. AND HE WHO UNDERSTANDS ME, UNDERSTANDS HIM WHO SENT ME.

46. MY TEACHING IS THE LIGHT, WHICH HAS COME INTO THE WORLD THAT WHOEVER BELIEVES IN ME SHOULD NOT BE LEFT IN DARKNESS.

47. AND IF ANY MAN HEARS MY WORDS AND DOES NOT KEEP THEM, I DO NOT CONDEMN HIM, FOR I AM NOT CALLED TO CONDEMN MEN, BUT TO SAVE THEM.

48. HE WHO DOES NOT UNITE WITH ME AND DOES NOT RECEIVE MY WORDS, HAS WITHIN HIM THE ONE WHO WILL CONDEMN HIM. THE UNDERSTANDING OF THE LORD, WHICH I HAVE EXPRESSED, CONDEMNS HIM TILL THE LAST DAY.

49. FOR I HAVE NOT SPOKEN OF MYSELF; BUT THE FATHER WHO SENT ME GAVE ME A COMMANDMENT, WHAT I SHOULD SAY AND SPEAK.

50. AND I KNOW THAT THIS COMMANDMENT IS THE ETERNAL LIFE. WHAT I SPEAK, I SPEAK, AS THE FATHER HAS TOLD ME: SO I SPEAK.

36. THUS SPOKE JESUS, AND HE WENT AWAY, AND HID HIMSELF FROM THEM.

42. BUT MANY OF THE RULERS BELIEVED IN HIS TEACHING, BUT DID NOT CONFESS IT ON ACCOUNT OF THE PASTORS, LEST THEY BE PUT OUT OF THE CHURCH,

43. FOR THEY VALUED MORE THE JUDGMENT OF MEN, THAN OF GOD.

THE ASSEMBLING AND PLOTTING OF THE HIGH PRIESTS

Matt. xxvi. 3. THEN ASSEMBLED THE CHIEF PRIESTS, THE SCRIBES, THE ELDERS OF THE PEOPLE IN THE YARD OF THE HIGH PRIEST CAIAPHAS,

4. AND CONSULTED HOW THEY MIGHT TAKE JESUS BY CUNNING, AND KILL HIM.

5. AND THEY SAID, ONLY NOT ON THE FEAST DAY, OR ELSE THERE WILL BE A NOISE AMONG THE PEOPLE.

14. THEN ONE OF THE TWELVE, JUDAS ISCARIOT, WENT TO THE CHIEF PRIESTS,

15. AND SAID, WHAT WILL YOU GIVE ME, IF I DELIVER HIM TO YOU? THEY PROMISED HIM THIRTY COINS.

16. AND FROM THAT TIME HE SOUGHT AN OPPORTUNITY TO BETRAY HIM.

17. ON THE FIRST DAY OF THE FEAST OF THE UNLEAVENED BREAD THE DISCIPLES CAME TO JESUS, AND SAID TO HIM, WHERE DOST THOU ORDER US TO PREPARE THE PASSOVER?

18. AND HE SAID, GO INTO THE CITY TO SOME MAN, AND SAY TO HIM, I HAVE LITTLE TIME: I WANT TO TAKE THE PASSOVER WITH THEE.

19. AND THE DISCIPLES DID AS JESUS HAD ORDERED THEM, AND THEY PREPARED THEM, AND THEY PREPARED THE PASSOVER.

20. IN THE EVENING HE SAT DOWN WITH HIS TWELVE DISCIPLES.

John xiii. 1. BEFORE THE FEAST OF THE PASSOVER JESUS KNEW THAT HIS HOUR HAD COME, THAT HE SHOULD DEPART FROM THIS WORLD TO HIS FATHER; AS HE LOVED HIS OWN, HE DID GOOD TO THEM UNTIL THE END.

2. AND DURING THE SUPPER, WHEN THE EVIL INTENTION TO BETRAY HIM HAD ALREADY ENTERED THE SOUL OF JUDAS ISCARIOT.

Matt. xxvi. 21. AND JESUS SAID, YOU KNOW YOURSELVES THAT ONE OF YOU, WHO ARE EATING WITH ME, WILL BETRAY ME.

22. AND THE DISCIPLES WERE VERY MUCH GRIEVED, AND BEGAN ONE AFTER ANOTHER TO SAY TO HIM, IS IT I, SIR?

23. AND HE ANSWERED THEM, HE WHO EATS WITH ME OUT OF THE SAME DISH, WILL BETRAY ME.

24. THE SON OF MAN GOES AWAY, AS IT IS WRITTEN,

John xiii. 18. HE WHO HAS EATEN WITH ME, WILL BETRAY ME.

Matt. xxvi. 24. BUT WOE TO THE MAN BY WHOM THE SON OF MAN IS BETRAYED! IT WOULD BE BETTER FOR HIM IF HE WERE NOT BORN.

26. AND WHEN THEY ATE, JESUS TOOK THE BREAD, AND, HAVING PRAYED TO GOD, BROKE IT, AND GAVE IT TO THE DISCIPLES, SAYING, TAKE, EAT; THIS IS MY BODY.

27. AND HE TOOK THE GLASS, AND, HAVING PRAYED TO GOD, HE HANDED IT TO THEM, AND SAID, DRINK ALL FROM IT.

28. THIS MY BLOOD OF MY NEW TESTAMENT, WHICH IS SHED FOR MANY FOR THE SAKE OF FORGIVENESS.

29. YOU KNOW YOURSELVES THAT I WILL NOT HENCEFORTH DRINK OF THE JUICE OF THE GRAPE, UNTIL THE DAY WHEN I DRINK ANOTHER WINE IN THE KINGDOM OF MY FATHER.

John xiii. 3. KNOWING THAT THE FATHER HAD GIVEN EVERYTHING INTO THE POWER OF THE SON, AND THAT HE CAME FROM GOD, AND WENT TO GOD,

4. JESUS ROSE FROM SUPPER, PUT OFF HIS GARMENTS, AND, TAKING A TOWEL, GIRDED HIMSELF WITH IT.

5. THEN HE POURED WATER INTO A PITCHER, AND BEGAN TO WASH THE DISCIPLES' FEET, AND TO WIPE THEM WITH THE TOWEL, WITH WHICH HE WAS GIRDED.

6. THEN HE WENT UP TO PETER, AND PETER SAID TO HIM, ART THOU REALLY GOING TO WASH MY FEET?

7. AND JESUS ANSWERED, THOU THINKEST STRANGE WHAT I AM DOING; BUT THOU WILT UNDERSTAND IT.

10. AND JESUS SAID TO HIM, YOU ARE CLEAN, BUT NOT ALL.

11. FOR HE KNEW HIM WHO WOULD BETRAY HIM; THEREFORE HE SAID, NOT ALL ARE CLEAN.

12. BUT WHEN JESUS HAD WASHED THEIR FEET, AND HAD DRESSED HIMSELF, HE SAT DOWN, AND SAID TO THEM AGAIN, DO YOU KNOW WHAT I HAVE DONE TO YOU?

13. YOU CALL ME TEACHER AND MASTER; AND YOU SAY WELL, FOR I AM INDEED A TEACHER.

14. IF, THEN, I, YOUR TEACHER AND MASTER, HAVE WASHED YOUR FEET, YOU ALSO OUGHT TO WASH ONE ANOTHER'S FEET.

15. I HAVE GIVEN YOU AN EXAMPLE, THAT YOU SHOULD DO AS I HAVE DONE.

16. YOU KNOW YOURSELVES, THE SLAVE IS NOT GREATER THAN HIS MASTER, NOR IS THE MESSENGER GREATER THAN THE COMMANDER.

20. YOU KNOW YOURSELVES THAT HE WHO WILL LISTEN TO WHAT I COMMAND, WILL LISTEN TO MY TEACHING, AND TO HIM WHO COMMANDS ME.

17. IF YOU KNOW THIS, YOU ARE HAPPY IF YOU DO IT.

18. I DO NOT SPEAK OF ALL, FOR I KNOW THOSE WHOM I HAVE CHOSEN. THUS THE SCRIPTURE IS FULFILLED, HE WHO ATE BREAD WITH ME HAS DESTROYED ME.

19. NOW I TELL IT TO YOU, THAT, WHEN IT COMES TO PASS, YOU MAY BELIEVE THAT MY TEACHING IS.

21. WHEN JESUS HAD SAID THIS, HE WAS TROUBLED IN SPIRIT, AND AFFIRMED, AND SAID, YOU KNOW YOURSELVES THAT ONE OF YOU WILL BETRAY ME TO BE KILLED.

22. AND AGAIN THE DISCIPLES BEGAN TO LOOK AT EACH OTHER, UNABLE TO GUESS WHOM HE MEANT.

23. ONE OF THE DISCIPLES, WHOM JESUS LOVED, WAS SITTING NEAR HIM.

24. SIMON PETER BECKONED TO HIM, THAT HE SHOULD ASK WHO IT WOULD BE.

25. HE MOVED UP TO JESUS, AND SAID TO HIM, WHO IS IT?

26. AND JESUS REPLIED, IT IS HE TO WHOM I SHALL GIVE A SOP, WHEN I HAVE DIPPED IT. AND WHEN HE HAD THE SOP, HE GAVE IT TO JUDAS ISCARIOT.

27. AND JESUS SAID TO HIM, WHATEVER THOU WILT DO, DO IT QUICKLY.

28. AND NOBODY GUESSED WHEREFORE HE SAID THIS.

29. THEY THOUGHT, BECAUSE JUDAS HAD THE MONEY, THAT HE COMMANDED HIM TO BUY WHAT WAS NEEDED FOR THE FEAST; AND OTHERS THOUGHT THAT HE COMMANDED HIM TO GIVE TO THE POOR.

30. AND HAVING RECEIVED THE SOP, JUDAS WENT OUT AT ONCE; AND IT WAS NIGHT.

31. WHEN JUDAS WAS GONE, JESUS SAID, NOW THE SON OF MAN IS RECOGNIZED, AND THAT GOD IS IN HIM.

32. AND GOD RECOGNIZES HIM IN HIMSELF, AND RECOGNIZES HIM DIRECTLY.

33. CHILDREN, ONLY A SHORT WHILE LONGER SHALL I BE WITH YOU; YOU WILL DISCUSS MY TEACHING, AND AS I TOLD THE JEWS, YOU WILL NOT GO WHITHER I LEAD; AND SO I TELL YOU NOW.

34. I GIVE YOU A NEW COMMANDMENT. LOVE ONE ANOTHER; AS I HAVE LOVED YOU, SO LOVE ONE ANOTHER.

35. BY THIS ALL MEN WILL TELL WHO ARE MY DISCIPLES, IF YOU LOVE ONE ANOTHER.

Matt. xxvi. 30. AND HAVING SUNG PSALMS, THEY WENT INTO THE MOUNT OF OLIVES.

31. THEN JESUS SAID, THIS NIGHT ALL OF YOU WILL BE ENTICED AWAY FROM ME, AS IT SAYS IN THE SCRIPTURE, I WILL KILL THE SHEPHERD, AND THE SHEEP WILL BE SCATTERED.

33. AND PETER REPLIED TO HIM, THOUGH ALL WILL BE ENTICED AWAY FROM THEE, I WILL NOT FALL INTO THE DECEPTION.

Luke xxii. 33. I AM READY TO GO WITH THEE, SIR, BOTH INTO PRISON, AND TO DEATH.

Matt. xxvi. 34. AND JESUS SAID TO HIM, I TELL THEE, PETER, BEFORE THE COCK CROWS, THOU WILT DENY ME THRICE.

35. AND PETER SAID TO HIM, THOUGH I SHOULD DIE WITH THEE, I WILL NOT DENY THEE. THE SAME SAID ALL THE DISCIPLES.

Luke xxii. 35. AND JESUS SAID TO THEM, WHEN I SENT YOU WITHOUT PURSE, AND BAG, AND SHOES, DID YOU LACK ANYTHING? THEY SAID, NOTHING.

36. AND HE SAID TO THEM, BUT NOW, HE WHO HAS PURSE, LET HIM TAKE ALSO HIS BAG; AND HE WHO HAS NOT, LET HIM SELL HIS GARMENT, AND BUY A KNIFE.

37. FOR I TELL YOU, THE SCRIPTURE WILL BE ACCOMPLISHED IN ME, AND HE WAS REGARDED AS A TRANSGRESSOR; AND AN END HAS COME ALL ABOUT ME.

38. THEY SAID, SIR, HERE ARE TWO KNIVES. AND HE SAID, VERY WELL.

John xviii. 1. WHEN JESUS HAD SAID THIS, HE WENT WITH HIS DISCIPLES OVER THE RIVER CEDRON, AND CAME TO THE VILLAGE OF GETHSEMANE, WHERE THERE WAS A GARDEN, WHICH HE ENTERED, AND HIS DISCIPLES.

Matt. xxvi. 36. AND JESUS SAID TO THE DISCIPLES, WAIT HERE, WHILE I PRAY.

37. AND TURNING TO PETER AND THE TWO SONS OF ZEBEDEE, HE BEGAN TO PINE AND BE SORROWFUL.

38. AND HE SAID TO THEM, MY SOUL IS HEAVY, EVEN UNTO DEATH; STAY HERE, AND DO NOT BE SORROWFUL AS I AM.

39. AND HE WENT AWAY A LITTLE DISTANCE, AND FELL INTO HIS FACE, AND PRAYED, SAYING, FATHER, EVERYTHING IS POSSIBLE TO THEE: LET THIS CUP PASS BY ME, NOT AS I WANT IT, BUT AS THOU WANTEST IT.

40. AND HE WENT UP TO HIS DISCIPLES, AND SAW THAT THEY WERE DISPIRITED. AND HE SAID TO PETER, COULD YOU NOT KEEP ONE HOUR FROM BEING DISPIRITED, AS I DO?

41. TAKE COURAGE AND PRAY, SO THAT YOU MAY NOT ENTER INTO TEMPTATION. THE SPIRIT IS STRONG, BUT THE FLESH IS WEAK.

42. AND HE WENT AWAY A SECOND TIME, AND BEGAN TO PRAY, SAYING, O MY FATHER, IF THIS CUP CANNOT PASS BY ME, UNLESS I DRINK IT, THY WILL BE DONE.

43. AND HE CAME AND FOUND THEM AGAIN DISPIRITED, FOR THEIR EYES WERE DIMMED.

44. AND HE LEFT THEM, AND WENT AWAY AGAIN, AND PRAYED FOR A THIRD TIME, SAYING THE SAME WORDS.

45. THEN HE RETURNED TO HIS DISCIPLES, AND SAID, SLEEP NOW, AND TAKE YOUR REST: THE HOUR IS NEAR WHEN THE SON OF MAN IS GIVEN OVER INTO THE HANDS OF WORDLY MEN.

TOLSTOY'S COMMENTARY

After this the pastors, the chief priests, sought with all their might to get at Jesus, so as to destroy him. They assembled in a council, and began to judge; they said, We must in some way put a stop to this man; he proves his teaching in such a way that, if we let him alone, all will believe in him and will abandon our faith. Even now half of the nation is believing in him. And if people will believe in his teaching, that man, the son of God, is not obliged to obey anyone, that all nations are brothers, that there is nothing special in our Jewish nation which distinguishes us from the other nations, then the Romans will completely vanquish us, and will destroy all our laws and our whole faith, and there will no longer be any Jewish kingdom.

And the pastors, chief priests, and learned men took counsel for a long time, and could not devise what to do with him, for they could not make up their mind to kill him.

Then one of them, Caiaphas, who was the high priest during that year, devised this: he said to them, We must remember that it is advantageous to kill one man, in order that a whole nation should not perish. If we let this man alone, the nation will perish—this I prophesy to you—and so it is best to kill Jesus. Even if the people will not perish, they will scatter and will abandon the one faith, if we do not kill Jesus, and so it is best to kill him.

When Caiaphas said this, all decided that there was nothing to reflect on, and that they ought by all means to kill Jesus. They would have taken him at once and killed him, but he hid from them in the wilderness.

But at this time the feast of the Passover was at hand, and many people used to gather in Jerusalem for the feast. And the pastors, the bishops, counted on this, that Jesus would come to the feast with the people. And so they announced to the people that if they saw Jesus they should bring him to them.

And, indeed, six days before the Passover Jesus said to his disciples, Let us go to Jerusalem; and he went with them.

And the disciples said to him, Do not go to Jerusalem.

And Jesus said to them, I cannot fear anything, for I am living in the light of the understanding. And as any man can walk in daytime, and not at night, that he may not stumble, so any man may live by the understanding, that he may not doubt or fear anything. Only he doubts and fears who lives in the flesh; but for him who lives in the understanding there is nothing doubtful or terrible.

And Jesus came into the village of Bethany, near Jerusalem, to Martha and Mary, and the sisters prepared a supper for him. And as they sat at supper, Martha served them, and Mary took a pound of costly, precious, perfumed oil, and rubbed Jesus' feet with it, and wiped them with her hair. And when the odor of the oil spread in the room, Judas Iscariot said, In vain has Mary wasted this oil. It would have been better if the oil had been sold for three hundred pieces, and the money given to the poor.

But Jesus said, You will have the poor with you, but me you will soon not have. She did well, for she has prepared my body for burial.

In the morning Jesus went to Jerusalem. There was a great multitude there for the feast. And when they saw Jesus they surrounded him, and broke off branches from the trees, and threw their garments on the road, and cried, Here he is, our true king, who has taught us about the true God. Jesus sat down on a young ass and rode on it, and the people ran before him, crying. And thus Jesus rode into Jerusalem. And when he entered into the city, all the people were agitated, and asked, Who is he? And those who knew him said, It is Jesus, the prophet out of Nazareth of Galilee.

And Jesus entered the temple, and again drove all the buyers and sellers out of it.

And the pastors, the bishops, saw all this, and said among themselves, See what this man is doing. All the people are following after him.

But they did not dare to take him away from the people, for they saw that the people clung to him, and they devised how they might take him by stratagem.

In the meantime Jesus was in the temple, teaching the people. Among the people there were not only Jews, but also pagan Greeks. The Greeks had heard of Jesus' teaching and understood that he was not teaching the truth to the Jews alone, but to all men, and so they wanted also to be his disciples; and they told so Philip, and Philip told Andrew. The disciples were afraid of bringing Jesus and the Greeks together. They were afraid that the people would be angered, because he did not recognize any difference between the Jews and the other nations, and so they could not for a long time make up their mind to tell Jesus so.

When Jesus heard that the Greeks wished to be his disciples, he said, I know that the people hate me, because I make no difference between Jews and Gentiles and because I recognize myself to be just like a Gentile; but now the time has come when the teaching of the son of God has to be recognized among all men. And if I perish for this, I must tell the truth. A grain of wheat brings fruit only when it perishes. He who is afraid for his carnal life loses the true life, and he who despises the carnal life will make this temporal life true, not in time, but in God.

And turning to Andrew and to Philip, he said, He who wants to serve my teaching, let him do the same as I. And he who does as I do, will be loved by my Father. Now it will be decided whether my life will be carnal or spiritual. Now, when that toward which I have been walking has come, shall I say, Father, free me from what I ought to do? I cannot say this, for I have been walking toward it. And so I say, Father, manifest thyself in me.

And, turning to the whole people, Jesus said, In the present alone is the power of the spirit over the flesh; in the present alone is the power of flesh vanquished. And if I lift myself up above the earthly life, I shall draw all toward me.

And they said to him, According to the law, we have heard, Christ is something especial and definite, which remains always the same, so how dost thou say that thou, Christ, wilt be lifted up as the son of man? What is meant by lifting up the son of man?

To this Jesus replied, To lift up the son of man means to live by that light of the understanding which is within you; to lift up the son of man above what is of earth means to believe in the light of the understanding, while there is this light, in order to be the son of the understanding. He who believes in my teaching does not believe me, but the spirit which gave life to the world. He who understands my teaching, understands the spirit which gave the light to the world. My teaching is the same light of life which has brought men out of the darkness. And if one hears my words and does not fulfill them, I do not condemn him, for my teaching does not condemn, but saves. He who does not receive my words is not condemned by my teaching, but by the understanding which is in him. It is this which condemns him. For I did not speak my own words, but what my Father, the spirit which is within me, has inspired. What I speak is what the spirit of the understanding has told me. And what I teach is the true life.

Having said this, Jesus went away, and again concealed himself from the chief priests.

Among those who heard the words of Jesus there were many powerful and rich men who believed in his teaching, but were afraid to acknowledge it before the chief priests, for not one chief priest acknowledged that he believed, for they judged in human, and not in divine fashion.

After Jesus had again concealed himself, the chief priests and the elders again met in the yard of Caiaphas and Passover how they might secretly seize Jesus and kill him. They were afraid to seize him publicly. And there came to counsel with them one of the first twelve disciples of Jesus, Judas Iscariot, who said, If you wish to seize Jesus secretly, so that the people may not see him, I shall find a time when there will be but a few with him, and will show you where he is, and then you can seize him. What will you give me for it? They promised him thirty dollars. He agreed to it, and after that tried to find a time to take the chief priests to Jesus, in order that they might seize him.

In the meantime Jesus concealed himself from the people, and only his disciples were with him. When the first day of the feast of the unleavened bread came around, the disciples said to Jesus, Where shall we celebrate the Passover?

Jesus said to them, Go to some person in the village and tell him that we have no time to prepare the Passover and ask him to allow us to take the Passover with him.

And so the disciples did. They asked the permission of a man in the village, and he let them in.

And they came and seated themselves at the table. Jesus knew that Judas Iscariot had already promised to betray him to death; but he did not accuse Judas, or avenge himself on him; as he had taught love to his disciples all his life, so he rebuked Judas in love even now.

When all twelve of them were seated at the table, he looked at them, and said, Among you sits he who has betrayed me. Yes, he who drinks and eats with me will cause my destruction.

And so they did not find out of whom he was speaking, and began to eat the supper. As they were getting ready to eat, Jesus took a loaf, broke it into twelve parts, and gave each disciple a piece, saying, Take it, and eat it. He who is betraying me, if he eats this piece, will be eating my body.

Then he filled a cup with wine, and offered it to his disciples, saying, Drink you all out of this cup.

And when they had all drunk, he said, He who is betraying me has drunk my blood. I will shed my blood that men may know my testament— to forgive others their sins. For I shall soon die and shall no longer be with you in the world, and shall unite with you only in God.

After this Jesus arose from the table, girded himself with a towel, took a pitcher of water, and began to wash the feet of all the disciples.

When he came up to Peter, Peter said, Art thou really going to wash my feet?

Jesus said to him, Thou thinkest it strange that I am washing thy feet; but thou wilt soon learn why I do it. I do it because not all of you are clean, and because among you is my betrayer, whose feet I want to wash also.

And when Jesus had washed the feet of all of them, he sat down again, and said, Do you understand why I did it? I did it, that you may do likewise to one another. If I, your teacher, do it, you certainly must serve all and not hate anyone. If you know this you are blessed. I am not speaking of all of you, for one of you, whose feet I have washed, and who has eaten bread with me, will betray me. Having said this, Jesus was troubled in spirit and continued that one of them would betray him. And again did the disciples look at each other, but they did not know of whom he was speaking. One of the disciples was sitting near Jesus, and Simon Peter beckoned to him to ask him who the traitor was. He asked him.

Jesus said, I will dip a piece, and he to whom I will give it is the traitor. And he gave it to Judas Iscariot, saying to him, Whatever thou wilt do, do it at once; and Judas understood that he ought to go away, and when he took the piece, he went away at once, and it was not possible to run after him, for it was night.

When Judas was gone, Jesus said, Now it is clear to you what the son of man is; now it is clear to you that God is in him, that he can forgive his enemies and do good. Children! I have but a little while to stay with you. Do not philosophize on my teaching, as I have told the pastors, but do what I do. I give you one new commandment: As I have loved you and Judas the traitor, so you love one another. Only thus shall you be distinguished: be distinguished from other men in that you love one another.

After this they went to the Mount of Olives. On the way Jesus said to them, Now the time comes when that will happen which is said in the Scripture, that the shepherd will be killed, and the sheep will scatter. And this will happen this very night: I shall be taken, and all of you will abandon me and run away.

And in reply Peter said to him, Even if all are frightened and run away, I will not deny thee. I am prepared to die with thee.

And Jesus said to him, But I tell thee that this very night, before cock-crow, when they will take me, thou wilt deny me, not once, but thrice.

But Peter said that he would not, and the disciples said the same.

And then, seeing that the disciples were with him, Jesus was tempted. He felt sorry, because they wanted to kill him without cause. And he said to his disciples, At first neither you nor I needed anything. You went without a scrip and without reserve footgear, and I commanded you to do so; but now, since they regard me as an outlaw, it can no longer be so, and you must provide yourselves with everything and with knives, lest you be destroyed without cause.

And the disciples said, We have two knives.

And Jesus said, Very well.

And they went beyond the river Cedron, where there was a garden, and entered that garden.

And Jesus said to his disciples, I am weakened, and I must pray. Be with me.

And he seated Peter and the sons of Zebedee near him, and began to groan and feel sorrowful, because he had fallen into an offence and wanted to struggle against evil.

He said, I am pained and grieved. Help me, rise in spirit together with me.

And he knelt down and prayed.

He said, My Father, spirit, thou art free: strengthen me that the offence of struggle may leave me; that everything may be as thou wishest, and not as I wish it, and that I may unite with thy will.

The disciples were not praying and were dispirited, and Jesus rebuked them, and said, Pray; be strong in spirit, lest you fall into the temptation of timidity or struggle. There is strength in the soul, but the body is powerless.

And he began to pray a second time, saying, Father, spirit, let everything be as thou wilt.

And again the disciples did not pray with him, but were dejected. And he prayed for a third time in the same way, and then, when he was strengthened in spirit, he said to his disciples, Now I shall soon be given into the hands of worldly men.

CHAPTER ELEVEN

The Farewell Discourse

John xiii. 36. AND PETER SAID TO JESUS, WHITHER DOST THOU GO? JESUS REPLIED, THOU WILT NOT BE ABLE TO FOLLOW ME, WHITHER I AM GOING NOW: BUT THOU WILT FOLLOW ME LATER.

37. AND PETER SAID, WHY DOST THOU THINK THAT I CANNOT FOLLOW THEE NOW, WHITHER THOU GUEST GOEST? I WILL LAY DOWN MY LIFE FOR THEE.

38. AND JESUS SAID, THOU SAYEST THAT THOU WILT LAY DOWN THY LIFE FOR ME, BUT BEFORE THE COCK WILL CROW, THOU WILT DENY ME THRICE.

John xiv. 1. DO NOT TROUBLE YOURSELVES IN YOUR HEARTS. BELIEVE IN GOD, AND BELIEVE IN MY TEACHING.

2. IN GOD'S WORLD ARE MANY DIFFERENT HOMES. IF IT WERE NOT SO, I SHOULD HAVE TOLD YOU, I GO TO PREPARE A PLACE FOR YOU.

3. AND IF I GO AND PREPARE A PLACE, I WILL COME BACK, AND WILL TAKE YOU WITH ME, THAT WHERE I AM, YOU MAY BE ALSO.

4. AND WHITHER I GO, YOU KNOW, AND YOU KNOW THE WAY.

5. AND THOMAS SAID TO HIM, SIR, WE DO NOT KNOW WHITHER THOU GOEST; HOW CAN WE KNOW THE WAY?

6. JESUS SAID TO HIM, I AM THE WAY, THE TRUTH, AND THE LIFE; NO ONE COMES TO THE FATHER, BUT BY ME.

7. IF YOU KNOW ME, YOU KNOW ALSO THE FATHER, AND NOW YOU WILL KNOW HIM AND SEE HIM.

8. PHILIP SAID TO HIM, SIR, SHOW US THE FATHER, AND WE SHALL BE CONTENTED.

9. AND JESUS SAID TO THEM, I HAVE BEEN SO A LONG TIME WITH YOU AND YET THOU DOST NOT UNDERSTAND MY TEACHING, PHILIP. HE WHO SEES ME SEES THE FATHER; HOW, THEN, DOST THOU SAY, SHOW ME THE FATHER?

10. DOST THOU NOT COMPREHEND THAT I AM IN THE FATHER, AND THE FATHER IN ME? THE WORDS WHICH I SPEAK I DO NOT SPEAK OF MYSELF: THE FATHER WHO IS IN ME DOES THE WORKS.

11. BELIEVE IN MY TEACHING THAT I AM IN THE FATHER, AND THE FATHER IN ME; OR ELSE, BY MY WORKS WILL YOU COMPREHEND MY TEACHING.

12. YOU KNOW YOURSELVES THAT HE WHO BELIEVES IN MY TEACHING WILL LIVE AS WELL AS I DO, AND EVEN BETTER, FOR I GO TO MY FATHER.

13. THAT IS, EVERYTHING WHICH YOU WILL WISH FOR ACCORDING TO MY TEACHING, MY TEACHING WILL GIVE YOU, SO THAT IN THE SON WILL THE FATHER HE KNOWN.

14. AND IF YOU ASK FOR ANYTHING IN MY NAME, MY TEACHING WILL GIVE IT TO YOU.

15. IF YOU LOVE MY TEACHING, KEEP MY COMMANDMENTS.

16. AND MY TEACHING WILL BE AN INTERCESSOR BEFORE THE FATHER, AND HE WILL GIVE YOU ANOTHER PROTECTOR, WHO WILL BE WITH YOU IN LIFE,

17. THE SPIRIT OF TRUTH, WHICH THE WORLD CANNOT RECEIVE, BECAUSE IT DOES NOT SEE IT AND DOES NOT KNOW IT. BUT YOU KNOW IT, BECAUSE IT IS WITH YOU AND IN YOU.

18. I WILL NOT LEAVE YOU AS ORPHANS: I STAY WITH YOU.

19. A LITTLE WHILE LONGER, AND THE WORLD WILL NOT SEE ME; FOR MY TEACHING LIVES, AND YOU WILL LIVE.

20. AT THAT TIME YOU WILL KNOW THAT I AM IN THE FATHER, AND YOU IN ME, AND I IN YOU.

21. HE WHO KEEPS MY COMMANDMENTS AND OBSERVES THEM, LOVES MY TEACHING. AND HE WHO LOVES MY TEACHING, IS LOVED BY THE FATHER, AND I LOVE HIM, AND WILL APPEAR TO HIM.

22. AND JUDAS, NOT ISCARIOT, SAID TO HIM, WHY, SIR, DOST THOU WANT TO MANIFEST THYSELF TO US, AND NOT TO ALL.

23. AND JESUS REPLIED TO HIM, HE WHO LOVES ME, FULFILLS MY TEACH-ING; AND MY FATHER WILL LOVE HIM, AND WE SHALL COME TO HIM, AND SHALL ABIDE IN HIM.

24. HE WHO DOES NOT LOVE ME, DOES NOT KEEP MY WORDS, MY WORD IS NOT MINE, BUT THE FATHERS WHO HAS SENT ME.

25. THIS DID I SAY, WHILE I WAS STILL WITH YOU.

26. AND THE INTERCESSOR, WHOM THE FATHER WILL SEND IN MY PLACE, WILL TEACH YOU EVERYTHING, AND WILL REMIND YOU OF EVERYTHING WHICH I TOLD YOU.

27. I WILL LEAVE YOU RESTFULNESS; NOT SUCH AS MEN GIVE DO I GIVE YOU: LET NOT YOUR HEART BE TROUBLED, AND DO NOT LOSE COURAGE.

28. YOU HAVE HEARD ME SAY TO YOU: I GO AWAY, AND COME TO YOU. IF YOU LOVE ME, YOU MUST REJOICE ME, YOU MUST REJOICE, FOR I TOLD YOU, I UNITE WITH THE FATHER, FOR THE FATHER IS GREATER THAN I.

29. I HAVE TOLD YOU BEFORE IT HAS HAPPENED, AND I TELL YOU NOW, THAT YOU MAY BELIEVE WHEN IT HAPPENS.

30. I HAVE BUT A LITTLE WHILE TO TALK WITH YOU, FOR THE POWER OF THIS WORLD IS NEAR; BUT IN ME IT HAS NOTHING.

31. BUT THAT THE WORLD MAY KNOW THAT I LOVE MY FATHER; AND AS THE FATHER COMMANDED ME SO I DO. AWAKEN, AND LET US GO OUT OF THIS WORLD.

John xv. 1. THE SON OF GOD IS THE TRUE ROOT, AND MY FATHER IS MY GARDENER.

2. EVERY SHOOT IN THE SON OF GOD, WHICH BEARS NO FRUIT, IS CUT OFF: AND EVERY SHOOT WHICH BEARS FRUIT IS CLEANED, THAT IT MAY BRING FORTH MORE FRUIT.

3. YOU ARE ALREADY CLEANED BY THE TEACHING WHICH I HAVE TAUGHT YOU.

4. ABIDE IN THE SON OF GOD, AND THE SON OF GOD IN YOU. AND AS A SHOOT CANNOT BRING FORTH FRUIT OF ITSELF, IF IT IS NOT ON THE ROOT, SO ARE YOU, IF YOU DO NOT ABIDE IN THE COMPREHENSION.

5. THE SON OF GOD IS THE ROOT, YOU ARE THE SHOOTS. HE WHO IS IN THE SON OF GOD, AND THE SON OF GOD IN HIM, BEARS MUCH FRUIT, SO THAT NOTHING CAN BE DONE WITHOUT THE COMPREHENSION.

6. HE WHO DOES NOT LIVE IN THE SON OF GOD IS CUT OFF LIKE A SHOOT, AND WITHERS; AND MEN GATHER THEM INTO HEAPS, AND BURN THEM.

7. IF YOU WILL ABIDE IN THE SON OF GOD, AND MY WORDS WILL ABIDE IN YOU, ASK WHATEVER YOU WISH, AND IT WILL DONE TO YOU.

8. FOR IN THIS IS THE DECISION OF MY FATHER, THAT YOU SHOULD BEAR FRUIT; THEN YOU ARE MY DISCIPLES.

9. AS THE FATHER HAS LOVED ME, SO I LOVED YOU. LIVE BY MY LOVE.

10. IF YOU KEEP MY COMMANDMENTS, THEN YOU LIVE BY MY LOVE. EVEN AS I HAVE KEPT MY FATHER'S COMMANDMENTS, AND SO LIVE BY HIS LOVE.

11. THIS I HAVE TOLD YOU THAT MY BLESSEDNESS MIGHT REMAIN IN YOU, AND THAT YOUR BLESSEDNESS MIGHT BE FULFILLED.

12. MY COMMANDMENT IS THAT YOU SHOULD LOVE ONE ANOTHER, AS I HAVE LOVED YOU.

13. THE TRUEST LOVE IS TO LAY DOWN ONE'S LIFE FOR THOSE WHO ONE LOVES.

14. YOU ARE LOVED BY ME, IF YOU DO WHAT I COMMAND YOU.

15. I DO NOT REGARD YOU AS SLAVES, FOR THE SLAVE DOES NOT KNOW WHAT THE MASTER DOES; BUT I REGARD YOU AS MY FRIENDS, FOR I HAVE EXPLAINED TO YOU EVERYTHING WHICH I KNOW FROM MY FATHER.

16. YOU (THE SHOOTS) HAVE NOT CHOSEN ME, BUT I HAVE SENT YOU FORTH AND PLACED YOU IN SUCH A WAY THAT YOU CAN GROW AND BRING FORTH FRUIT, AND THAT YOUR FRUIT MAY REMAIN, THAT WHATEVER YOU MAY ASK OF THE FATHER, LIVING BY ME, HE MAY GIVE YOU.

17. THIS I COMMAND YOU, LOVE ONE ANOTHER.

18. IF THE WORLD HATES YOU, KNOW THAT IT HATED ME BEFORE, AND STILL HATES ME.

19. IF YOU WERE OF THE WORLD, THE WORLD WOULD LOVE ITS OWN; BUT YOU ARE NOT OF THE WORLD, FOR I HAVE SEPARATED YOU FROM THE WORLD, AND SO THE WHOLE WORLD HATES YOU.

20. REMEMBER THE WORDS WHICH I TOLD YOU, THE SLAVE IS NOT GREATER THAN HIS MASTER. IF THEY HAVE PERSECUTED ME, THEY WILL PERSECUTE YOU ALSO. IF YOU KEEP MY WORD, THEY WILL KEEP YOURS ALSO.

21. BUT ALL THIS THEY WILL DO TO YOU BECAUSE OF MY TEACHING, FOR THEY DO NOT KNOW HIM THAT SENT ME.

22. IF I HAD NOT COME AND SPOKEN TO THEM, THEIR ERRORS WOULD NOT BE APPARENT TO THEM; BUT NOW THEY HAVE NO EXCUSE FOR THEIR ERROR.

23. HE WHO DOES NOT LOVE MY TEACHING DOES NOT LOVE MY FATHER ALSO.

24. IF I HAD NOT LIVED AMONG THEM AS NO OTHER MAN LIVED BEFORE, THEIR ERROR WOULD NOT BE APPARENT TO THEM; BUT NOW THEY HAVE SEEN, AND HATE BOTH ME AND THE FATHER.

25. THUS THE WORLD HAS COME TO PASS, THAT IS WRITTEN IN THEIR LAW, THEY HATED ME WITHOUT A CAUSE.

26. WHEN THE INTERCESSOR COMES, WHOM I WILL SEND YOU FROM THE FATHER, THE SPIRIT OF TRUTH, HE WILL CONFIRM MY TEACHING.

27. AND YOU WILL CONFIRM THAT YOU ARE BY PRINCIPLE WITH ME.

John xvi. 1. THIS I HAVE TOLD YOU THAT YOU SHOULD NOT BE OFFENDED.

2. THEY WILL PUT YOU OUT OF THE ASSEMBLIES. NAY, THE TIME COMES WHEN EVERY ONE WHO KILLS YOU WILL THINK THAT HE IS WORKING FOR GOD.

3. ALL THIS WILL THEY DO, BECAUSE THEY HAVE KNOWN NEITHER THE FATHER, NOR MY TEACHING.

4. BUT I TOLD YOU THIS, THAT WHEN THE TIME COMES YOU MAY REMEMBER WHAT I TOLD YOU. IN THE BEGINNING I DID NOT TELL YOU THIS, BECAUSE I WAS WITH YOU.

5. NOW I GO AWAY TO HIM WHO SENT ME, AND NOBODY ASKS ME, WHITHER DOST THOU GO?

6. BUT WHEN I HAVE SAID THESE THINGS TO YOU SORROW HAS FILLED YOUR HEART.

7. BUT I TELL YOU TRUTH: IT IS USEFUL FOR YOU THAT I GO AWAY. IF I DO NOT GO AWAY, THE INTERCESSOR WILL NOT COME TO YOU: BUT IF I GO AWAY, HE WILL COME TO YOU.

8. HE WILL COME, AND THERE WILL APPEAR FOR MEN ERROR, AND RIGHTEOUSNESS, AND CONDEMNATION.

9. THE ERROR IS, THAT THEY HAVE NOT BELIEVED IN MY TEACHING.

10. THE RIGHTEOUSNESS IS IN THIS, THAT I LEAD TO THE FATHER, AND THAT THEY HAVE NOT UNDERSTOOD MY TEACHING.

11. AND THE JUDGEMENT IS IN THIS, THAT DEATH IS CONDEMNED.

12. THOUGH I SHOULD LIKE TO TELL YOU MANY THINGS NOW, YOU CANNOT UNDERSTAND THEM.

13. BUT WHEN THE SPIRIT OF TRUTH COMES, HE WILL SHOW YOU THE PATH TO ALL TRUTH; FOR HE WILL NOT SPEAK OF HIMSELF; BUT WHATEVER HE WILL HEAR, THAT HE WILL SPEAK, AND ANNOUNCE TO YOU IN ANY CASE.

14. HE WILL JUDGE JUST AS I DO, FOR HE WILL TAKE OF MINE, AND WILL ANNOUNCE IT.

15. ALL THAT THE FATHER IS, IS MINE; THEREFORE I SAID THAT HE WILL TAKE OF MINE, AND WILL ANNOUNCE IT TO YOU.

16. AT TIMES YOU WILL NOT SEE ME FOR A LITTLE WHILE; AND AGAIN YOU WILL SEE ME FOR A LITTLE WHILE BECAUSE I SHALL GO TO THE FATHER.

17. AND THE DISCIPLES SAID AMONG THEMSELVES, WHAT DOES THIS MEAN WHICH HE SAYS, YOU WILL NOT SEE ME, BECAUSE I GO TO THE FATHER?

18. AND THEY SAID, WHAT DOES THIS MEAN, IT WILL BE, IT WILL NOT BE? WE DO NOT KNOW WHAT HE SAYS.

19. JESUS SAW THAT THEY WANTED TO ASK HIM, AND SAID TO THEM, YOU ARE TRYING TO MAKE OUT WHAT I SAID, YOU WILL NOT SEE ME, AND AGAIN YOU WILL SEE ME.

20. YOU KNOW YOURSELVES THAT YOU WILL WEEP AND LAMENT, BUT THE WORLD WILL REJOICE; YOU WILL BE SORROWFUL; BUT YOUR SORROW WILL BE TURNED INTO JOY.

21. A WOMAN WHEN SHE IS IN CHILD LABOR IS SORROWFUL, WHEN HER HOUR HAS COME; BUT AS SOON AS THE CHILD IS BORN, SHE DOES NOT REMEMBER THE PAINS FOR JOY THAT A HUMAN IS BORN INTO THE WORLD.

22. AND SO YOU WILL HAVE SORROW; BUT I WILL HAVE SORROW SEE YOU AGAIN, AND YOUR HEART WILL REJOICE, AND NO MAN WILL TAKE YOUR JOY FROM YOU.

23. AND IN THAT DAY YOU WILL ASK ME NOTHING. YOU KNOW YOURSELVES THAT EVERYTHING WHICH YOU WILL ASK OF THE FATHER FOR THE SPIRIT'S SAKE, WILL BE GIVEN TO YOU.

24. HITHERTO YOU HAVE NOT ASKED ANYTHING FOR THE SAKE OF THE SPIRIT. ASK, AND YOU WILL RECEIVE, SO THAT YOUR JOY WILL BE FULL.

25. I TELL YOU THIS IN AMBIGUOUS WORDS; BUT THE TIME WILL COME WHEN I WILL NOT SPEAK TO YOU IN AMBIGUOUS WORDS, BUT WILL DIRECTLY SPEAK TO YOU ABOUT THE FATHER.

26. ON THAT DAY YOU WILL ASK ACCORDING TO MY TEACHING; AND I DO NOT SAY THAT I WILL ASK MY FATHER FOR YOU.

27. THE FATHER HIMSELF LOVES YOU, BECAUSE YOU HAVE LOVED ME, AND HAVE BELIEVED THAT THE COMPREHENSION IS GOD;

28. THAT I AM THE COMPREHENSION, COME INTO THE WORLD FROM THE FATHER, AND THAT I AGAIN LEAVE THE WORLD, AND GO TO THE FATHER.

29. THE DISCIPLES SAID TO HIM, NOW THOU SPEAKEST PLAINLY, AND NOT AMBIGUOUSLY.

30. NOW WE UNDERSTAND THAT THOU KNOWEST EVERYTHING, AND THAT WE NEED NOT ASK THEE ANY MORE. NOW WE BELIEVE THAT THE COMPREHENSION IS FROM GOD.

31. JESUS REPLIED TO THEM, NOW YOU BELIEVE:

32. BUT THE TIME WILL COME AND IS COMING, WHEN YOU WILL BE SCATTERED, EVERY MAN IN HIS OWN, AND WILL LEAVE ME ALONE. BUT I AM NOT ALONE, FOR THE FATHER IS WITH ME.

33. ALL THIS I HAVE TOLD YOU THAT YOU MIGHT HAVE RESTFULNESS THROUGH MY TEACHING. IN THE WORLD THERE WILL BE CALAMITIES; BUT HAVE NO FEAR: I HAVE OVERCOME THE WORLD.

John xvii. 1. HAVING SAID THIS, JESUS LIFTED UP HIS EYES TO HEAVEN, AND SAID, FATHER, THE HOUR HAS COME, RECOGNIZE THY SON, THAT THY SON MAY RECOGNIZE THEE:

2. AS THOU HAST GIVEN HIM POWER OVER ALL FLESH, THAT HE MAY GIVE THE TRUE LIFE TO EVERYTHING THOU HAST GIVEN HIM.

3. THE TRUE LIFE CONSISTS IN KNOWING THE ONLY TRUE GOD, AND JESUS CHRIST, WHOM THOU HAST SENT.

4. I HAVE RECOGNIZED THEE ON EARTH; I HAVE THOU THE WORK WHICH THOU COMMANDEDST ME TO DO.

5. AND NOW, O FATHER, RECOGNIZE ME AS IF I WAS BEFORE THE WORLD WAS.

6. I HAVE SHOWED THY PURPOSE TO THE MEN OUT OF THE WORLD, WHOM THOU GAVEST ME. THEY WERE THINE, BUT THOU GAVEST THEM TO ME; AND THEY HAVE KEPT THY PRECEPTS.

7. NOW THEY HAVE LEARNED THAT ALL THINGS WHICH THOU HAST TAUGHT ME ARE FROM THEE.

8. WHAT THOU HAST TAUGHT ME, I HAVE TAUGHT THEM. AND THEY HAVE UNDERSTOOD AND KNOW WELL THAT I COME FROM THEE, AND HAVE BELIEVED THAT THOU HAST SENT ME.

9. I PRAY THEE FOR THEM: NOT FOR THOSE THE WORLD BUT FOR THOSE WHOM THOU HAST GIVEN ME, FOR THEY ARE THINE.

10. AND EVERYTHING OF MINE IS THINE, AND THINE IS MINE, AND THOU HAST RECOGNIZED MY TEACHING IN THEM.

11. FOR THEY ARE IN THE WORLD, AND I GO TO THEE. HOLY FATHER, KEEP THEM IN THEE, THOSE THAT THOU GAVEST ME, THAT THEY MAY BE ONE WITH US.

12. WHEN I WAS WITH THEM IN THE WORLD, I KEPT THEM IN THEE. I KEPT THOSE WHOM THOU GAVEST ME, AND NONE OF THEM PERISHED, EXCEPT THE SON OF PERDITION, AS IT IS SAID IN THE SCRIPTURE.

13. NOW I GO TO THEE; AND I SPEAK THIS IN THE WORLD, THAT THEY MAY HAVE MY JOY, THAT IT MAY FULFILLED IN THEM.

14. I HAVE TAUGHT THEM THE COMPREHENSION OF THEE, AND THE WORLD HATES THEM, BECAUSE THEY ARE NOT OF THE WORLD, EVEN AS I AM NOT OF THE WORLD.

15. I DO NOT ASK THEE TO TAKE THEM OUT OF THE WORLD OF THE FLESH, BUT TO KEEP THEM FROM THE EVIL.

16. THEY ARE NOT OF THE WORLD OF FLESH, EVEN AS I AM NOT OF THE WORLD OF FLESH.

17. HOLY FATHER, KEEP THEM IN TRUTH. THY COMPREHENSION IS TRUTH.

18. AS THOU HAST SENT ME INTO THE WORLD, EVEN SO I SEND THEM INTO THE WORLD.

19. AND FOR THEM I PURIFY MYSELF, THAT THEY ALSO MAYBE PURIFIED IN THE TRUTH.

20. I DO NOT PRAY FOR THEM ALONE, BUT FOR THOSE ALSO WHO BELIEVE IN ME ACCORDING TO THEIR COMPREHENSION,

21. THAT THEY ALL MAY BE ONE; EVEN AS THOU, O FATHER, ART IN ME, AND I IN THEE, THAT THEY ALL MAY BE ONE IN US: THAT THE WORLD MAY BELIEVE THAT THOU HAST SENT ME.

22. AND I HAVE TAUGHT THEM THE RECOGNITION WHICH THOU HAST TAUGHT ME, THAT THEY MAY BE ONE, EVEN AS WE ARE ONE:

23. I IN THEM, AND THOU IN ME, THAT WE MAY BE UNITED IN ONE, AND THAT THE WORLD MAY KNOW THAT THOU HAST SENT ME, AND LOVEST ME.

24. FATHER, I WISH THAT THOSE WHOM THOU HAST GIVEN ME SHOULD BE WITH ME WHERE I AM, THAT THEY MAY KNOW THAT THOU HAST SENT ME, FOR THOU LOVEDST ME BEFORE THE BEGINNING OF THE WORLD.

25. O RIGHTEOUS FATHER, THE WORLD DID NOT KNOW THEE; BUT I HAVE KNOWN THEE, AND THESE HAVE KNOWN THAT THOU HAST SENT ME.

26. AND I HAVE EXPLAINED THEE TO THEM, AND AM EXPLAINING THEE, THAT THE LOVE WITH WHICH THOU LOVEST ME MAY BE IN THEM, AND I IN THEM.

TOLSTOY'S COMMENTARY

The personal life is a deception of the flesh. The true life is the life which is common to all men.

When Jesus, feeling himself prepared for death, went out, in order to deliver himself, Peter stopped him and asked him whither he was going. Jesus replied, I go whither thou canst not follow me. I am prepared for death, but thou art not yet prepared for it. Peter said, Nay, I am even now prepared to give my life for thee. Jesus replied, A man can make no promises. And he said to all the disciples, I know that death awaits me, but I believe in the life of the Father, and so am not afraid of it. Let not my death agitate you, but believe in the true God and in the Father of life, and then my death will not appear terrible to you. If I am united with the Father of life, I cannot be deprived of life. It is true, I do not tell you what and when and where my life after death will be, but I point out to you the way to the true life. My teaching does not say what kind of a life it is going to be, but it reveals the only true way of life. It consists in this, that we should unite with the Father, for the Father is the principle of life. My teaching is this, that we should live in the will of the Father and do his will for the life and good of all men. Your teacher after me will be your recognition of the truth.

By keeping my teaching, you will always feel that you have the truth, that the Father is in you and you are in the Father. And by recognizing the Father of life in you, you will experience that peace which nothing will take away from you. And so, if you know the truth and live in it, neither my death, nor yours can trouble you. Men imagine themselves as separate beings, each with his own will of life, but that is only a deception. The only true life is the one which recognizes the will of the

Father as the principle of life. My teaching reveals this unity of life and represents life not as separate shoots, but as one tree, on which all the shoots grow. Only he lives who lives in the will of the Father, as a shoot on a tree; but he who wants to live by his own will, like a shoot broken off, dies. If you will live in the will of the Father, you will have everything you wish, for life is given to man for the good. The Father has given me life for the good, and I have taught you to live for the good. If you will fulfill my commandments you will be blessed. The commandment which expresses my whole teaching is only this, that we should love one another. But love consists in sacrificing our carnal life for another. There is no other definition of love. By keeping my commandment of love, you will not fulfill it as slaves, who do their master's will without understanding it, but you will live like free men, even as I, for I have explained to you the meaning of life which flows from the recognition of the Father of life. You have accepted my teaching, not because you have chosen it by chance, but because it is the only true one, and the one with which alone men are free.

The teaching of the world consists in doing evil to men; but my teaching consists in loving one another, and so the world hates you, even as it has hated me.

The world does not understand my teaching, and so it will persecute you and cause you harm, imagining that it thus serves God; so do not marvel at it, and understand that it must be so. The world, which does not understand the true God, must persecute you, and you must affirm the truth. You will be grieved, because they will kill me; but I shall be killed for establishing the truth. Thus my death is necessary in order that truth may be established. My death, when I will not recede from the truth, will confirm you, and you will know wherein the lie is, and wherein the truth, and what comes from the knowledge of the lie and of the truth.

You will understand that the lie is this, that men believe in the carnal life, and do not believe in the life of the spirit; that the truth is in the union with the Father; and that this results in the victory of the spirit over the flesh. When I shall no longer be in the carnal life, my spirit will be with you. But, like all men, you will not always feel in yourselves the power of the spirit. At times you will weaken and lose the power of the spirit: you will fall into temptation; at other times you will awaken to the true life. You will be overcome by the enslavement of the flesh, but that will be only temporary; you will suffer for awhile, and then you will again be regenerated in spirit, even as a woman who suffers in labor and then feels joy, because she has brought a man into the world. The same you will feel when, after the enslavement of the flesh, you will rise in spirit: you will then feel such bliss that there will be nothing for you to wish for.

Know in advance, and know this, in spite of persecutions, and inner struggles, and dejection of spirit, that the spirit is alive in you, and that the one true God is the understanding of the will of the Father, as I have revealed it. And turning to the Father, the spirit, Jesus said, I have done what thou commandedst me: I revealed to people that thou art the beginning of everything, and they understood me; I taught them this, that they all have come from the one principle of endless life, and that, therefore, they are one and, as the Father is in me, and I in the Father, so they are one with me and with the Father. I revealed this to them, that, as thou, loving them, hast sent them into the world, they also must live in the world by love.

And Peter said to Jesus, Whither dost thou go?

Jesus replied, Thou wilt not be able to go whither I am going; but later thou wilt go thither thyself.

And Peter said, Why dost thou think that I am not able to follow thee; I will give my life for thee.

And Jesus said, Thou sayest that thou wilt give thy life for me, but thou wilt deny me thrice before cockcrow.

And Jesus said to his disciples, Let not your spirit be troubled and lose courage, but believe in the true God of life and in my teaching. The life of the Father is not only the one which is on earth; there is also another life. If there were only the life which is here, I should have told you that, when I die, I shall go to the bosom of Abraham and prepare there a place for you, and will come and take you, and we will be in bliss together in the bosom of Abraham. But I show you only the way to life.

Thomas said, But we do not know whither thou goest, and so we cannot know the path. We must know what will be there after death.

Jesus said, I cannot show you what will be there; my teaching is the way, the truth, and life, and it is impossible to unite with the Father of life, except through my teaching. If you will fulfill my teaching, you will know the Father.

Philip said, But who is thy Father?

And Jesus said, The Father is that which gives life. I do the will of the Father, and so thou canst understand from my life wherein the will of the Father is. I live through the Father, and the Father lives in me, and everything I do and say, I do by the will of the Father. This is my teaching, that I am in the Father, and the Father in me. If you do not understand the teaching itself, you see me and my works, and so you can understand what the Father is. And you know that he who will follow my teaching can do the same as I do, and even more, for I shall die, and he will still live. He who will live according to my teaching will have everything he wishes, for then the son will be the same as the Father.

Whatever you may wish according to my teaching you will have; but you must love my teaching for that. My teaching will give you an intercessor and comforter in my place. This comforter will be the recognition of the truth, which the men of the world do not understand, but you will know it in yourselves. You will never be alone, if the spirit of my teaching is with you. I shall die, and the men of the world shall not see me; but you will see me, because my teaching lives, and you will live by it. And if my teaching will be in you, you will understand that I am in the Father, and the Father in me. He who will fulfill my teaching will feel the Father in himself, and my spirit will live in him.

And Judas, not Iscariot, said to him, But why cannot all live by the spirit of truth?

And Jesus replied to him, Only him who fulfills my teaching does the Father love, and only in him can my spirit take up his abode. He who does not fulfill my teaching is not loved by my Father, because this teaching is not mine, but the Father's. This is all I can tell you now. But my spirit, the spirit of truth, who will take up his abode in you after me, will reveal everything to you, and you will recall and understand much of what I have told you.

Thus you may always be calm in spirit, not with that worldly peace which men of the world seek, but with the peace of the spirit, with which you will no longer have any fear. And so, if you will fulfill my teaching, you will have no cause for grieving at my death. I will come to you as the spirit of truth, and together with the recognition of the Father will take up my abode in your heart. If you fulfill my teaching, you must rejoice, for instead of me the Father will be in your heart, and that is better for you.

My teaching is the tree of life. The Father is he who tends the tree. He cleans and watches the branches on which there is any fruit, so that they may bring forth more.

Keep my teaching of life, and life will be in you. And as a shoot does not live of itself, but of the tree, even so you must live by my teaching. My teaching is the tree, and you are the shoots. He who lives by my teaching of life brings forth much fruit, and outside of my teaching there is no life. He who does not live by teaching withers and perishes, and the dry branches are cut off and burned. If you live by my teaching and fulfill it, you will have everything you wish: for the will of the Father is that you should live the true life and have what you wish. As the Father has given me the good, even so I give you the good. Keep this good. I live, because my Father loves me, and I love the Father, and you must live by the same love. If you live by it, you will be blessed. My commandment is that you should love one another as I love you. There is no other love than that we should sacrifice our life for the love of others, even as I have done.

Let us love one another, for love is from God. And he who loves was born of God and knows God. And he who does not love does not know God, because God is love. God's love for us has shown itself in this, that he has sent his son, such as he himself is, that we might live through him.

His love for us is seen in this, that it is not we who have come to love God, but God loves us, and we must love one another. God can never be seen. If we love one another, God remains in us, and his love is accomplished in us. We recognize one another only because we remain in him, and he in us, because he has given us his spirit.

Love is accomplished in us, when we are sure and calm on the day of death, for such as God is, we are in this world. Love does not know fear; on the contrary, complete love destroys fear, for fear causes resistance, struggle. And he who fears is not perfect in love.

We love God only because he has loved us first. (Consequently we first know love toward men.) And so, if one says, I love God, but will not love my brother, he lies, for he who does not love his brother, whom he sees, cannot love God, whom he has not seen and cannot see. The commandment is for one who loves God to love his brother.

You are equal to me if you do what I have taught you. I do not regard you as slaves, who are commanded, but as equals, for I have explained to you everything which I know about the Father. You do not choose my teaching of your own will, but because I have pointed out to you this only truth, by which, if you live in it, you will have everything you wish. The whole teaching is in this, that we should love one another. If the world shall hate you, you must not wonder, for it hates my teaching. If you were one with the world, the world would love you; but I have separated you from the world, and for this it will hate you. If they have persecuted me, they will persecute you also.

They will do all this, because they do not know the true God. I have explained to them, but they would not even listen to me. They have not understood the Father. They have seen my life, and my life has shown them their error, and for this they have hated me even more. The spirit of truth, which will come to you, will confirm the same. And you will confirm it. I tell you this in advance, that you may not be deceived, when they shall persecute you. They will make you apostates. All will think that killing you they do something pleasing to God. They cannot help doing it, for they do not understand my teaching, nor the true God. All this I tell you in advance, that you may not marvel, when all this shall happen.

And so I now go to this spirit who has sent me, and now you understand that you must not ask whither I go. Before this you were grieved, because I did not tell you whither, to what place, I go. But I tell you truly that it is good for you that I am going away. If I do not die, the spirit of truth will not appear to you; and if I die, it will take the abode in you. He will take his abode in you, and it will be clear to you wherein the truth is, wherein the solution is. The lie is this, that men do not believe in the life of the spirit. The truth is this, that I am one with the Father. The solution is this, that the power of the carnal life is destroyed.

I could tell you many things more, but it is hard for you to understand them. But when the spirit of truth shall take his abode in you, he will show you the whole truth, for he will not tell you anything new, that which is his, but that which is from God, and he will in all conditions of life show you the way. He will also be of the Father, as I am of the Father, for he will speak the same as I speak. But when I, the spirit of truth, shall be in you, you will not always see me. At times you will hear me, and at other times you will not.

And the disciples said among themselves, What does this mean which he says, At times you will see me, and at other times you will not see me? What does this mean: at times you will, and others you will not? What does he say?

Jesus said to them, Do you not understand what is meant by, At times you will see me, and at other times you will not see me? You know how it always is in the world, that some are sorrowful and lamenting, while others rejoice. You will be sorrowful, and your sorrow will pass into joy. When a woman bears a child, she is sorrowful in her labor, but when the labor is over she does not remember her pain for joy, because a man is born into the world.

Even so you will grieve, and suddenly you will see me: the spirit of truth will enter into you, and your sorrow will be changed into joy. Then you will no longer ask anything of me, for then you will have everything you wish. Then a man will have from his Father everything he wishes in his spirit. Before this you asked nothing for the spirit, but then you will ask what you want for the spirit, and everything will be given you, so that your blessedness will be complete. Now I, a man, cannot explain all this in words; but when I shall live in you as the spirit of truth, I will clearly announce to you about the Father. Then everything you will ask of the Father in the name of the spirit will be given you not by me, but by your Father, for he loves you, because you have received my teaching. You have understood that the understanding proceeds in the world from the Father and returns from the world to the Father.

Then the disciples said to Jesus, Now we understand, and we have nothing more to ask. We believe that thou art from God.

And Jesus said, I told you all this that you may have assurance and rest in my teaching. No matter what calamities may befall you in the world, fear nothing, for my teaching has conquered the world.

After this Jesus lifted up his eyes to heaven, and said, My Father, thou hast given thy son the freedom of life, that he may know the true life. Life is the knowledge of the true God, of the understanding discovered by me. I have revealed you to men on earth. I have done the work which thou commandedst me. I have declared thy essence to men on earth. They were thine even before this: they have understood that everything they have, that their life, is only from thee; and that I have taught them not of me, but that I and they have proceeded from thee. I pray thee for those who recognize thee. They understand that all mine is thine, and thine mine. I am no longer in the world, but return to thee; but they are in the world, and so I pray thee, Father, keep thy understanding in them. I do not ask thee that thou shouldst take them out of the world, but that thou shouldst deliver them from evil. Confirm them in thy truth. Thy understanding is truth.

My Father, I wish that they should be such as I am, that they should understand, even as I do, that the true life began before the beginning of the world; that they should all be one, as thou, O Father, art in me, and I in thee—that they should be one in us; that I in them and thou in me should unite into one; and that men should understand that they were not born of themselves, but that thou, loving, hast sent them into the world, as thou hast sent me.

Righteous Father! The world has not known thee, but I have known thee, and they know thee through me. I have explained to them what thou art. Thou art this, that love, with which thou lovest me, should be in them. Thou hast given them life, consequently thou lovest them. I have taught them to know this and to love thee in such a way that thy love for them should return from them to thee.

CHAPTER TWELVE

THE VICTORY OF THE SPIRIT

Matt. xxvi. 46. AWAKEN, LET US BE GOING: HE WILL BETRAY ME IS ALREADY HERE.

47. AND AS HE HAD SAID THIS, JUDAS, ONE OF THE TWELVE, CAME, AND WITH HIM A GREAT MULTITUDE WITH KNIVES AND CLUBS, SENT BY THE CHIEF PRIESTS AND ELDERS.

48. HE WHO BETRAYED HIM HAD AN UNDERSTANDING WITH THEM BEFORE-HAND; HE SAID TO THEM, HE WHOM I SHALL KISS, AS I GO UP TO HIM, IS HE: SEIZE HIM.

49. AND GOING UP AT ONCE TO JESUS, HE SAID, HAIL, TEACHER, AND KISSED HIM.

50. AND JESUS SAID TO THEM, DIDST THOU COME FOR THIS? THEN THEY CAME UP, AND TOOK HIM.

John xviii. 10. THEN PETER DREW HIS SWORD AND STRUCK THE HIGH PRIEST'S SERVANT, AND CUT OFF HIS EAR.

Luke xxii. 51. AND JESUS SAID, STOP IT.

Matt. xxvi. 52. AND HE SAID TO PETER, PUT UP THE SWORD INTO ITS PLACE, FOR THOSE WHO TAKE UP THE SWORD WILL PERISH BY THE POWER OF THE SWORD.

55. THEN JESUS SAID TO THE PEOPLE, WHY HAVE YOU COME OUT WITH KNIVES AND CLUBS, TO TAKE ME AS A THIEF? I SAT DAILY WITH YOU IN THE TEMPLE, TEACHING YOU, AND YOU DID NOT TAKE ME.

Luke xxii. 53. NOW IS YOUR HOUR AND POWER OF DARKNESS.

Matt. xxvi. 56. THEN ALL THE DISCIPLES RUN AWAY.

John xviii. 12. THEN THE SOLDIERS, AND THE CAPTAIN, AND THE SERVANTS TOOK JESUS, AND BOUND HIM,

13. AND FIRST LED HIM AWAY TO ANNAS, WHO WAS CAIAPHAS FATHER-IN-LAW, FOR CAIAPHAS WAS THE HIGH PRIEST THAT YEAR.

14. CAIAPHAS WAS HE WHO COUNSELED THE JEWS THAT IT WAS USEFUL TO DESTROY ONE MAN FOR THE NATION.

Mark xiv. 53. AND THEY LED JESUS INTO THE HOUSE OF THE HIGH PRIEST, AND ALL THE CHIEF PRIESTS AND ELDERS AND SCRIBES WERE GATHERED THERE.

Matt. xxvi. 58. AND PETER FOLLOWED JESUS AFAR OFF TO THE HIGH PRIEST'S YARD, AND WENT IN, AND SAT DOWN WITH THE HIGH PRIEST'S SERVANTS, TO SEE HOW WOULD IT END.

69. AND A GIRL CAME UP TO PETER, AND SAID, ART THOU WITH JESUS OF GALILEE?

70. AND PETER DENIED BEFORE THEM ALL, AND SAID, I DO NOT KNOW WHAT THOU SAYEST.

71. AND WHEN HE WENT INTO THE VESTIBULE, A WOMAN SAW HIM, AND SAID TO THOSE WHO WERE THERE, THIS MAN WAS WITH JESUS OF NAZARETH.

72. AND AGAIN HE DENIED WITH AN OATH, SAYING THAT HE DID NOT KNOW THIS MAN.

73. A LITTLE WHILE PASSED, AND MEN CAME UP TO PETER, AND SAID, NO DOUBT THOU ART ONE OF THESE, FOR WE CAN TELL THEE BY THY SPEECH.

74. THEN PETER BEGAN TO SWEAR AND CURSE, THAT HE DID NOT KNOW THAT MAN. AND IMMEDIATELY THE COCK CREW.

75. AND PETER THOUGHT OF THE WORDS WHICH JESUS HAD TOLD HIM, BEFORE COCK CREW THOU WILT DENY ME THRICE. AND HE WENT OUT, AND WEPT BITTERLY.

John xviii. 19. THE HIGH PRIEST THEN ASKED JESUS ABOUT HIS DISCIPLES AND HIS TEACHING.

20. JESUS ANSWERED HIM, I HAVE SPOKEN OPENLY TO THE WORLD; I HAVE ALWAYS TAUGHT IN THE ASSEMBLIES, IN THE TEMPLE WHERE ALL GATHER, AND HAVE SAID NOTHING IN SECRET.

21. WHY ASKEST THOU ME? ASK THOSE WHO HAVE HEARD WHAT I HAVE SAID TO THEM; THEY KNOW WHAT I HAVE TOLD THEM.

22. ONE OF THE HIGH PRIEST'S SERVANTS WAS STANDING NEAR BY. WHEN JESUS SAID THIS, HE BOXED JESUS' EARS, AND SAID, DOST THOU ANSWER THE HIGH PRIEST SO?

23. JESUS SAID TO HIM, IF I HAD SPOKEN EVIL, SHOW WHAT IS EVIL; AND IF I HAVE SPOKEN WELL, WHY DOST THOU STRIKE ME?

Matt. xxvi. 59. BUT THE CHIEF PRIEST AND THE WHOLE COUNCIL SOUGHT ACCUSATIONS AGAINST JESUS, SO AS TO PUT HIM TO DEATH.

60. BUT THEY DID NOT FIND ANY, BECAUSE MANY ACCUSED HIM FALSELY, AND THE ACCUSATIONS DID NOT AGREE. THEN THERE CAME TWO FALSE WITNESSES.

61. THEY SAID, WE HAVE HEARD THIS MAN SAY, I WILL DESTROY THIS HANDMADE TEMPLE, AND IN THREE DAYS I WILL BUILD ANOTHER, WHICH IS NOT MADE BY HANDS.

62. THE HIGH PRIEST AROSE, AND SAID TO JESUS, WHY DOST THOU NOT ANSWER TO WHAT THEY SHOW AGAINST THEE?

63. JESUS WAS SILENT AND MADE NO REPLY. AND THE HIGH PRIEST SAID TO HIM AGAIN, IN THE NAME OF THE LIVING GOD I ADJURE THEE, TELL US, ART THOU THE CHRIST, THE SON OF GOD?

64. AND JESUS SAID TO THEM, THAT I AM. AND I WILL TELL YOU ALSO THAT FROM NOW ON YOU WILL ALL UNDERSTAND THE SON OF MAN, WHO IS EQUAL IN POWER WITH GOD IN HEAVEN.

65. THEN THE HIGH PRIEST TORE HIS CLOTHES, AND SAID, THOU ART BLASPHEMING. WHAT NEED HAVE WE OF WITNESSES? YOU HAVE HEARD HIM BLASPHEME.

66. WHAT SHALL YOU DECIDE ABOUT HIM? AND ALL DECIDED THAT HE WAS GUILTY OF DEATH.

67. THEN THEY BEGAN TO SPIT INTO HIS FACE.

Luke xxii. 63. AND THE MEN THAT HELD HIM, STRUCK AND SCRATCHED HIM.

64. AND COVERING HIS EYES, THEY STRUCK HIM IN THE FACE, SAYING, NOW GUESS WHO HAS STRUCK THEE.

65. AND MANY OTHER CURSES DID THEY PRONOUNCE AGAINST HIM.

Matt. xxvii. 1. WHEN THE MORNING CAME, ALL THE ELDERS OF THE PEOPLE, THE CHIEF PRIEST, AND THE LEARNED TOOK COUNSEL AGAINST JESUS TO PUT TO DEATH.

2. AND HAVING BOUND HIM, THEY TOOK HIM TO PONTIUS PILATE THE GOVERNOR.

John xviii. 28. AND THEY LED JESUS FROM CAIAPHAS TO THE COURT; BUT THEY THEMSELVES DID NOT ENTER THE COURT, LEST THEY SHOULD BE DEFILED AND COULD NOT EAT THE PASSOVER.

29. PILATE CAME OUT TO THEM, AND SAID, OF WHAT DO YOU ACCUSE THIS MAN?

30. AND THEY SAID TO HIM IN REPLY, IF HE WERE NOT A MALEFACTOR, AND HAD NOT DONE ANY EVIL, WE SHOULD NOT HAVE BROUGHT HIM BEFORE THEE.

31. THEN PILATE SAID TO THEM, TAKE HIM, AND JUDGE HIM ACCORDING TO YOUR LAW. AND THEY SAID, IT IS NOT LAWFUL FOR US TO PUT ANY ONE TO DEATH.

32. THUS WAS THE SAYING OF JESUS FULFILLED, WHICH SHOWED BY WHAT DEATH HE WOULD DIE.

Luke xxiii. 2. AND ALL BEGAN TO ACCUSE HIM, WE THINK THAT THIS MAN IS PERVERTING THE NATION, AND FOR BIDDING MEN TO GIVE TRIBUTE TO CÆSAR, CALLING HIMSELF KING AND CHRIST.

John xviii. 34. JESUS REPLIED TO THEM, THOU THYSELF CONSIDEREST ME A KING, OR THOU SAYEST ONLY WHAT OTHERS HAVE SAID OF ME.

35. PILATE ANSWERED, I AM NOT A JEW; THY OWN NATION AND THY CHIEF PRIESTS HAVE DELIVERED THEE TO ME. AND I ASK WHAT THOU HAST DONE.

36. JESUS ANSWERED, MY KINGDOM IS NOT OF THE EARTH. IF MY KINGDOM WERE OF THE EARTH, MY SERVANTS WOULD FIGHT FOR ME, THAT I SHOULD NOT BE DELIVERED TO THE CHIEF PRIEST: BUT YOU SEE THAT MY KINGDOM IS NO SUCH.

38. AND PILATE ENTERED THE COURT, AND CALLED JESUS, AND SAID TO HIM, THOU ART THE KING OF THE JEWS.

37. PILATE SAID TO HIM, DOST THOU CONSIDER THYSELF A KING? JESUS SAID TO HIM, THOU CALLEST ME KING. I CAME INTO THE WORLD TO CON-FIRM THE TRUTH; EVERY MAN WHO LIVES BY THE TRUTH UNDERSTANDS MY VOICE.

38. PILATE SAID TO HIM, WHAT IS THE TRUTH? AND WHEN HE HAD SAID THIS, HE WENT OUT AGAIN TO THEM, I FIND NO GUILT IN HIM.

Mark xv. 3. BUT THE CHIEF PRIESTS ACCUSED HIM OF MANY THINGS.

Luke xxiii. 5. AND THE CHIEF PRIESTS WERE PERSISTENT, AND SAID, HE HAS WITH HIS TEACHING STIRRED UP THE NATION THROUGHOUT JUDEA, BEGINNING WITH GALILEE.

Mark xv. 4. AND PILATE BEGAN ONCE MORE TO ASK HIM, SAYING, WHY DOST THOU NOT ANSWER? THOU SEEST HOW THEY ACCUSE THEE.

5. BUT JESUS DID NOT ANSWER WITH A SINGLE WORD, SO THAT PILATE MARVELED VERY MUCH.

Luke xxiii. 6. WHEN PILATE HEARD OF GALILEE, HE ASKED WHETHER THE MAN WAS GALILEAN.

7. WHEN HE HEARD THAT HE BELONGED TO HEROD'S JURISDICTION, HE SENT HIM TO HEROD, WHO WAS AT THAT TIME AT JERUSALEM.

8. AND WHEN HEROD SAW JESUS, HE WAS VERY GLAD, FOR HEROD HAD HEARD SO MUCH OF HIM AND HAD FOR A LONG TIME WANTED TO SEE HIM. HEROD THOUGHT THAT HE WOULD SEE HIM DO SOME MIRACLE.

9. AND HE QUESTIONED HIM A GREAT DEAL; BUT HE DID NOT ANSWER HIM.

11. AND HEROD WITH HIS SOLDIERS, THINKING LITTLE OF HIM IN A RED ROBE, AND SENT HIM BACK TO PILATE.

12. AND FROM THAT DAY PILATE AND HEROD BECAME FRIENDS, FOR BEFORE THEY WERE AT ENMITY.

Luke xxiii. 13. BUT PILATE, WHEN HE HAD CALLED TOGETHER THE CHIEF PRIESTS AND THE RULERS AND THE PEOPLE,

14. SAID TO THEM, YOU HAVE BROUGHT THIS MAN TO ME, BECAUSE HE PERVERTS THE PEOPLE; AND HERE I HAVE EXAMINED HIM IN YOUR PRESENCE, AND HAVE FOUND NO FAULT IN HIM, OF WHICH YOU ACCUSE HIM;

15. NOR HAS HEROD FOUND ANY, FOR I SENT YOU TO HIM; AND YOU SEE THAT NOTHING HAS BEEN FOUND FOR WHICH HE SHOULD BE WORTHY OF DEATH.

16. AND SO PUNISH HIM, AND SET HIM FREE.

Mark xv. 13. BUT THEY CRIED, CRUCIFY HIM.

Matt. xvii. 15. AT THE FEAST THE GOVERNOR WAS IN THE HABIT OF RELEAS-ING ONE OF THE PRISONERS, WHOM THEY WANTED.

16. AND THEY HAD THEN A PRISONER, CALLED BARABBAS.

Luke xxiii. 19. BARABBAS HAD CAUSED SEDITION AND MURDER IN THE CITY, AND WAS SITTING IN PRISON.

Matt. xxvii. 17. AND PILATE SAID TO THEM, WHOM DO YOU WANT ME TO RELEASE TO YOU, BARABBAS OR JESUS, WHO IS CALLED CHRIST?

18. FOR HE SAW THAT THE CHIEF PRIESTS HAD DELIVERED HIM OUT OF ENVY.

Mark xv. 11. BUT THE CHIEF PRIESTS INCITED THE PEOPLE TO CRY, THAT HE SHOULD RATHER RELEASE BARABBAS TO THEM.

12. AND PILATE REPLIED TO THEM, WHAT, THEN, DO YOU WANT ME TO DO WITH HIM WHOM YOU CALL THE KING OF THE JEWS?

13. AND THEY CRIED AGAIN. CRUCIFY HIM.

Luke xxiii. 20. AND PILATE AGAIN TRIED TO PERSUADE THEM THAT THEY SHOULD RELEASE JESUS.

21. BUT THEY CRIED AGAIN, CRUCIFY HIM.

22. AND HE SAID TO THEM FOR THE THIRD TIME, WHAT WRONG HAS HE DONE TO YOU? I HAVE FOUND NO CAUSE FOR WHICH HE SHOULD BE PUT TO DEATH; PUNISH HIM, AND LET HIM GO.

John xix. 4. I WILL LET HIM OUT OF THE COURT, FOR I FIND NO FAULT IN HIM.

6. WHEN THE CHIEF PRIESTS AND THEIR SERVANT SAW HIM, THEY CRIED, CRUCIFY HIM, AND PILATE SAID, TAKE HIM AND CRUCIFY HIM, FOR I FIND NO FAULT IN HIM.

7. THE JEWS ANSWERED HIM, WE HAVE A LAW, AND BY OUR LAW HE OUGHT TO DIE WHO MAKES HIMSELF THE SON OF GOD.

8. WHEN PILATE HEARD THIS, THAT JESUS WAS THE SON OF GOD, HE WAS DISTURBED EVEN MORE.

9. AND HE RETURNED TO THE COURT, AND SAID TO JESUS, WHO ART THOU? BUT JESUS MADE NO ANSWER.

10. PILATE SAID TO HIM, DOST THOU NOT ANSWER ME? DOST THOU NOT KNOW THAT I CAN CRUCIFY OR RELEASE THEE?

11. AND JESUS ANSWERED, THOU HAST NO POWER OVER ME, IF THOU ART NOT TAUGHT BY GOD.

12. PILATE WAS ANXIOUS TO RELEASE HIM; BUT THE JEWS SAID, IF THOU LETTEST HIM GO, THOU ART NOT CÆSAR'S FAITHFUL SERVANT; WHOEVER MAKES HIMSELF A KING IS CÆSAR'S ADVERSARY.

Matt. xxvii. 24. WHEN PILATE SAW THAT HE COULD DO NOTHING, BUT THAT THE CRY WAS GROWING LOUDER, HE TOOK WATER, WASHED HIS HANDS BEFORE THE MULTITUDE, AND SAID, I AM INNOCENT OF THE BLOOD OF THIS JUST MAN. YOU SEE YOURSELVES.

25. AND ALL THE PEOPLE CRIED, HIS BLOOD IS ON US AND OUR CHILDREN.

Luke xxiii. 23. AND THEY DRIED LOUDER STILL, THAT HE BE CRUCIFIED, AND THE VOICES OF THE CHIEF PRIESTS PREVAILED.

John xix. 13. WHEN PILATE UNDERSTOOD THAT SAYING, HE BROUGHT OUT JESUS, AND SAT DOWN IN HIS JUDGEMENT SEAT.

1. THEN PILATE TOOK JESUS, AND HAD HIM FLOGGED.

2. AND THE SOLDIERS WHO FLOGGED HIM PUT A CROWN ON HIS HEAD, AND A RED ROBE ON HIM.

Matt. xxvii. 29. AND GAVE HIM A STICK IN HIS HAND, AND BOWED BEFORE HIM, MOCKING HIM.

30. AND THEY BOXED HIS EARS AND BEAT HIM ON THE HEAD, AND SPIT ON HIM, AND SAID HAIL, KING OF THE JEWS.

John xix. 14. IT WAS THE SIXTH HOUR, AND PILATE SAID, THIS IS YOUR KING.

15. THEY CRIED, TAKE HIM AND CRUCIFY HIM. PILATE SAID, YOU WANT ME TO CRUCIFY YOUR KING. THE CHIEF PRIESTS REPLIED, WE HAVE NO KING BUT CÆSAR.

5. JESUS CAME OUT IN HIS CROWN AND RED ROBE, AND SAID TO THEM, BEHOLD THE MAN!

16. THEN PILATE DELIVERED HIM TO THEM TO BE CRUCIFIED.

Matt. xxvii. 31. AND THEY TOOK OFF HIS RED ROBE, AND PUT ON HIS OWN GARMENT, AND LED HIM AWAY TO CRUCIFY HIM.

John xix. 17. AND HE CARRIED HIS CROSS TO THE PLACE CALLED GOLGOTHA.

18. AND THERE THEY CRUCIFIED HIM, AND TWO OTHERS WITH HIM, ON EITHER SIDE ONE, AND JESUS IN THE MIDDLE.

Luke xxiii. 34. JESUS SAID, FATHER, FORGIVE THEM, FOR THEY DO NOT KNOW WHAT THEY DO.

Mark xv. 29. AND THE PEOPLE MOCKED HIM: THEY CAME UP, AND SHOOK THEIR HEADS, SAYING, AND THOU WOULDST DESTROY THE TEMPLE, AND BUILD IT UP AGAIN IN THREE DAYS;

30. SAVE THYSELF, AND COME DOWN FROM THE CROSS.

31. AND THE CHIEF PRIESTS AND LEARNED MEN LAUGHED AMONG THEM-SELVES, SAYING, HE HAS SAVED OTHERS, BUT CANNOT SAVE HIMSELF.

32. LET CHRIST, THE KING OF THE JEWS, COME DOWN FROM THE CROSS AND WE WILL BELIEVE HIM.

Matt. xxvii. 43. HE TRUSTED ALL THE TIME IN GOD; LET HIM SAVE HIM-SELF NOW, FOR HE SAYS THAT HE IS THE SON OF GOD.

Luke xxiii. 36. AND THE SOLDIERS ALSO MOCKED HIM.

Matt. xxvii. 44. AND ONE OF THE ROBBERS, WHO WERE CRUCIFIED WITH HIM, MOCKED HIM.

Luke xxiii. 39. AND ONE OF THE ROBBERS WHO WERE HANGED WITH HIM, SCOLDED HIM, SAYING, IF THOU ART CHRIST, SAVE THYSELF AND US.

40. BUT THE OTHER STOPPED HIM, SAYING, DOST THOU NOT FEAR GOD? THOU ART PUNISHED ENOUGH.

41. WE DESERVE IT, BUT HE HAS DONE NO WRONG.

42. AND HE SAID TO JESUS, REMEMBER ME, LORD IN THY KINGDOM.

43. AND JESUS SAID TO HIM, THOU SPEAKEST TRULY: NOW THOU ART IN PARADISE WITH ME.

Matt. xxvii. 46. ABOUT THE NINTH HOUR, JESUS SAID IN LOUD VOICE, ELI, ELI, LAMA SABACHTHANI? WHICH MEANS, MY GOD, MY GOD, IN WHAT HAST THOU LEFT ME?

47. SOME OF THOSE STOOD NEAR HEARD IT, AND SAID, HE IS CALLING ELIJAH.

49. AND OTHERS SAID, LET BE, LET US SEE WHETHER ELIJAH WILL COME.

John xix. 28. THEN JESUS CALLED OUT, I WANT TO DRINK.

Matt. xxvii. 48. AND A MAN TOOK A SPONGE, AND FILLED IT WITH VINE-GAR, AND PUT IT ON A REED, AND GAVE HIM THIS VINEGAR TO DRINK.

John xix. 30. AND WHEN JESUS HAD PARTAKEN OF THE VINEGAR,

Luke xxiii. 46. HE SAID IN A LOUD VOICE, FATHER, INTO THY HANDS I GIVE MY SPIRIT.

John xix. 30. IT IS FINISHED: AND HE BOWED HIS HEAD, AND GAVE UP THE GHOST.

TOLSTOY'S COMMENTARY

Having said this, Jesus went with his disciples into the garden of Gethsemane. And when he came into the garden, he said, Let us stay here, I want to pray.

And he went up to Peter and the two sons of Zebedee and was sorrowful and grieved. And he said to them, My heart is heavy, I shall be sorrowful before my death. Stay here, and be not dispirited, as I am.

And he went a little distance away, and lay down on the ground on his face, and began to pray, and said, My Father, spirit, let it not be as I wish it, that I should not die, but do as thou wishest: let me die, but to thee, as a spirit, everything is possible, and so let me not be afraid of death and have the temptation of the flesh.

Then he got up, and went up to his disciples, and saw that they were dispirited, and said to them, Can you not for one hour be strong in spirit, so as not to fall into the temptation of the flesh? The spirit is strong, but the flesh is weak.

And again Jesus went away from them, and began to pray, and said, Father, if I must die, let me die, let thy will be done.

And having said this, he again walked over to his disciples, and he saw that they were even more dispirited than before, and were ready to weep. And he went away from them again, and said for the third time, Father, thy will be done.

Then he returned to the disciples, and said to them, Sleep awhile and rest yourselves, for now the son of man will soon be delivered into the hands of the men of the world. Then wake up, for he who will betray me is coming already.

And when he had said this, Judas, one of the twelve disciples, suddenly appeared, and with him there was a large crowd of people with clubs and knives.

Judas knew that Jesus and his disciples frequently came to this garden, and so he brought there the guards and the servants of the chief priests. He said to them, I will bring you where he is with the disciples, and that you may be able to recognize him, watch whom I shall kiss first, for it is he.

And he went up to Jesus, and said, Hail, teacher, and kissed him.

And Jesus said to him, Didst thou come for this?

Then the guards surrounded Jesus, and wanted to take him. And Peter took a knife away from one of the servants of the chief priests, and cut off his ear.

Jesus said, We must not resist evil; let this be. And he said to Peter, Give the sword back to him from whom thou tookest it; he who takes up the sword will perish by the sword.

After this Jesus turned to the whole crowd, and said, Why did you come against me with weapons, as against a robber? Have I not been everyday amidst you in the temple, teaching you? Why did you not take me then? You could do nothing to me in the light of the day, for your power is only in the darkness.

When his disciples saw that he was taken, they fled. Then the chief commanded the soldiers to take Jesus and bind him, and to take him first to Annas, who was Caiaphas's father-in-law, for Caiaphas was the high priest in that year, and was living with his father-in-law. It was the same Caiaphas who had been planning to destroy Jesus. He considered it useful for the nation to destroy Jesus, for if he did not destroy Jesus, it would have been worse for the whole nation.

And Jesus was brought into the yard of the house, where the high priest was living.

While they were leading Jesus there, one of the disciples, Peter, walked behind, to see where they were going to take him. When they took him into the courtyard of the high priest, Peter went there himself to see how it would all end. And a girl in the yard saw Peter, and said to him, Art thou also with Jesus of Galilee?

Peter was frightened, lest he should be also accused, and said in a loud voice before all the people, I do not know what thou sayest.

Then, when Jesus was taken into the house, and Peter entered the vestibule with the people, and a woman was warming herself at the fire, and Peter went up to her, the woman looked at him, and said to the people, Behold, this man looks as though he belonged to Jesus of Nazareth.

Peter was frightened even more than before, and swore that he had never been with Jesus, and did not know what kind of a man Jesus was.

A little while later some men walked over to Peter, and said, It looks, though, as if thou wert one of these seditious people; we can tell by thy speech that thou art from Galilee.

Then Peter began to curse and swear that he had never seen or known Jesus. And the moment he had said this, a cock crew. And Peter recalled the words which Jesus had spoken, when Peter swore that though all might deny him, he would not deny him. Jesus had said, Tonight thou wilt deny me thrice before cockcrow. And Peter went away from the yard, and wept bitterly.

And the pastors, chief priests, scribes, and rulers assembled at the house of the high priest. And when all were assembled, they brought Jesus, and the chief priests asked him what his doctrine consisted in, and who his disciples were.

And Jesus replied, I have always spoken before all, and have never concealed anything from men. What askest thou me about? Ask those who have heard and understood my teaching, and they will tell thee.

When Jesus said this, one of the chief priests' servants struck Jesus in the face, and said, With whom art thou speaking? Is this the way to answer a chief priest?

Jesus said, If I spoke badly, say so; but if I did not speak badly, why do you beat me?

The pastors, the chief priests, tried to accuse Jesus, and at first did not find any good cause for which he might be sentenced. Then they found two false witnesses. These false witnesses said of Jesus, We ourselves heard this man say, I will destroy this handmade temple of yours, and in three days will build you up another temple of God, one which is not made by hand.

But even this was not sufficient cause for an accusation. And so the chief priest called out Jesus, and said, Why dost thou not reply to their testimony?

Jesus was silent, and said nothing.

Then the chief priest said to him, Tell me, then, art thou the Christ, the son of God?

Jesus answered him, and said, Yes, I am Christ, the son of God. And you will soon see for yourselves that the son of God is equal to God.

Then the chief priest called out, Thou blasphemest God, and now we need no further proofs: we have all heard thee blaspheme God.

And the chief priest turned to the assembly, and said, You have heard yourselves that he blasphemes God, so what do you sentence him to?

And all said, We condemn him to death.

And then all the people and the guards pressed forward toward Jesus, and began to spit into his face, and strike him, and scratch him. They covered his eyes, and boxed his ears, and asked, Well, prophet, canst thou guess who has struck thee?

And Jesus was silent.

After they had mocked him, they bound him and took him before Pontius Pilate.

And he was brought to the court. Pilate, the governor, came out to them, and asked, Of what do you accuse this man?

They said, This man is doing evil, and so we have brought him before thee.

Pilate said to them, If he does evil, judge him yourselves according to your law.

And they said, We have brought him to thee that thou shouldst put him to death, for we may not kill.

And so that which Jesus had wished was fulfilled: he had said that he must be prepared to die on the cross at the hands of the Romans, and not by his own death, or at the hands of the Jews.

When Pilate asked him of what they accused him, they said that he was guilty in that he created sedition among the people, forbidding them to pay taxes to Cæsar, and calling himself Christ and king.

Pilate listened to them, and commanded that Jesus be brought to the court. When Jesus came in to him, Pilate asked him, Art thou the King of the Jews?

Jesus said, Why dost thou ask? Dost thou ask in thy own name whether I am the King of the Jews, or dost thou ask whether what they say of me is true?

Pilate said, I am not a Jew, and it makes no difference to me what thou callest thyself, but I ask thee only what thou hast done? Didst thou call thyself king?

Jesus replied, I taught the kingdom which is not of earth.

To this Pilate replied, Still thou considerest thyself a king.

Jesus said, Not only I, but even thou canst not help considering me a king. All I teach is to reveal the truth to you. And every man who lives by the truth will understand me.

Pilate did not wish to listen to Jesus, and said, Thou speakest of truth; what is truth? And having said this, he turned around and went again to the chief priests, and said to them, In my opinion this man has done no wrong.

And the chief priests were persistent, and said that he had done much wrong and was creating sedition in all of Judea as far as Galilee.

Then Pilate began to question Jesus once more in the presence of the chief priests, but Jesus made no reply.

Thou seest how they accuse thee, so why dost thou not justify thyself?

But Jesus kept silence, and did not say another word, so that Pilate marveled at him.

Pilate happened to think that Galilee was under Herod's jurisdiction, and so he asked, Is he from Galilee?

He was told, Yes.

Then he said, If he is from Galilee, he is under Herod's jurisdiction, and I will send him to Herod.

Herod was at that time in Jerusalem, and Pilate sent Jesus to Jerusalem to Herod, that he might get rid of him. When Jesus was brought to Herod, Herod was very glad to see him. He had heard a great deal about Jesus, and wanted to know what kind of a man he was. Herod called him up, and began to question him concerning everything he wanted to know, but Jesus did not answer him. But the chief priests and teachers accused him fiercely, as before Pilate, saying that he was a rioter. And Herod regarded Jesus as a worthless man, and, to rail at him, ordered his servants to put a red robe on him, and sent him back to Pilate.

Herod was satisfied that Pilate had respected him by sending Jesus to his court, and so they made peace, for they had been at odds before. When Jesus was brought back to Pilate, Pilate once more called the chief priests and rulers of the Jews, and said to them, You brought this man to me, saying that he created sedition among the people, and I questioned him in your presence, and do not see that he is a rioter. I sent him with you to Herod, and you see that nothing harmful was found there against him, and so it is my opinion that there is no cause for putting him to death, and that it would be better to set him free.

When the chief priests heard this, they cried out, No, put him to death, put him to death in Roman fashion. Crucify him.

Pilate heard what they said, and replied to the chief priests, Very well; but it is your habit to pardon a criminal at your feast. There is a murderer and rioter, Barabbas by name, who is sitting in my prison. One of the two you must release: whom will you pardon, Jesus or Barabbas?

Pilate wanted to save Jesus, but the chief priests instructed the people to cry, Barabbas, Barabbas!

And so Pilate said, And what will you do with Jesus? And they cried again, In Roman fashion, on the cross, crucify him!

And Pilate tried to persuade them, saying, Why do you urge me so? He has not done anything for which he should be put to death, and he has done you no wrong. I will release him, for I see no guilt in him.

The chief priests and their servants cried, Crucify him, crucify him!

And Pilate said to them, If so, take him and crucify him, for I see no fault in him.

The chief priests replied, We demand that which comes to him for calling himself the son of God.

When Pilate heard these words, he was troubled, for he did not know what was meant by the words, Son of God. And he went back to the court, and called Jesus, and asked him, Who art thou, and whence dost thou come?

But Jesus made no reply to him.

Then Pilate said, Why dost thou not answer? Dost thou not see that thou art in my power, and that I can crucify or release thee?

Jesus answered him, The evil is that thou hast the power; if thou wert not entrusted with power, the Herodians would not have enticed thee and led thee into offense, both thee, and themselves and the teachers with thee.

Pilate wished to release Jesus, but the Jews said to him, If thou lettest Jesus go, thou wilt prove that thou art not a faithful servant of Cæsar, for he who makes himself a king is Cæsar's enemy.

When Pilate heard these words, he understood that he could not help but put Jesus to death.

Then Pilate went out to the Jews, took some water, washed his hands before the people, and said, I am not guilty of the blood of this righteous man.

And the whole people cried out, Let the blood be on us and on our children.

Thus the chief priests prevailed. Pilate sat down in his judgment seat, and ordered Jesus to be flogged. When he was flogged, the soldiers who flogged him put a crown on his head, and gave him a stick into his hands, and threw a red robe over his shoulders, and began to mock him. They bowed before him in mockery, and said, Rejoice, King of the Jews; and they struck his face and head, and spit into his face.

Pilate said to them, How can you have your king crucified?

But the chief priests cried out, Crucify him; our king is Cæsar—crucify him.

Jesus came out in the crown and the red robe, and said, Behold, here is a man.

Then Pilate ordered that he be crucified.

The red robe was taken off Jesus and his own was put on him, and he was told to carry his own cross to the place called Golgotha, in order that they might crucify him there. And he carried his cross and came to Golgotha. And there they stretched Jesus out on the cross, and two men with him, one at each side of him, and Jesus in the middle.

As they were crucifying Christ, he said, Father, forgive them, for they do not know what they are doing.

And when Jesus was already hanging on the cross, the people surrounded him, and mocked him.

They came up, and shook their heads, and said, Well, thou wouldst destroy the temple of Jerusalem and build it up again in three days, so save thyself and come down from the cross.

And the chief priests and pastors stood there, and mocked him, and said, Thou hast saved others, but thou canst not save thyself. Show us that thou art Christ, come down from the cross, and then we will believe thee. He has been saying that he is the son of God, and that God would not leave him, so why has God left him now?

And the people and chief priests and soldiers mocked him, and so did one of the robbers who were crucified with him.

One of the robbers, mocking him, said, If thou art Christ, save thyself and us.

But the other robber heard this, and said, Dost thou not fear God? Thou art thyself on the cross, and yet railest at an innocent man. Thou and I are being punished for what we have done, but this man has done no wrong.

And turning to Jesus, this robber said to him, Sir, remember me in thy kingdom.

And Jesus said to him, Thou art blessed with me at once.

In the ninth hour Jesus, being worn out, cried out in a loud voice, Eli, Eli, lama sabachthani, which means, My God, my God, in what hast thou left me?

And when they heard this among the people, they began to speak and laugh, He is calling Elijah the prophet; let us see how Elijah will come.

Then Jesus said, I want to drink, and a man took a sponge, dipped it in vinegar, for a vat of it was standing near by, and raised it up to Jesus on a reed.

Jesus sucked the sponge, and said in a loud voice, It is finished. Father, into thy hands I give up my spirit.

And inclining his head, he gave up the ghost.

Conclusion to the
Investigation of the Gospel

With the words, It is finished, the Gospel is ended. To those who saw the divinity of Jesus in this, that he was not like other men, the resurrection may have been convincing, that is, may have proved to them that he was not like other men, and only that he was not like other men, and nothing else; but only to those who saw Jesus die, and were convinced that he was dead, and then saw him alive, and were convinced that he was alive. But, according to the description of the evangelists, except Luke, who suddenly mentions his ascension in the presence of five hundred men, there were no such people, for according to their description he came as a dream, as a vision.

Let us even assume that he came in the flesh, and that Thomas put his fingers into his wounds, what did this prove to Thomas? That he was not like other men. But what follows from his not being like other men? Only this, that other people, such as all are, would find it very hard or impossible to do what a special being did. But if even it were necessary to convince people that he was not like other men, his appearance to Thomas and ten other men and later to five hundred men could not have convinced others, who had not seen this resurrection; it was only the disciples who told of the resurrection, but one can tell anything one wishes; to believe the stories of the disciples, one must have the assurance that these stories are true. And to confirm the truth of their stories the disciples tell that tongues of fire descended upon them, and that they themselves wrought miracles, healed, and raised from the dead. Again, that the tongues came down and that the disciples raised from the dead and healed, the disciples of the disciples prove by new miracles, and so until the present relics and saints heal and raise from the dead; and it turns out that the divinity of Christ is based on the story of unusual events. But the stories of unusual events are based on stories of other unusual events, and the last unusual events have not been seen by men in their sound senses.

Very well, Christ was raised from the dead, made his appearance, and flew to heaven: has this explained anything? Has it added anything to his teaching? Nothing, absolutely nothing, except the necessity of inventing new, unnecessary miracles, in order to confirm this invented, unnecessary miracle. We have seen and read the teaching about Christ's life previous to the resurrection, and in the most corrupt parts of this teaching there shines always the light of the truth which he announced to the world. No matter how crudely the recording evangelists understood the teaching, they rendered the words and actions of the man Jesus, and the light startles us. Now what is added to the teaching after the resurrection by what Christ did and said after the resurrection?

He appears for some reason to Mary Magdalene, out of whom he had cast seven devils, and tells her not to touch him, for he has not yet entered to his Father.

Then he appears to the women, and tells them that he will come to his brothers.

Then he appears to his disciples, and explains something to them of Moses in the whole Scripture.

And now they see him, and now they do not see him. Then he appears to his disciples, rebukes them for not believing, shows them his side, and breathes on them, and this causes the sins to be remitted to those to whom they remit them. Then he appears to Thomas, and says nothing. Then he catches fish, a large amount of them, with his disciples, and says three times to Peter, Feed my sheep, and predicts Peter's death.

Then he appears to a crowd of five hundred at once, and again he says nothing. Then he says that to him is given power in heaven and on earth, and that therefore they must bathe people in the name of the Father, the Son, and the Holy Ghost, and that he who is bathed will be saved, and that those to whom they will transmit this spirit will take up snakes and drink poison without harm, and speak in all languages, which they naturally have never done. Then he flies to heaven. He said nothing more. What sense was there in his resurrection, since he did and said only these foolish things?

And so:

1. The resurrection, like any story about something incomprehensible, cannot prove anything.

2. The resurrection, like any miracle, if a man has seen it, can prove only that something contrary to the laws of reason has happened, and that a man who has been subject to a miracle has been subject to something unusual, and nothing else. But if on the basis of a miracle the conclusion is drawn that a man who is not subject to the laws of reason is an unusual man, such a conclusion is correct only for those who contemplate the miracle, and only as long as they contemplate it. A story about a miracle cannot convince any one, so that the truth has to be confirmed by a miracle which has taken place with the one who tells about it. The confirmation of the truth of a miracle by another miracle inevitably leads to the fabrication of new miracles, up to our own time, in order to confirm the truth of the narrator, though in our time we see clearly that there are no miracles, and that, as miracles are invented for the present time, they must have been invented for the past. The story about the miracle of Christ's resurrection betrays its untruth in that it sharply differs in its primitiveness, insignificance, and, simply, stupidity from all previous descriptions of Christ's life, and shows clearly that the story of Christ's real life had for its foundation actual life, full of depth and holiness; but the story of the resurrection and the supposed actions and speeches after it no longer had life for its basis, and is altogether a fabrication. No matter how crude and primitive the description of Christ's life is, the holiness of his life and the elevation of his personality shines through the crudeness and primitiveness of the writers; but when there is no longer anything real at the basis of the description, but only mere inventions, this primitiveness and crudeness appear in all their nakedness. They have evidently managed to raise him from the dead, but they cannot make him say or do anything worthy of him.

3. The miracle of the resurrection is directly opposed to the teaching of Christ, consequently it was hard to make Christ say anything characteristic of him after the resurrection, since the very idea that he could rise from the dead is contrary to the whole meaning of his teaching. We must fail to understand his whole teaching, in order that we may conceive of the possibility of his resurrection in the body. He even directly denied the resurrection, explaining how we were to understand the resurrection of which the Jews spoke.

How the dead are raised, he said, Moses showed in the bush, when he called God the God of Abraham, and the God of Isaac, and the God of Jacob; God is not a God of the dead, but of the living; for to God all are living. He said, The spirit brings to life, and the flesh is of little avail. He said, I am the living bread, which has come down from heaven. He said, I am the way, the truth, and the life. He said, I am the resurrection and the life. And him who taught that he was that which was sent from God into the world, to give life to men; that which gave life; that which is the spirit; that which does not die; that which will return to men as the spirit of truth—him they understood to say that he was to rise from the dead in the flesh. Indeed, what could that Jesus do, who was glad to return to the Father, that Jesus who, dying, said, Into thy hands I give up my spirit? What could he do and say, when he was imagined to have risen from the dead in the flesh, except what was contrary to his teaching? And so it was.

This legend of the resurrection, which is expressed in the last chapters of the gospels, which did not have Christ's life and words for its basis, and which wholly belongs to the views held by the recorders of the gospels on the life and teaching of Jesus, is remarkable and instructive in that these chapters clearly show the depth of the layer of misunderstanding, with which the whole description of Jesus' life and teaching is covered. It is as though a precious painting were covered with a thick layer of paint, and those spots, where the paint got on the bare wall, showed clearly the depth of the layer which covered the picture itself. The story of the resurrection gives the key for the understanding and explanation of all miracles, of which the Gospel is full, and of those contradictory words and conceptions by which the meaning of the best passages of the teaching is frequently destroyed.

It is not known who wrote the fourth gospel, and the history of criticism has come to the conclusion that we shall never find that out. There may be more or less probable suppositions as to time, place, persons; suppositions as to what gospel, or what part of what gospel, is copied from another, but their origin is unknown. We cannot judge of the historical trustworthiness of the Gospel, but we are able to judge of the quality of the books themselves. We can judge as to what formed the foundation of the Christian beliefs of men, and what did not have any influence on the beliefs.

From this side we see in the gospels two sharply distinguished parts of the expositions: one the exposition of the teaching; the other, an attempt at proving the truth of the teaching, or, more correctly, the importance of the teaching, such as are the miracles, prophecies, and predictions. The teaching has passed the centuries unimpaired—all agree on this. The proofs, which, no doubt, were proofs, now form the chief stumbling-block in the acceptance of the teaching.

To this part belong all the miracles and the chief miracle, the resurrection. In the description of the resurrection, as in an event fabricated without any foundation, it is easiest of all to follow out the methods of the formation of such legends, and the causes of their acceptance, and the methods of their exposition, and their significance, and their consequences. The origin of the legend of the resurrection was a confirmation of the veracity of the writers (except Luke), and it is written down in the gospels so clearly that every unbiassed man cannot help but see the most natural germ of the legend, such as around us spring up everyday in the stories of miraculous relics, saints, magicians. The stories and articles of spiritualism, of the girl who materialized and danced, are told more definitely and more circumstantially than the story of the resurrection. Nothing could be clearer than the history of the growth of this legend. On the Sabbath they went to see the grave. The body was not there. Evangelist John tells that they said that the disciples had taken out the body. Women come to the grave, one of them Mary Magdalene, out of whom seven devils have been cast, and she is the first to say that she saw something at the grave, something like a gardener, or an angel, or him himself. The story passes from gossips to gossips, and then to the disciples. Eighty years later they tell that such and such a man saw him there and then, but all the accounts are contradictory and indefinite. The disciples do not invent them—so much is evident—but none of the men who revere his memory dare contradict what, in their opinion, tends to add to his glory, and, above all, to convince others that he is from God, and that God produced a miracle in his honor. It seems to them that this is the best proof, and the legend grows and spreads.

The legend aids in the dissemination of the teaching, but the legend is a lie, while the teaching is truth. And so the teaching is no longer transmitted in all the purity of the truth, but intermingled with the lie. One lie provokes another for its confirmation. New false legends of miracles are told in confirmation of the first false legend. There appear legends of miracles wrought by the followers of Christ and of miracles which preceded him—of his procreation, his birth, his whole life—and the whole teaching is mixed with lies. The whole exposition of his life and teaching is covered up by a thick layer of paint of the miraculous, which dims the teaching. New believers join Christ's faith, not so much in consequence of his teaching, as of the faith in the miraculousness of his life and actions. And there comes that terrible time, when there appears the conception of faith, not of πίστις, of which Christ speaks (the inward inevitableness of conviction, which becomes the basis of life), but as a consequence of an effort of will, when one can say, I command you to believe, I want to believe, you must believe. There comes the time, when all the false legends take the place of the teaching, all are gathered into one, are formulated, and are expressed as dogma, that is, as decrees. The crowd, the rude crowd, takes possession of the teaching, and smearing it over with the false legends, obscures it.

But, in spite of all the efforts of the crowd, the chosen people see the truth through all the mire of lies and carry it in all its purity through the ages, by the side of the lies, and in this form the teaching reaches us. He who in our day, be he Catholic, Protestant, Orthodox, Milker, Stundist, Khlyst, Eunuch, Rationalist, or of any other creed, reads the Gospel, finds himself in a strange position. He who does not purposely shut his eyes cannot help but see that, if there is not everything in it which we know and live by, there is at least something very wise and significant. But this wisdom and significance is expressed in such a monstrously bad way, as Göthe says, that one cannot find a worse written book than the Gospel, and is buried in such a lumber of monstrous, stupid, even unpoetical legends that one does not know what to do with this book. There is no other interpretation in this book than what the different churches give to it. These interpretations are all filled with absurdities and contradictions, so that in the beginning one is confronted with an alternative: either, as the Russian proverb has it, to get furious at the lice and chuck the fur coat into the stove, that is, to reject the whole as absurd, as ninety-nine of every hundred men actually do, or to subvert reason, as the church commands us to do, and accept everything stupid and unimportant with what is wise and important, which is actually done by the remaining hundredth of men, who either have no vision, or know how to squint in such a way that they do not see what they do not wish to see. But this alternative is not firmly grounded. It is enough to show these people what they did not wish to see, and they involuntarily reject with the lie the truth which was mixed in with it. What is terrible in this case is this, that the lie, which is smeared in with the truth, is not smeared in by the enemies of truth, but by its first friends: that this lie was considered of importance and served as the first instrument for the dissemination and propagation of truth is proved by this, that the lie about Christ's resurrection was, during the times of the apostles and the martyrs of the first centuries, the chief proof of the truth of Christ's teaching. It is true, this same fable of the resurrection was also the chief cause of unbelief in the teaching. The pagans in all the lives of the first Christian martyrs call them men who believe in this, that their crucified one rose from the dead, and quite legitimately rail at them for this.

But the Christians did not see this, just as the popes in Kíev do not see that their straw-stuffed relics are on the one hand an incitement to faith, and on the other an obstacle to it. Then, during the first times of Christianity, it cannot be denied that they were necessary; I am even willing to admit that they coöperated in the dissemination and confirmation of faith. I can imagine how, thanks to faith in the miracle, men came to see the importance of the teaching and turned to it. The miracle was not a proof of the truth, but of the importance of the matter. The miracle attracted attention—the miracle was an advertisement. Everything which happened was foretold; a voice speaks from heaven, the sick are healed, the dead rise—how, then, can one help directing his attention to the teaching, and trying to grasp it? Its truth enters the soul, but the miracles are only an advertisement. Thus the lie was useful. But it could be useful only in the first time, and only because it attracted men to the truth. If there had been no lie, the teaching might have been disseminated more quickly still. But there is no need of considering what might have happened. The life of that time concerning the miracles may be compared with this, as if a man sowed a forest, and in the sowing put up a sign saying that God sowed this forest, and that he who does not believe that there is a forest here will be eaten up by monsters. Men are to believe it, and must beware of tramping down the forest. This might have been useful and necessary in its time, when there was not any forest there, but when the forest grows up, it is evident that that which was useful became unnecessary and harmful, as a lie. The same is true of the belief in miracles, which is connected with the teaching: the belief in them aided in the propagation of the faith—they may have been useful; but the teaching has been disseminated and confirmed, and the belief in miracles has become useless and harmful. So long as they believed in miracles and in the lie, it happened that the teaching itself took such firm root that its stability and dissemination became an essential proof of its truth. The teaching has passed unimpaired through the ages—all agree to this—and the external, miraculous proofs of its truths now form the chief stumbling-block in accepting the teaching. To us now the proofs of the truth and importance of Christ's teaching are only an obstacle which prevents our seeing the significance of Christ.

Its existence of eighteen hundred years among billions of people sufficiently attests its importance. Maybe it was necessary to say that the forest was planted by God and that a monster guarded it and God defended it; maybe it was necessary to say so as long as there was no forest; but now I live in this forest of eighteen hundred years of existence, when it has all grown up and surrounds me on all sides. I need no proofs that it exists: it does exist. So let us leave out what was necessary at some past period, in order to make the forest grow—to form the teaching of Christ.

Many things were necessary, but the question is not the investigation of how the teaching was formed; the question is as to the significance of the teaching. It is the business of history to investigate how the teaching was formed; but for the understanding of the meaning of the teaching we do not need any reflections on the methods used for the confirmation of the truth of the teaching. These two parts are sharply separated in all the gospels; as I have said, the four gospels are like a wonderful painting which for temporary purposes is all covered up with a deep layer of paint. This paint is continued to both sides of the painting: the layer over the bare wall—previous to the birth of Christ—all the legends about John the Baptist, about the procreation, and about the birth; then follows the layer over the painting—miracles, prophecies, and predictions; and then the layer over the bare wall again—the legends of the resurrection and the acts of the apostles, etc. Knowing the thickness of the layer and its composition, we must scratch it off where it runs over the bare wall and is particularly evident in the legend of the resurrection, and carefully scrape it off from the whole painting, and then only shall we understand the painting in all its significance, and it is this that I have been trying to do.

My idea is as follows: The Gospel consists of two distinct parts so far as purposes are concerned. One is the exposition of Christ's teaching; the other is the proof of the importance and divinity of this teaching. All the churches agree on this. The proofs of the importance and divinity of Christ's teaching are based on the consciousness of the truth of Christ's teaching (on which all the churches also agree) and on external historical proofs of the significance, importance, and divinity of the teaching, such as were collected in the gospels in the first time of the teaching and such as, by their essence, could have been convincing only to the eyewitnesses, but in our time attain, the opposite result, by repelling from the understanding of and belief in the teaching of the church, not the enemies of Christ, but the men who are sincerely devoted to the teaching. Nor can the churches help admitting that the aim of these proofs of the importance is the conviction of the truth of the teaching, and if there presents itself another, not an internal, but an external, historical proof of the importance of the teaching, which is complete, incontrovertible, and clear, then we must reject those proofs which call forth incredulity and which serve as an obstacle in the propagation of the teaching, and hold on to the incontrovertible and clear external proof of the importance. Such a proof, which did not exist in the first times, is the dissemination of the teaching itself, which penetrates all human knowledge, serves as a foundation of human life, and is constantly expanding. Thus, in order that we may understand the teaching, we not only can, but must inevitably put aside from the teaching all those proofs of its truth, which give way to other indubitable proofs, and which give nothing for the understanding of the teaching and serve as a chief obstacle to its acceptance. Even if these proofs were not harmful, they are no longer necessary, since they have an entirely different purpose and can add nothing to the teaching.

AFTERWORD

THE UNDERSTANDING OF LIFE IS THE DOING OF GOOD

FIRST EPISTLE OF JOHN

The announcement of good by Jesus Christ is the announcement of the understanding of life.

The understanding of life is this, that the principle of life is the perfect good. And so the life of man is just such perfect good. In order that we may attain this principle, we must understand that the spirit of life in man came from this principle. Man, who did not exist before, was called to life by this principle. This principle has given the good to man, and so the quality of this principle is the good.

Not to deviate from the principle of his life, a man must keep the only, understandable quality of this principle—the beneficence of love. And so man's life must consist in the good, that is, in doing good, in love, but good can be done to men only.

All the personal lusts do not correspond to the principle of the good, and so man must sacrifice them and all his carnal life for the principle of beneficent love for his neighbors.

From the understanding of life, as revealed by Jesus Christ, results the love of our neighbors. There are two proofs of the truth of this understanding: one is this, that if we do not recognize it, the principle of life presents itself as a deceiver that gave to men an unsatisfactory striving toward life and the good; the other is this, that man in his heart feels that love and doing good to his neighbor is the one true, free, and eternal life.

Chap. I. 1, 2, 3. This is the announcement about the understanding of life, wherein men have communion with the Father of life, and so eternal life.

4. This is the announcement of good.

5. The understanding of life consists in this, that God is life and the good, and that in life and in the good there is no death or evil.

6. If we should say that we have united with God and live in evil and death, we should either be deceived, or not be doing what we ought to.

7. Only if we live the life which he lives, do we unite with him.

Chap. II. 1. We have a teacher in this life in Jesus Christ the righteous.

2. He has delivered us and the whole world from untruth.

3. Hereby do we know the teaching of Jesus Christ, if we keep his commandments.

4. He who says that he knows the teaching of Jesus Christ, and does not keep his commandments, is a cheat, and the truth is not in him.

5. But he who keeps his commandments has the love of God. Through the love alone do we know that we are united with God.

6. He who says that he is united with Jesus Christ must live as Jesus lived.

9, 10, 11. He who says that he is in the life and the good, and hates his living brother, is not in the life and the good, but in death and evil, and does not know himself what he is doing; and blind is he who hates the life which is in him.

15. In order that one may not be blind, one must remember that everything of the world is a lust of the flesh or vanity, and all this is not of God;

16. That it passes away and dies;

17. But that he who does the will of God, love, abides forever.

23. Only he who recognizes his spirit as the son of God unites with the Father.

24. And so keep that understanding that according to the spirit you are the sons of God the Father, and then you will have eternal life.

Chap. III. 1. God has given you the possibility of being his sons, and such as he is.

2. Thus we in this life become the sons of God. Though we do not know what we shall be, we know that we are like him, and that we unite with him.

3. The hope in this eternal life frees man from error and makes him pure, even as the Father is.

4. Whoever commits a sin acts contrary to the will of God.

5. Jesus Christ appeared to teach us the liberation from sin and the union with God.

6. And so he who has united with him can no longer sin. Only he who does not know him commits sin.

7. And he who lives in God does righteousness.

8. He who has not united with God does not do righteousness.

9. Whoever acknowledges his birth from God cannot lie.

10. And so men are divided into those who are of God and those who are not: into those who know the truth and love their brothers, and into those who do not know the truth and do not love their brothers.

11. For according to the announcement of Jesus Christ we cannot help but love our brothers.

14. From the announcement of Jesus Christ we know that we pass from death to life, for we love our brothers, and that he who does not love a brother is in death.

15. We know that he who does not love his brother does not love life. And he who does not love life cannot have life.

16. From his announcement we know love to be this, that life is given to us, and so we know that we must lay down our life for a brother.

17. So that if a man who has life and sees that his brother is in need, and does not lay down his life for his brother, the love of God is not in him.

19. And he who loves thus has a peaceful heart, for he is united with God.

20. If his heart struggles he subdues his heart to God.

21. For God is more important than the desires of the heart. But if the heart does not struggle, he is blessed.

22. For he does everything he can, the very best he can, and he does what he is commanded to do.

23. But he is commanded to believe that he is the son of God, and to love his brother.

Chap. IV. 4. Those who act so unite with God and become higher than the world, for what is in them is greater and more important than the whole world.

7. And so we shall love one another. Love is of God, and every one who loves is a son of God, and knows God.

6. And he who does not love, does not know God, for God is love.

9. That God is love we know from this, that he sent his spirit, such as he himself is, into the world, and gave us life through it.

10. We were not, and God did not need us, but he gave us life, the good, consequently he loves us.

12. No one can know God. What we can know of him is that he loves us and through this love gave us life.

11. And so, to be in communion with God, we must be the same as he, and do the same that he is doing, that is, love men.

12. If we love one another, God is in us, and we in him.

16. Understanding God's love to us, we believe that God is love and that he who loves is united with God.

17. And understanding this, we are not afraid of death, for we have become in this world like God.

18. Our life has become love and is freed from fear and from all sufferings.

19. We love, because he loves.

20. And we must love, not God, whom we cannot love, because no man sees him, but the brother, whom we can love. He who says that he loves God, and hates his brother, is deceiving, for if he does not love his brother, whom he sees, how can he love God, whom he does not see?

21. For we have the commandment to love God in our brother.

Chap. V. 3, 4. The love of God is, that we keep his commandments. His commandments are not hard for him who, recognizing his birth from God, becomes above the world. Our faith rises above the world. Our true faith is that which Jesus, the son of God, has taught us.

8. And the spirit is in us and confirms us in the truth of his teaching.

9. If we shall believe in what men affirm, how, then, can we fail to believe in the spirit which is in us?

10. He who believes that the spirit of life in him is a spirit that has come down from above, has satisfaction in himself. But he who does not believe that life is a spirit that has come down from above, from the Father, makes God a deceiver.

11. The spirit confirms that the life in us is the eternal life.

12. He who believes that this spirit is the son of the eternal spirit and like him, has eternal life.

14. He who believes in this has no obstacles in life and everything he wishes according to the will of God is accomplished for him.

18. And so, he who believes that he is the son of God does not live in the lie and is pure from evil.

19. For he knows that the world is a deception.

20. That in himself (in man) there is understanding, so that he may find out that truth exists. But the truth is that only the spirit, the son of the Father, exists.

THE END

SUGGESTED READING

BERLIN, ISAIAH. *The Hedgehog and the Fox: An Essay on Tolstoy's View of History.* New York: Simon & Schuster, 1970.

GAY, PETER. *The Enlightenment: The Rise of Modern Paganism.* New York: W. W. Norton, 1995.

TOLSTOY, LEO. *Anna Karenina.* Trans. Constance Garnett. New York: Barnes & Noble, 2003.

———. *A Confession and Other Religious Writings.* Trans. Jane Kentish. New York: Penguin, 1988.

———. *The Kingdom of God Is Within You.* Trans. Constance Garnett. New York: Barnes & Noble, 2004.

TROYAT, HENRI. *Tolstoy.* Trans. Nancy Amphoux. New York: Grove, 2001.

WARE, TIMOTHY. *The Orthodox Church: New Edition.* New York: Penguin, 1993.